Reshaping housing policy

Reshaping housing policy
Subsidies, rents and residualisation

Peter Malpass

R

Routledge
London and New York

First published 1990
by Routledge
11 New Fetter Lane, London EC4P 4EE

Simultaneously published in the USA and Canada
by Routledge
a division of Routledge, Chapman & Hall, Inc.
29 West 35th Street, New York, NY 10001

© 1990 Peter Malpass

Typeset by Ponting–Green Publishing Services, London

Printed and bound in Great Britain
by Mackays of Chatham PLC, Kent

British Library Cataloguing in Publication Data

Malpass, Peter
  Reshaping housing policy : subsidies, rents and
  residualisation.
  I. Title
  363.5'56'0941

  ISBN 0–415–03069–2
  ISBN 0–415–03070–6 pbk

Library of Congress Cataloging in Publication Data

Also applied for

Contents

Tables and figures

Tables

Figures

Stillman School's a West Indian study: some racial considerations in West Indian ...

The family of the early industrial ...

The natural history of the record, 1951 to 1954.

He and seven other families: a case study of well-off families and work.

Grandsons: the popular conception that ...

Industrial capitalism I: small-scale enterprise in the planning and present-day economy in Lessan, 1956.

Household structure and kin marriage rates in rural society, in Britain.

Class consciousness, class conflict in rural Southern England and the rise of ...

Acknowledgements

The research on which this book draws was supported for several years by Bristol Polytechnic, and during that time I received considerable help and advice from numerous colleagues. In particular David Garnett and Alan Murie were generous with their time and comments. Latterly I was encouraged by Murray Stewart and Michael Harloe to press ahead with publication. I also wish to acknowledge the help derived from the opportunity to present papers to Housing Studies Group seminars at Bristol, Cambridge, and Glasgow.

The Chartered Institute of Public Finance and Accountancy (CIPFA) were remarkably trusting in lending me a huge quantity of data on local-authority rents and housing-revenue accounts, without which the research would have been much more difficult to conduct. CIPFA staff were also always very helpful in answering requests for clarification.

I am grateful to the Institute of Housing for the opportunity to become involved in discussions about the new regime for local-authority housing finance.

On the production side I must express thanks to Chris Wade for drawing up the figures, to Angela Findlay for transforming the manuscript into publishable form, and to Robert for lending me his calculator for so long. Finally I owe a continuing debt to my wife, Mina, for her understanding and support, and to Robert and Alexander for their grasp of the need for so much quiet when 'Daddy's working'.

Peter Malpass
January 1989

Introduction

During the 1980s the pattern of housing provision in Britain has been changing rapidly and in ways not previously experienced. In addition the whole nature and tenor of public debate about housing is now markedly different from that of the 1960s and 1970s. Whilst a number of different factors have contributed to the pace and character of these changes, it is clear that government policies have had an important part to play. Three consecutive election victories, together with continuity of leadership have given the Conservative Party the opportunity to pursue radical measures in key areas of social and economic policy. Reshaping housing policy has been, and remains, an important part of the wider strategy to transform British society. Between 1980 and 1986 there were ten Acts of Parliament directly affecting housing, and yet this stream of legislation has been followed by the Housing Act, 1988, which is itself only the first of a two-part programme of reform designed to effect a permanent restructuring of housing provision.

The significance of these developments should not be underestimated, for what has been happening in recent years represents more than a change of emphasis; it is a challenge to some long-established and hitherto widely accepted assumptions about the nature and direction of housing and housing policy in Britain. The Thatcherite approach to housing can be summarised by saying that, first, the government appears to be determined to explore the limits to the growth of home ownership. This remains the overwhelmingly favoured form of tenure, to which an ever increasing proportion of the population is encouraged to aspire. However, in some respects expansion is becoming more difficult than in the past, because the great majority of established households who are willing and able to buy houses has already done so. Further proportionate growth in home ownership depends upon drawing in more and more low-income purchasers for whom the much vaunted benefits of ownership may not be readily obtainable and for whom investment in housing may not be the best use of their limited income. An additional consideration, which is likely to become more significant as the end of the century draws nearer, is a possible slackening of demand,

1

reflecting the declining numbers of people in the twenty-to-thirty age range (due to birth rate trends in the late 1960s and 1970s). Nevertheless, the government remains committed to further expansion of home ownership, and retains a battery of valuable incentives designed to attract more and more people into house purchase.

Second, the governments led by Margaret Thatcher have displayed an attitude and level of hostility towards local authority housing which represents a departure from the approaches of previous governments over a long period, arguably since the First World War. Hitherto it was accepted by governments of both left and right that local authority housing had a continuing long-term role to play, and that councils should continue to act as major providers of new rented housing. As a result, although there were changes of emphasis in housing policy, the stock of dwellings owned by local authorities continued to grow throughout the period 1919–79. A measure of the determination and achievement of the right during the 1980s is that the sixty-year growth of council housing has been stopped and, more significantly, put into reverse. The number of dwellings owned by local authorities in Great Britain declined by 673,000 between 1979 and 1986 (from 31.5 per cent to 26.7 per cent), and now the role of local authorities as providers of housing is being openly and officially questioned. This is more than a shift of emphasis; it is a challenge to local authority housing in principle.

Third, having reversed the growth of council housing the government has now embarked on an attempt to stem the long decline of private renting. Deregulation of private sector rents and the erosion of security of tenure are coupled with measures to reprivatise the housing associations, which since the mid-1970s have come to be seen as part of the public sector.

All this amounts to a concerted attempt to achieve a more fully privatised, market-based housing system in which local authorities would have a minimal role as providers of housing, acting instead primarily as enablers of provision by other agencies. Persistent themes in recent housing debates refer to the residualisation of local authority housing and the erosion of local autonomy in the face of growing central government assertiveness. In pursuing its housing objectives since 1980 the government has deployed a number of innovative policy instruments which lend support to interpretations of this kind. Given the radicalism and scope of the government's policies there is a temptation to identify 1979 as a key turning point and to see developments in the 1980s in isolation from what went before. The tendency to treat the election of the first Thatcher government as a watershed event is reinforced by the subsequent pace of change which sometimes makes it difficult to keep up with what is happening now, without trying to relate it to past experience. Whilst it may be convenient to concentrate on contemporary developments, explanations which fail to take account of the longer term are likely to be less than adequate. It is during periods of rapid change that it is especially necessary to retain a sense of historical perspective and to identify the continuities as well as the discontinuities.

In this respect the title *Reshaping Housing Policy* should be seen as referring both to contemporary developments and to processes which are much longer term, with their roots embedded in earlier decades. This book adopts a historical approach to the problem of how to understand the present. In doing so it deals mainly with the period since 1945 and concentrates on issues of rents and subsidies, especially in the local authority sector, as a way of examining longer-term trends. Questions of rents and subsidies lie at the heart of the politics of housing. The issues of how much tenants should pay for their accommodation, and how subsidies, if any, should be structured and delivered, have never been far below the surface of domestic British politics in the twentieth century, and at certain times they have given rise to great set-piece conflicts. For instance, in 1915 it was private tenants' protesting against unjustified rent increases which brought about emergency legislation to impose rent controls on landlords. On the other hand, in 1972 it was council tenants who opposed a Conservative government's attempt to raise rents and reduce and redistribute subsidies. In the early 1980s a major restructuring of local authority housing finance, again involving very large rent increases, attracted much less public criticism, partly because of the controversy surrounding the simultaneous implementation of the local authority tenants' right to buy. In the late 1980s the rents issue has returned to prominence once more, initially in relation to the deregulation of the private sector but also in the context of a wider recasting of local-authority housing finance. Higher rents in all sectors is a central element in the strategy to restructure the housing system, but it is not a straightforward uncomplicated policy for there are obstacles and contradictions to be confronted, as later chapters will demonstrate.

Despite the importance and political salience of these issues the academic literature on council rents and subsidies policy is sparse, the most recent extended discussion being Parker's work published in 1967.[1] The main aim here is to provide both an account of rents and subsidies policies in the postwar period, and a perspective on current policy changes which is informed by a number of more general themes such as residualisation, continuity in policy and the complexity of central–local relations. On the specific subject matter of rents and subsidies policies the objective is to provide an alternative to those accounts which emphasise the frequent and detailed changes in legislation. The analysis is structured around a framework which recognises the similarities as well as the differences, the continuities as well as the changes, and which refers to the gradual, yet strikingly consistent, departure from a system based on historic cost pricing with general subsidies, and the subsequent search for a politically acceptable and durable pricing system based on some measure of current value, supported by means-tested assistance for the least well off.

It is argued that this reshaping of rents and subsidies stretching back to the mid-1950s represents a residualisation of housing policy, in the sense that it has made council housing simultaneously more expensive for better-off tenants and yet more affordable for the least well off. Thus one of the aims of the book is to develop an understanding of residualisation as a process which was well established before the collapse of the so-called post-war consensus in the mid-1970s or the advent of Thatcherism after 1979.

This is linked to the second theme, that of the importance of continuity in policy development. There are two points to be made here. The first is that identification of consistency in the direction of rents and subsidies policies since the mid-1950s is not to equate continuity with sameness, but to argue that developments in policy can be seen as representing further steps towards established objectives. The second point, following directly from the first, is that there is a distinction between *policy objectives* and *policy instruments*, and there may be continuity of objectives throughout periods of radical change in the instruments used to pursue these objectives. Equally, there may be important changes of policy objectives without recourse to legislation. In this sense, then, what is being argued here is that it can be misleading to concentrate exclusively on major legislative events in attempting to understand policy development.

The third theme refers to the importance of both central and local government in explanations of housing policy processes, and in particular the richness and complexity of central–local relationships. It is tempting, especially in the 1980s, to characterise relations between central and local government in terms of conflict, with central government becoming increasingly assertive and local authorities suffering severe erosion of their cherished automony. Whilst this is not wrong it is only part of the whole picture. Local autonomy remains significant, and elected representatives' commitment to retaining some control over policy and resources in their own areas continues to be a factor which central government has to take into account. However, it is not just a question of local automony and local resistance to central policy. In addition, it is necessary to recognise wide variation in circumstances from one authority to another. This means that central policy has different meaning for different authorities, and that the constraining power of central policy will vary too, with the likely result that local circumstances will continue to vary and that variation may actually increase. The distinctive feature of this book is that it draws on research on rents and subsidies policy which looks at both central and local levels, using information covering a wide range of authorities over a long period of time. The results help to explain why successive governments have been drawn into new legislation on rents and subsidies, and why they have found it so difficult to devise lasting solutions.

Structure of the book

The book falls into three parts. The first three chapters are broadly introductory, the middle four chapters present the historical narrative of events since 1945, and the last two chapters are concerned with prospects for the future.

Chapter 1 outlines the main features of recent housing policies which have prompted references to the impending residualisation of council housing and looks at the evidence on the changing social composition of the council sector. This is followed by a review of the literature dealing with residualisation, marginalisation, and related attempts to conceptualise changes in housing provision.

Chapter 2 provides an overview of developments in public housing since 1919, referring to rent levels and pricing policies between the wars as well as more general indicators of changing roles for and perceptions of municipal housing provision over the period as a whole.

Chapter 3 is an important chapter, setting up the conceptual framework which underpins the historical account in subsequent chapters. It introduces the terminology necessary for understanding local authority housing finance and explains the basic principles upon which rents and subsidies policies have been built at different times.

Chapters 4 and 5 deal with the quarter century after the Second World War, during which time there were several changes in the level and method of calculation of housing subsidies, all within the framework of historic cost pricing, as explained in Chapter 3. The importance of these chapters is the elaboration of the way in which the flexibility of historic cost pricing permitted a major change of policy in 1955, and how flexibility had given way to rigidity and demands for change by the end of the 1960s.

Chapter 6 looks at the period 1972–9, during which an attempt was made to establish a new legislative framework, based on 'fair rents', deficit subsidy, and rent rebates. This controversial measure was abandoned in 1974, to be replaced by a temporary system, pending new proposals for reform. It is shown that the proposals eventually produced were very similar in certain respects to the system introduced in 1972.

Chapter 7 examines the restructuring of rents and subsidies arrangements in the early 1980s including the subsidy system introduced in the Housing Act, 1980, the housing aspects of the block-grant changes in the Local Government, Planning and Land Act, 1980, and the new housing benefit arrangements. An important part of the chapter is analysis of the implementation of the system and the variation in its impact at local level.

Chapter 8 draws out from the preceding historical account a discussion of the issues to be confronted and the problems to be overcome in devising an efficient, equitable, and durable system of local authority housing finance, in a situation where local circumstances are highly variable, and most tenants rely on housing benefit. It goes on to provide a description and critical evaluation of the government's proposals for reform of local authority housing finance. The final chapter draws together the themes of the book, arguing that the policies on rents and subsidies that were effective in the long period when governments were seeking to expand home ownership and residualise public housing are no longer appropriate in an era when the transition to a residualised public sector is approaching completion.

Reference

1 Parker, R., *The Rents of Council Houses*, Bell, London, 1967.

Chapter one

Towards a 'residual' public sector?

The decline of council housing

Council housing in Britain is in decline. The extent and rate of decline vary in different parts of the country, but the signs are unmistakable and much discussed. Comparison with the period immediately after the Second World War highlights the bleakness of the present situation. Forty years ago the public sector was the fastest growing part of the housing system, favoured by the then Labour government as the main provider of new homes to tackle the huge post-war housing problem. In 1945 Aneurin Bevan, the Minister of Health (then responsible for housing), told the House of Commons:

> we shall ask the local authorities to be the main instruments for the housing programme. It is a principle of the first importance that the local authorities must be looked to as the organisations and the source for the building of the main bulk of the housing programme. The local authorities are admirably suited for this purpose.[1]

Contrast this with the view of the Conservative Minister of Housing in 1987, William Waldegrave:

> I can see no arguments for generalised new build by councils, now or in the future... The next great push after the right to buy should be to get rid of the state as a big landlord and bring housing back to the community [sic].[2]

In the late 1940s the level of output of council houses was high, quality was good, in the sense that most new housing was in the form of two-storey, three-bedroomed houses of generous proportions, and the image of council housing was generally positive. Forty years later the position could hardly be more different: output is barely a tenth of the level achieved in 1948; new building increasingly emphasises small, one-bedroomed flats for the

7

elderly and so called 'special needs' groups; there are serious problems of disrepair; and the popular image of council housing has become much less attractive. For many years council housing benefited from comparisons with extensive areas of rundown private rented housing, where bathrooms, inside toilets and piped hot water were often lacking. In this context local authorities were providing modern, high-quality, high-amenity accommodation. Now, however, the picture is very different, partly because of the reduction in numbers of older houses lacking basic amenities and partly because council housing itself is no longer uniformly modern. In addition, a significant and highly visible proportion of the municipal stock built in the 1960s and 1970s is widely seen as providing an undesirable and unsatisfactory residential environment. In particular the construction of high-rise blocks of flats has been seen as contributing to the 'delegitimation' of council housing as a whole.[3] Thus, whereas in the past the typical council house was a traditionally built, brick-and-tile, semi-detached, three-bedroomed house with a garden on a low-density estate, public perceptions are now more likely to contain negative imagery such as high-rise, system-built flats, on high-density estates plagued by crime and vandalism.

The decline of council housing is a complex process and can be measured in a variety of ways. The most obvious indicators of decline refer to the total size of the stock, in both absolute and proportionate terms. The public sector reached its maximum size in 1979, when it contained over 6.5 million dwellings in Great Britain as a whole. By December 1986 the figure had fallen to under 5.9 million.[4] Figure 1.1 shows the decline of council housing as a percentage of the total; from a peak of 31.7 per cent in the late 1970s it had declined to 26.7 per cent in 1986. It is worth noting here that the figures for England alone show that owner occupation has been consistently higher, and council housing consistently lower, than in Great Britain as a whole. By 1986 council housing represented only 24.4 per cent of the stock in England compared to 49.4 per cent in Scotland.

Measures of housing quality refer to the type and size of dwellings, and the state of repair. The best available statistics on dwelling type show that the proportion of flats in the council stock in England and Wales increased from 31.3 per cent in 1976 to 35.0 per cent in 1986.[5] A key factor in the increasing proportion of flats in the public sector in recent years has been the sale of dwellings under the right to buy. According to Forrest and Murie flats were heavily underrepresented in sales under the right to buy and accounted for only 5 per cent of all sales in the period 1981–5.[6] They also show that in Birmingham 98 per cent of sales up to May 1986 were houses as distinct from flats and other dwelling types, and that 35 per cent of the stock of houses had been lost through sales.[7] Meanwhile, the proportion of flats has been increasing because of a shift in the pattern of new building; Chartered Institute of Public Finance and Accountancy (CIPFA) statistics

Figure 1.1 Housing tenure in Great Britain, 1960–87

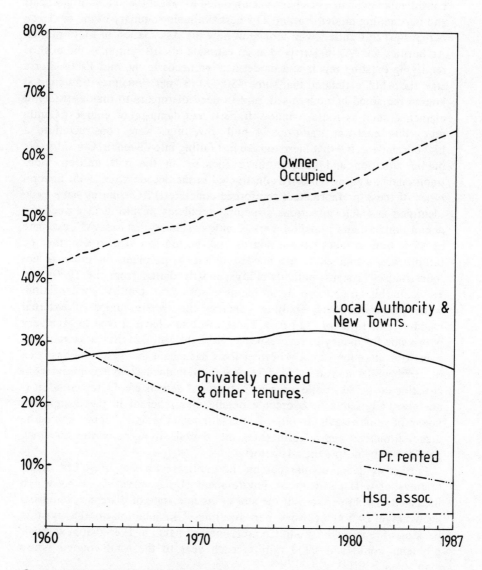

Source: *Annual Abstract of Statistics*, HMSO

suggest an increase of 48 per cent in the number of one-bedroomed flats in England and Wales in the period 1976–1986.[8]

If we turn to the question of the physical state of public sector housing, considerable evidence has been accumulated to reveal the extent of disrepair and outstanding modernisation. The best available summary of the evidence is that by Ted Cantle,[9] who looked at how the Association of Metropolitan Authorities (AMA) had arrived at an estimate of £19 billion as the cost of rectifying existing repair and modernisation needs in the mid-1980s. For a start the AMA estimated that some 450,000 (37 per cent) pre-1939 council houses remained unmodernised, and in need of repairs to major structural elements, such as roofs, window frames, and damp-proof courses. Cantle notes that post-war traditionally built dwellings were constructed to a higher standard, but that these too are fast falling into disrepair. Considerable public attention and concern have focused on the half million 'non-traditional' dwellings, mostly constructed in the decade after 1945. Several types of these prefabricated, reinforced-concrete (PRC) houses have been identified as liable to serious structural problems, resulting in a need for demolition or major remedial work. Cantle concludes that the AMA estimate of £5 billion to rectify these houses may be too low. Up to a further £5 billion was estimated to be needed to tackle problems in more recent industrialised systems-built dwellings, mostly dating from the 1960s and 1970s. In this group there are problems of structural stability, condensation, water penetration, and spalling concrete (i.e. where lumps of external cladding panels simply fall off). These dwellings have proved to give very poor value for money in two respects. First, the fact that they have required expensive attention so early in their lives has meant that new debt has been incurred whilst considerable debt charges remained from the initial construction costs. Second, even where structural defects can be remedied, it is not always possible to overcome deficiencies inherent in the design and layout of some estates. In other words, although the flats themselves can be made attractive and comfortable, the overall living environment may continue to be deeply unsatisfactory.

Further evidence of disrepair in the public sector was presented in the findings of a Department of Environment (DoE) survey in 1985 which indicated that 85 per cent of the stock was in a state of disrepair, requiring an average £4,500 of work per dwelling.[10] In addition to the existing backlog of repairs, the Audit Commission estimated in 1986 that new repair problems could add £900 million each year to the total council house maintenance bill.[11]

The decline of council housing is also a social and political phenomenon, in the sense that is has been downgraded from an important element in the solution of housing problems to a position where it is officially and widely seen as part of the problem; indeed for some people council housing seems to be the housing problem.

Twenty years ago, for instance, the development of new estates by local authorities was seen as an essential component of the policy response to the problems of the overall shortage, the lack of basic amenities, and the widespread disrepair in the private rented sector. In the late 1980s, however, the debate about housing supply has become side-tracked into disputes about private development in the London green belt and official references to disrepair concentrate on the problems in the public sector. Whilst it is, of course, true that the underlying housing situation in Britain has changed since the 1960s, it is also true that there has been a continuing and largely successful attempt to shift the terms of public debate against local authority housing and in favour of private market based alternatives.

For example, in January 1987 John Patten (then Minister of Housing, Urban Affairs and Construction) wrote a piece for the *Guardian*[12] which dwelt at length on the failings of local authorities as providers and managers of housing. The initial assumption underlying the article was that council housing was a failed solution, characterised by a whole litany of deficiencies: poor design and layout, serious disrepair, rising rent arrears, increasing numbers of void properties, and unmanageably large housing departments. 'Above all there is the growing dissatisfaction among many tenants of many estates about the conditions in which they live, and about their lack of control over their own environment and housing.' Patten described council housing as an 'extreme' solution to the problem of providing social rented housing and his successor later described the extent of council housing in Britain as an 'oddity'.[13]

The impact of ministerial criticisms of council housing is heightened by the fact that they often follow statements in praise of owner occupation and the government's record in promoting opportunities for ownership. An example is provided by the statement released by Nicholas Ridley, Secretary of State for the Environment, during the 1987 general election campaign.[14] He began by saying, 'The Housing Policy we have pursued has given us a flourishing owner occupation sector. The Right to Buy has been an unqualified success. People want to be home owners.' But he went on to say,

Monopoly provision by local authorities has not succeeded. There have been serious problems of management. Local authority rent arrears now total over £200 million. Thousands of dwellings are left empty. Performance on repairs is poor and insufficient attention is paid to the wishes of the tenants. Many estates are plagued by vandalism. For many there is no escape from these conditions. In many areas tenants have become totally dependent on their council.

After the election the newly appointed Minister of Housing, William Waldegrave, addressed the Institute of Housing, and again councils were unfavourably compared with the market:

What we now have to do is to change the ethos of the rented sector, to get some of the same sense of commitment on the part of tenants to their property that owner occupation achieves, or to get people off that most deadly of all social drugs, the drug of dependence – on the state, or bureaucracy, or whoever.[15]

Statements of this kind are clearly intended to undermine council housing, both to justify alternative policies and to divert consumers into other, apparently more successful tenures. It is important also to recognise that the attack on council housing is part of a wider campaign against local government itself.[16] Whereas central government claims credit for what it sees as the successful parts of its housing policy (such as the right to buy), responsibility for the perceived failings of council housing is placed firmly on the local authorities themselves. Thus in an interview in *Roof* John Patten rejected poverty as a cause of rent arrears, arguing instead that managerial inefficiency and a lack of political will were the real causes.[17]

Local authority housing management has been the target of considerable criticism in recent years. It was perhaps inevitable in the context of an increasingly aged stock and a much reduced supply of new housing that attention would shift to the management of the existing stock. The complaints of the tenants have been seized upon by a government opposed not just to the way council housing is managed but to the very existence of a substantial municipal housing service. Support for the government's attack on standards of housing management has come from the Audit Commission which published a report bluntly titled *Managing the Crisis in Council Housing*.[18] This report called for a range of improvements in housing management, including a strengthening of the position of the chief officer in relation to the elected representatives, referring to 'political interference' in day-to-day management activities. The Commission claimed that, if its proposals were implemented by local authorities, then there would be substantial savings and benefits; 'excessive' administration costs could be reduced by up to £100m. per year, the number of empty properties could be reduced by up to 25,000, use of bed-and-breakfast hotels for the homeless could be reduced by a quarter and rent arrears could be cut by £100m. or more. This severe criticism of current local authority performance was followed up in a further report focusing on housing maintenance.[19] The Commission's assessment of the problem was that many authorities had neglected repairs over a long period, they continued to operate very slow and inefficient repairs services, and they charged rents that were too low to ensure an adequate standard of maintenance.

Further criticism of local authorities' housing management practices has come from the DoE-sponsored Priority Estates Projects (PEP). The critique formulated within PEP has been most forcefully expressed by Anne

Power who argues that local authorities have concentrated on building up a large stock of houses, paying too little attention to the management of their housing, with the result that services are fragmented, bureaucratic, and remote from tenants.[20] Power also argues that 'it was inevitable that local authorities would first be overtaken by the scale of their operation and then be prevented by the very scale from responding to the crisis it provoked.'[21]

Whilst for Anne Power the problem is primarily one of management, other academic commentators joining in the campaign of denigration of council housing have developed different themes. Most notably, Alice Coleman places the emphasis on design and its impact on behaviour.[22] Her research purported to show that certain designs were closely associated with a high incidence of 'social malaise' (as she defined it). The study attracted considerable criticism from other researchers,[23] mainly in terms of research method and the validity of the conclusions. In addition, it is important to consider Coleman's underlying analytical method. She starts from a behavioural definition of the problem of council housing – litter, graffiti, vandalism, etc. She then proposes that design might be a key influence on behaviour and, having convinced herself that it is, she goes on to argue that the sorts of designs that her research shows to be 'disadvantaging' are the result of the utopian idealism of central government bureaucrats, working through local housing authorities. The main purpose of Coleman's book is to attack council housing as such by seeking to demonstrate that public provision leads to inappropriate design, whereas the private market produces housing which is socially successful. For her the speculatively built 1930s semi-detached house represents the high point of residential design.[24]

A different line of attack is adopted by Minford, Peel, and Ashton.[25] These authors are much more explicit than Coleman in suggesting a return to a free market in all rented housing. Their criticism of council housing is that it emerged as a response to the reduction in the supply of private sector rented housing, following misguided state-imposed rent controls, and that over time the public sector has become a major barrier to labour mobility. Minford *et al.* identify the relatively low levels of council rents (45 per cent below market level, according to their calculations) and restrictions on access to the local authority sector as two key causes of distortion in the housing and labour markets. In addition to deregulation of rents in all tenures, their prescription for housing policy involves measures to reduce substantially the size of the public sector, including the introduction of a new statutory ground for eviction, namely that tenants are deemed to have the capacity to find alternative accommodation in the private sector.

In the face of attacks of this kind and the continuing decline of council housing, the response from defenders of the public sector has been muted. As Pahl pointed out some fifteen years ago, compared to the National Health Service and the education system, council housing has lacked its champions.[26] As a result its detractors have been largely unchallenged and

13

public housing has become labelled as a failure. In this context debate has moved away from issues of growth and development, turning instead to questions of contraction and residualisation. For instance, in the book referred to above, Minford *et al.* openly call for council housing to be confined to a minimal role of providing for 'renters of the last resort', defined by the authors as the poor, the old, the handicapped, and the unfortunate.[27] In various ways the reshaping of housing policy in the 1980s has been, and is, designed to bring about just this sort of residual public sector.

Housing policy in the 1980s

Reference has been made above to the undermining of council housing in the political rhetoric of ministerial speeches. This section reviews the policies that lie behind the decline and residualisation of council housing.[28] The broad housing policy objectives for the 1980s were set out by Michael Heseltine in a speech in June 1979, shortly after his appointment as Secretary of State for the Environment.[29] Addressing the Institute of Housing Annual Conference he identified four objectives:

(i) to increase individual freedom of choice and sense of personal opportunity. This, he explained, meant expansion of opportunities for home ownership, claiming 'Dreams are going to come true for many more people'.
(ii) continuing improvement in the quality of housing.
(iii) greater value for money (to be achieved partly by removing restraints on private house builders).
(iv) better use of resources, by concentrating them where housing needs are most acute.

Notably absent from this and subsequent statements of policy objectives have been references to building targets and homelessness. Heseltine pointedly refused to estimate future housing requirements, preferring to concentrate on 'what the country can afford' and the need to create a climate in which private builders could flourish.[30] The most recent statement of housing objectives, in the White Paper of 1987,[31] showed some changes of emphasis compared with the early 1980s, referring to new life for the 'independent' rented sector and a different (i.e. diminished) role for local authorities, but there was still no reference to homelessness. Indeed, critics were quick to point out that the word homelessness did not appear anywhere in the White Paper.

The decline of council housing in the 1980s has to be seen in the context of a growing commitment to private market solutions, and gathering, wider hostility to local government as such. Policies directly aimed at the council housing sector can be divided into three categories:

(i) measures designed to privatise the existing stock;
(ii) restriction on capital investment by local authorities;
(iii) changes in the terms on which tenants rent their homes.

After taking office in May 1979 the new Conservative government lost no time in moving towards implementation of its first wave of policies directly affecting council housing. In anticipation of the introduction of a statutory right for council tenants to buy their homes the Secretary of State announced that local authorities were to be permitted to sell at discounts of up to 50 per cent less than the market value. The actual right to buy was introduced as the centrepiece of the Housing Act, 1980, and took effect from October 1980. Secure tenants of three years' standing were given the right to buy at a discount of 33 per cent, increasing by 1 per cent for each additional year's tenancy, up to a maximum of 50 per cent after twenty years. In addition, tenants were entitled to a mortgage from their local authority. As Table 1.1 shows, there was a rapid increase in sales in 1980, 1981 and 1982, reflecting pent-up demand, but in subsequent years the rate of sales declined to less than half the 1982 peak.

The figures below indicate that sales exceeded new building in each year after 1980, something which had never happened before, but in addition it is worth pointing out that in the early 1980s, when private-sector building was experiencing a slump in output, the sale of council houses served to sustain a rapid growth in owner occupation. In the period 1980–4 sales exceeded new building by private developers, something else which had never happened before.

Table 1.1 Sales and new building by local authorities 1979–87

	All sales	New building
1979	41,665	69,734
1980	81,485	70,824
1981	102,825	49,407
1982	201,880	30,176
1983	145,585	29,823
1984	103,180	29,185
1985	92,295	23,478
1986	88,748	18,532
1987	105,567	16,089

Source: *Housing and Construction Statistics*, HMSO.

The sale of council housing has been a major factor in the changing character of public housing in the 1980s. In the United Kingdom as a whole over one million dwellings have been sold so far. However, the real impact is not to be measured in aggregate terms but in the uneven pattern of sales both within and between the regions. The fullest analysis and discussion is that provided by Forrest and Murie,[32] and it is sufficient here to note that their research confirms earlier predictions that the best and most desirable dwellings, on the most attractive estates, would sell in greater numbers than the flats and dwellings in unattractive locations; and that purchasers are not representative of council tenants as a whole but on the contrary they tend to be middle-aged people in relatively well-paid employment. Thus the right to buy has tended to remove selectively the better-off tenants and the better parts of the housing stock, leaving behind the poorer tenants and those living in dwellings that no one wants to buy, even at a discount. In order to maintain demand and spread sales across the wider spectrum of dwellings discounts were increased, first in 1984 and then again in 1986. The Housing and Building Control Act, 1984, reduced the residential qualification from three years to two, providing tenants with a 32 per cent discount after two years' occupation; at the same time the maximum discount was raised up to 60 per cent for tenants of thirty or more years. In 1986 the Housing and Planning Act raised the level of subsidy on flats to 44 per cent after two years, raising it by 2 per cent per year to a maximum of 70 per cent after just fifteen years.

The Housing and Planning Act, 1986, also launched, in a rather tentative fashion, the second wave of privatisation: estate sales and further diversification of control. Local authorities were given additional powers to dispose of blocks or whole estates to private developers who required vacant possession. The Act made it possible for authorities to remove tenants, even against their will, in order to dispose of blocks or estates, although tenants were to be given suitable alternative accommodation. This development was clearly not consistent with the language of tenants' rights associated with sales to individual occupiers. It was a response to the problem of how to continue the break-up of public housing, given that some estates had proved to be so unattractive to tenants. It was also a response to the recognition, on the one hand, that such estates often required massive investment, if not complete redevelopment, and, on the other hand, a reluctance to sanction the public expenditure needed to enable local authorities to carry out the work themselves.

By 1987 over 150,000 dwellings had been sold in block schemes. The majority of these were in two areas, Thamesmead in south-east London and Cantril Farm (renamed Stockbridge Village) in Knowsley, but other estates had been sold with vacant possession for refurbishment and resale by property developers such as Regalian, a company which has very profitably exploited opportunities offered by right-wing Conservative boroughs like Wandsworth.[33]

In addition to disposals initiated by local authorities themselves, the 1986 Act required councils to give a reasoned response to proposals from tenants wishing to take over management or ownership of their estates. In the Housing White Paper of 1987 the government tried to link the idea of tenant power and choice to the disposal of estates in proposals to require local authorities to sell to new landlords. Ministerial statements referred to the introduction of a 'right' for tenants to transfer to a new landlord, but the publication of the Housing Bill made it clear that in fact what was being proposed was a right for landlords to buy selected parts of the public sector. Part IV of the Housing Act, 1988, set out the arrangements by which approved landlords can exercise their right to acquire parts of the municipal housing stock, unless a majority of the tenants vote against the sale.

Further erosion of the public-sector stock is envisaged in Part III of the Act, which established powers for the Secretary of State to set up Housing Action Trusts (HATs). These bodies are designed to take over those parts of the local authority stock which are deemed to be so problematic as to be beyond the abilities of the local authorities to deal with them. The first six HATs were announced in July 1988,[34] following delay associated with opposition from local authorities and particularly from tenants in one area, Hulme, in Manchester, which had been widely seen as a prime target for HAT treatment. The first set of HATs take 24,500 dwellings out of local authority ownership. With a budget of £125m. for the first three years, the HATs are charged with the task of improving the environment so that estates can be resold, to individual home owners, new landlords or con-ceivably back to the local authority (if it can afford to repurchase at the new, post-improvement value).

Taken together, the right to buy, the change of landlord scheme, and HATs represent a comprehensive package of measures designed to carry forward the break-up of public sector housing. An interesting development prompted by the publication of the White Paper in 1987 has been the interest shown by many local authorities in the idea of transferring the whole of their housing stock to a new organisation set up by the authority for the purpose, or to an existing housing association. Amongst the first to pursue this route were Rochford, Salisbury, Torbay, Gloucester and Ynys Mon, but in the early months of 1988 several dozen more authorities were reported to be drawing up detailed plans to dispose of all their houses, and around two hundred (50 per cent of English and Welsh authorities) had sought advice from central government.[35] Whether this is seen as going beyond the intentions of the government, or as subverting those intentions by seeking to keep the stock together, is open to debate, but it implies that the break-up of the public sector is likely to proceed further than most would have thought possible before the 1987 general election.

One of the arguments advanced by supporters of the wholesale transfer of local authority housing to new bodies is that such moves could provide access to investment capital, thereby facilitating the new building and renovation which are so difficult within the confines of the public sector. As soon as the Conservatives took office in 1979, the constraints on local authority capital expenditure began to tighten. The determination of the new government was shown by its decision, after the start of the financial year 1979–80, to reduce capital allocations approved for that year by the previous Labour government. This was followed by a moratorium on local authority capital spending in the second half of 1980–1. The housing strategies and investment programme system (HIPs), which had been presented as a means of facilitating forward planning and local autonomy in capital spending when it was introduced in 1977–8, was rapidly turned into a mechanism for constraining investment. It has been argued, for instance by Leather, that from an initial justification in terms of both planning and control elements HIPs 'have evolved into a narrower mechanism for short-term financial control and the imposition of national housing policy objectives at local level.'[36] In practice HIPs have given local authorities freedom to spend less and less as Table 1.2 shows.

Table 1.2 Housing strategies and investment programme (HIP) allocations 1978–9 to 1987–8

1978–9	£2,432m	1983–4	£1,769m
1979–80	£2,837m	1984–5	£1,771m
1980–1	£2,186m	1985–6	£1,572m
1981–2	£1,761m	1986–7	£1,361m
1982–3	£1,847m	1987–8	£1,262m

The figures in the table are cash amounts, taking no account of inflation, which means that in real terms local authorities' ability to borrow for housing purposes has been cut by much more than the 50 per cent implied in the comparison of figures for 1978–9 and 1987–8. In addition, local authorities' freedom to determine spending patterns within the agreed allocations has been eroded by the emergence of 'top slicing', a procedure whereby the Department of Environment (DoE) removes a sum from the total investment allocation before the remainder is distributed to local authorities. This top slice is then distributed in relation to specific schemes approved by DoE through its Estate Action Unit (formerly the Urban Housing Renewal Unit). A different sort of earmarking of HIP resources emerged in the Housing Defects Act, 1984, which placed a statutory duty on authorities to assist owners of certain types of defective, prefabricated reinforced-concrete (PRC) dwellings purchased under the right to buy. In aggregate financial terms these two examples are not particularly significant (although at the local level they can be). However, a third illustration of the erosion of the HIP system refers to the government's pre-election treatment of improvement grant spending in 1982–3, when there was a selective relaxation of controls on capital spending, resulting in a considerable increase in improvement grant expenditure, some of which had to be met out of reduced 'normal' HIP allocations in later years.

In addition to controls via HIPs, the government has operated a system of increasingly severe constraints on local authority freedom to dispose of capital receipts arising from the sale of houses and land. Housing capital receipts have become a very important aspect of local housing finance in the 1980s, as well as providing the largest proportion of receipts from all asset sales. Forrest and Murie have calculated that in the period 1980–1 to 1985–6 housing capital receipts generated over £9b., compared with less than £7.4b. from all other privatisation schemes put together.[37] The government's own estimate of housing capital receipts is £12.5b. in the period 1981–2 to 1987–8.[38] Following the introduction of the right to buy, local authorities began to take in large capital sums (reflecting the popularity of building society mortgages amongst people buying their council houses). Initially authorities were permitted to augment their HIP allocation by up to 50 per cent of receipts accrued from previous years. By the end of 1984 the total of accrued capital receipts was estimated at £5b., and authorities began to spend. The government responded by imposing a tighter limit of 40 per cent on both current and accrued receipts in 1984–5, and from 1985–6 authorities were permitted to spend only 20 per cent of their receipts. However, receipts continued to pour in and, even after using some £4.5b. to repay outstanding debts, local authorities in England and Wales still held £4.4b.in cash at the end of 1987–8.[39]

Government constraints on borrowing through the HIP system and expenditure of capital receipts indicate a determination to limit investment in public housing, and a disregard for local autonomy in the face of overriding commitment to control of public expenditure. Local authorities have been given clear signals that 'The Government does not expect local authorities to add significantly to the stocks of rented housing in their direct ownership.'[40] Capital controls must be seen as a major factor in the declining levels of new building by local authorities throughout the decade (see Table 1.1. above). New building by local authorities has reached its lowest level since 1924, and since 1983–4 local authority output has been overtaken by that of the housing associations.

However, whilst the centrally imposed constraints on investment have been real and severe, there is no way of telling what the level of investment would have been in the absence of those constraints. The point to note here is that, whereas some authorities have undoubtedly been frustrated in their expenditure aspirations, others have consistently underspent their allocations, and in aggregate there has been a marked change in the pattern of local-authority capital expenditure. Overall, authorities have tended to spend more on repairing existing stock and less on new building.

In areas of less pressing housing need, where, as it happens, capital receipts have tended to be highest, some authorities have been tempted by the revenue advantages of capital receipts and have not been constrained by the 20 per cent limit. By writing off old debt authorities reduce revenue costs, and by lending their capital receipts they generate income for the housing revenue account in the form of interest. Each of these alternatives to investment in new housing has the effect of helping create a surplus on the housing revenue account, and in recent years over 100 authorities have regularly transferred such surpluses into their rates funds (see Chapter 7). It is therefore wrong to interpret the decline in new building simply in terms of central government suppression of local aspirations.

The third area of housing policy directly focused on council housing covers rents, subsidies, and social security assistance with housing costs. Since this is the subject of extended discussion in later chapters, it can be dealt with briefly here. It is sufficient to note that in the early 1980s there was a major restructuring of policy on subsidies, away from general subsidy and towards income-related assistance via the social security system. The effect was to make council housing more expensive for better-off tenants without affecting the position of the least well off. This sharp increase in the real level of unrebated rents in the early 1980s has to be seen alongside the simultaneous introduction and promotion of the right to buy at heavily discounted prices. Higher rents were designed to provide an incentive for better-off tenants to buy their homes, and some supporters of the government have urged greater use of this device.[41] A policy of higher, un-subsidised, council rents, set alongside a policy of discounted sales and mortgage costs subsidised through tax relief, clearly signalled to the better-off tenants that they were unwelcome in a public sector which was seen as appropriate only for those who could not aspire to home ownership.

At the same time this shift in policy changed the terms on which the less well off related to their local authority landlords. Higher rents and more widespread reliance on income-related assistance meant that increasing numbers of tenants confronted their landlord not as people with money in their hand to pay the agreed rent, but as claimants, dependent upon means-tested rebates. This can be seen as having a pauperising effect, and for very large numbers of council tenants their homes have become a form of welfare benefit in kind, since their rent is now paid direct to the authority by the Department of Social Security (DSS).

In addition to these three areas in which government policy has directly and adversely affected council housing, it is important to recognise the wider context of approval and support for home ownership and private renting. The residualisation of council housing is reinforced and intensified by positive endorsement of alternative market-based tenures. Here it is appropriate to refer to the growth and extent of support for home ownership, most obviously through the provision of tax relief on mortgage interest, amounting to £4,750m. in 1987–8, to which can be added the estimate of £3,500m. represented by the exemption of owner-occupied dwellings from capital gains tax.[42] These sums dwarf the amounts of public expenditure on council housing, despite the rhetoric of targeting on people in need, and represent a major redistribution of financial support for housing. The aggregate value of tax relief has grown enormously since the late 1970s during a period when the official measure of public expenditure (excluding tax relief) has declined by no less than 68 per cent (between 1979–80 and 1987–8).[43] Whereas in the past, before the Second World War, it was reasonably accurate to distinguish between subsidised council housing and unsubsidised private housing, that distinction is no longer credible.[44]

In addition to the overwhelmingly positive tone of housing policy in relation to home ownership, it is also necessary to mention the various measures to encourage the 'independent' rented sectors, i.e. private commercial renting and the housing associations. It is highly improbable that renting in its nineteenth-century form can be revived on any scale (even if it were desirable), but the government has introduced specific forms of assistance in addition to rent deregulation in the Housing Act, 1988. First, in the Local Government Act, 1988, local authorities have been given powers to provide financial assistance for the provision of private rented housing and, second, in the 1988 Budget the Chancellor announced tax incentives to private investors through the extension of the business-expansion scheme to cover investment in private rented housing. However, the government recognises that the numerical impact of these schemes is likely to be slight, and the main element in its policy for the independent rented sector involves a much expanded role for housing associations. The new model form of landlordism is based on private finance provided by institutional investors (building societies, pension funds, etc), with housing associations providing the housing management function, and local authorities providing development land at peppercorn rents,[45] or transferring existing estates.

All of these policies together add up to a package which is overwhelmingly biased in favour of home ownership and private renting, and against council housing. But what does this imply for consumer preferences and the social composition of the public sector?

The social composition of council housing

Given the continuing decline of municipal housing and the relative attractions of home ownership, it is hardly surprising that fewer and fewer people aspire to be council tenants, nor that local authorities have increasingly become landlords to people with little real choice in the housing market. A succession of surveys of public opinion has revealed growing numbers of people expressing a clear preference for owner occupation.[46] Table 1.3 indicates the trend in responses to a question about preferred tenure in two years' time.

Table 1.3 Trends in attitudes towards housing tenures, 1967–86

Year	Preferred Tenure (%)			
	Owner occupation	Council renting	Private renting	Don't know
1967	66	23	11	–
1975	69	21	8	3
1978	72	19	5	3
1983	77	16	5	2
1986	77	17	4	3

Sources: 1967–83, *Housing Tenure*, Building Societies Association, London, 1983, p.10
1986, *Housing and Savings 1986*, Technical Report and Tables, BMRB, London, 1986, Table 11

Respondents were also asked in which tenure they expected to be in ten years' time. In 1975, 62 per cent expected to be home owners in ten years, but by 1986 the proportion had risen to 80 per cent. Amongst younger people both the preference for and expectation of home ownership are more marked than amongst people over retirement age. In 1986, 93 per cent of people aged 25–34 expected to own a home within ten years. Amongst council tenants of all ages in the 1986 survey, 46 per cent expected to be home owners within ten years, compared with 44 per cent who expected still to be renting from the local authority. However, it is important to add that no fewer than 77 per cent of council tenants expressed themselves to be either satisfied or very satisfied with their present accommodation.

Changes in consumer preference and demand have contributed to a shifting pattern in social composition of council tenants. In recent years a number of writers have drawn attention to a variety of indicators of change in the social and economic status of council tenants. The importance of this evidence lies in both the picture that it reveals of council housing in the 1980s – a tenure in which large numbers of poor households live – and the contrast with earlier post-war decades. Taking income evidence first, Gray quotes *Family Expenditure Survey (FES)* data for England and Wales which suggest that in 1953–4 only 16 per cent of families in the bottom quarter of the income distribution were council tenants, compared with 43 per cent in 1976.[47] In 1953 local authorities owned about 18 per cent of the stock, and 29 per cent in 1976, and Gray concludes that:

> even taking into account the growth of the sector during this period, the income characteristics of local authority tenants have undergone drastic changes, from being biased away from the lowest income groups in the mid-1950s to strongly emphasise this very group twenty years later.[48]

Robinson and O'Sullivan[49] also drew on *FES* data to compare 1968 and 1978. Their analysis showed that the percentage of households from the bottom three deciles in local authority housing was substantially greater in 1978, and that the increase was particularly marked in the bottom decile, where the percentage rose from 32.5 per cent in 1968 to 56.1 per cent in 1978.

Another analysis of *FES* data, this time by Bentham, dealt with the period 1953–83.[50] He showed how the income gap between council tenants and home owners had widened during this period. The median income of council tenants had declined from only a little below the overall median in 1953 to only 58 per cent of the overall figure by 1983. Bentham calculated that the median income of council tenants had fallen from 89 per cent of the median for home owners in 1953 to 45 per cent in 1983, despite a substantial increase in home ownership drawing in more low-income purchasers. Bentham also looked at income distribution within and between tenures. Table 1.4 shows that whereas in 1953–4 under half of council tenants were in the first two income quartiles, by 1983 the figure was 75 per cent. The proportion in the lowest quartile more than doubled on these figures, whilst the proportion in the highest quartile fell by almost two-thirds. Meanwhile, purchasing owner occupiers had become more markedly concentrated in the highest quartiles.

The 1986 *FES* confirms the contrast between council tenants and owner occupiers: in that year 58.9 per cent of council tenants were in the lowest three income deciles, compared with just 14 per cent of home owners, and the gross normal household weekly income of council tenants was £124.30 on average, whereas for purchasing owners the figure was £343.79[51]

Hamnett's study of tenure differences in terms of socio-economic groups provides an alternative approach.[52] Despite reservations about the data, he showed that, 'Skilled manual workers have moved increasingly into the owner occupied sector, leaving behind them a council sector increasingly dominated by the semi-skilled, the unskilled and the economically inactive.' In the period 1961–81 there was a three-fold increase in the proportion of households counted as economically inactive in the population as a whole, but in the council sector the increase was more than five-fold, from 4.8 per cent in 1961 to 28.0 per cent in 1981.

Table 1.4 Distribution of household income by tenure (percentage of households)

Income quartile	Local authority tenants	Privately Rented		Owner occupiers	
		Unfurnished	Furnished	Purchasing	All
1953–4					
1(lowest)	18.7	31.0	26.0	8.5	19.9
2	28.7	25.8	29.1	20.6	19.6
3	28.8	23.5	26.6	32.1	25.9
4	23.8	19.7	18.3	38.3	34.6
1983					
1	44.3	47.2	41.2	2.3	12.2
2	30.6	25.9	29.6	15.0	21.4
3	17.0	15.6	21.6	34.3	29.8
4	8.1	11.3	7.5	48.4	36.6

Source: G. Benthan, 'Socio-tenurial polarisation in the United Kingdom, 1953–83: the income evidence', *Urban Studies*, vol. 23, no. 2, 1986.

Forrest and Murie state that by 1984 more than half (53 per cent) of households in council housing were headed by an economically inactive person, and that overall nearly two-thirds of council housing heads of households were not working.[53] Two significant factors here are the high incidence of unemployment amongst council tenants and the increase in the proportion of elderly tenants. In 1981 in England council housing comprised just over 28 per cent of the total stock, but 36 per cent of household heads over the age of 60 were in this tenure,[54] and it has been claimed that retired people provide up to a quarter of all new council tenants.[55] Table 1.5 shows how the elderly have become heavily over-represented in local authority housing since the early 1970s. These figures also indicate important changes in younger age groups, with the under 25s becoming over-represented, whilst there have been reductions in the proportions of people aged 30 to 59 who are council tenants.

Table 1.5 Proportions of households of different ages in local authority housing

Age of head of household	1971	1985
	%	%
24 and under	21	32
25–29	24	24
30–44	29	19
45–59	35	27
60–69	32	37
70–79	31	36
80 and over	31	39
All households	31	28

Source: *Social Trends 1988*, HMSO, London, 1988, Table 8.20

Another set of indicators to be considered is provided by the social security statistics. Forrest and Murie have brought together figures for the period 1967 to 1984, showing that in that time the proportion of supplementary benefit claimants who were council tenants rose from 45 per cent to 61 per cent, whereas the proportion who were owner occupiers rose only from 17 per cent to 21 per cent despite the considerable growth in home ownership.[56] Table 1.6 breaks down supplementary benefit claimants into various categories, showing that in each group council tenants predominate. The slight decline between 1984 and 1986 reflects the contraction of the public housing sector.

Table 1.6 Supplementary benefit recipients by tenure, 1972, 1984, and 1986

Tenure	All recipients	Supplementary pensions	Unemployed	Sick and disabled	Single-parent families
1972					
No.(000s)	2,482	1,796	269	183	164
	%	%	%	%	%
Owner occupiers	17	18	14	14	7
Local authority tenants	55	53	53	60	63
Private tenants	29	29	33	26	30
1984					
No.(000s)	3,389	1,550	1,069	151	425
	%	%	%	%	%
Owner occupiers	21	22	22	22	14
Local authority tenants	61	61	55	65	75
Private tenants	17	16	23	13	12
1986					
No.(000s)	3,650	1,556	1,226	174	501
	%	%	%	%	%
Owner occupiers	22	22	23	24	13
Local authority tenants	60	62	52	63	74
Private tenants	18	16	24	13	13

Sources: 1972 and 1984, R. Forrest and A. Murie, *Selling the Welfare State*, Routledge, 1988, p. 68
1986, *Social Security Statistics 1987*, DHSS, HMSO, London.

A more striking contrast between the two main tenures is obtained by looking at the proportions of owners and council tenants claiming supplementary benefit. According to Forrest and Murie the proportion of home owners claiming supplementary benefit rose from just 4 per cent to 5 per cent between 1979 and 1984, despite a very substantial increase in the total number of owners. At the same time the proportion of claiming council tenants rose from 21 per cent to 34 per cent, in a shrinking sector.[57]

A final source of information about the composition of council tenants is the *London Housing Survey, 1986–7*, which showed that, amongst other things, in London as a whole 4 per cent of all households were headed by single parents, but in the council sector the proportion was 9 per cent.[58] On ethnic origin the report showed that nearly half (48 per cent) of Afro-Caribbean households were in council housing, and that this group was underrepresented in owner occupation.[59]

All the indicators referred to in this discussion reflect the tendency of council housing to become the tenure of the least well off and others who are socially and economically disadvantaged. This is not to imply that all council tenants are poor, nor that there are no poor home owners. In the case of owner occupation the emphasis on increasing house prices and access to wealth accumulation should not be allowed to obscure the fact that there is very considerable variation in the incomes of owners, both within and between different regions. The dominant feature of home owner-ship is its heterogeneity, embracing rich and poor. Council housing, on the other hand, is becoming increasingly homogeneous by comparison, with fewer and fewer tenants on above-average earnings and increasing propor-tions of tenants who are outside the workforce altogether.

The final point to make here is to reiterate that the social composition of council housing has been changing for many years and in response to a variety of forces, some of which are relatively specific to housing, whilst others are to do with wider processes of social and economic change. Following sections discuss, first, the housing policies which can be seen to have contributed to the residualisation of council housing and then different perspectives on the interpretation of observable trends.

Perspectives on change in housing provision and housing policy

Recognition that fundamental changes are taking place in the structure of housing provison and housing policy in Britain, and in other advanced capitalist countries, has led to various interpretations of the processes involved. It is important to avoid over-emphasising the role of policy in the explanations of both the nature and pace of change, as Ball has persuasively argued.[60] He suggests that much conventional analysis of housing grossly overrates the power of the state to transform the situation of consumers, and that there is too much emphasis on policy, to the exclusion of wider socio-economic factors. He links this to the suggestion that housing research and analysis have been dominated by the consumption perspective and a misunderstanding of tenure categories. Marcuse[61] and Harloe [62] have made similar points, and the following discussion aims to locate changes in housing in a wider context.

Some writers have discussed the shifting pattern of housing consumption in terms of social polarisation. In an important early contribution in this vein Murie and Forrest argued that housing-market restructuring, aided by housing and taxation policies, was having a significant effect in sorting the population into two socially distinct tenures.[63] The polarisation theme has continued to feature in their work[64] and is central to the comparative study of British and French social housing by Willmott and Murie.[65] Other writers to explore this idea are Hamnett[66] and Somerville,[67] and it is clear that the notion of polarisation provides a very useful way of describing the social consequences of changes which go far beyond housing. Nevertheless it remains essentially descriptive. An alternative approach is to look not at who lives where but at the way in which changing modes of provision determine differences in access to housing. The progressive and accelerating growth of owner occupation, and the corresponding decline of council housing, have been discussed in terms of commodification,[68] which refers to the tendency for market-based commodity relations to spread out and extend into more and more areas of life, as part of the constant search for new markets and the maintenance of the dominance of capitalist ideology. The development of council housing meant that access to a substantial proportion of the housing stock was determined by some measure of need rather than ability to pay. Privatisation through council house sales is clearly important in recommodifying housing consumption, but so too is the restructuring of rents and subsidies policy in a way that moves rents towards market levels. In other words, the commodification process includes not only the promotion of home ownership but also the public sector itself.

However, the future of public housing has been most widely discussed in terms of residualisation. This term is derived from the social policy literature, and in a wider sense it refers to the erosion of the universalist welfare state, a process which has gathered strength in Britain since the advent of Thatcherism. It is interesting to note that, in outlining the residual model of social welfare in the early 1970s, Titmuss linked it to the ideas and beliefs of right-wing economists such as Hayek, Friedman, and followers of the Institute of Economic Affairs, who were to become so influential with the government a decade later.[69] The residual model of social welfare is based on the view that the market and the family should be the main providers of all needs and services, and that the state has a minimal role to play in direct provision, catering only for those who cannot support themselves in the market place or who have no family to support them. It is an approach in which individuals' welfare would closely reflect their position in the labour market. The role of the state, on this view, is to complement the market rather than to compete with it. Thus *residualisation* refers to the processes of moving towards a residual safety-net type of state welfare provision, and in relation to housing it refers to the way in which the local authority sector has begun to take on this role.

One of the earliest references to this idea was Harloe's suggestion that council housing might acquire a residual role, which he described as an 'ambulance service concentrating its efforts on the remaining areas of housing stress and dealing with a variety of "special needs" such as the poor, the homeless, one-parent families, battered wives and blacks.'[70] Subsequent references linking council housing and various uses of residualisation have become common in the housing literature.[71]

Because of the differences in usage it is appropriate to expand a little on what is meant by residualisation. In one sense a residue is what remains after a process of reduction. Discussion of the prospects for a residual public sector emerged during the early 1980s when council house sales were rising rapidly and commentators began to envisage a very much diminished sector, on the scale of public housing in the United States.[72] Others argued that, whilst British council housing might decline numerically, the size of the sector was not as important as who lived in it.[73] On this view a residual public sector was one which catered wholly or largely for people who were so disadvantaged in the housing market that they had effectively no choice but to seek housing from the local authority. Whether the residual public sector was large or small, growing or shrinking, would depend on the factors determining the total size of the group of people who were excluded from the private housing market. The two key sets of factors involved are, first, the state of the economy and the labour market, and second, housing policy and the willingness to subsidise private housing market consumption.

In their discussion of changes in the social relations of housing tenure Forrest and Murie place the emphasis on the restructuring of the labour market, arguing that the declining demand for living labour is producing a larger group of people who are more or less permanently excluded from the labour force. For these authors it is a section of the working class which is being residualised, or marginalised:

An approach to residualisation which emphasises economic and occupational change and powerlessness provides an opportunity to see changes in management style, size and quality of stock or level of subsidy as symptoms or consequences of the powerlessness of those using the service to resist reductions in standards or to achieve high standards. The economic and political powerlessness of this group is both a factor in their becoming and remaining tenants and in the quality and terms of the service they receive. It is important to recognise that the marginalised poor have always tended to be in the worst housing in each tenure and to have the greatest difficulty in negotiating access to and through the housing market. What is new in the present situation is the level of concentration in the public sector especially as the private rented sector declines and the impact of this trend in a period in which the 'residuum' is increasing in size as a consequence of economic and employment changes.[74]

Forrest and Murie take the view that the concept of marginalisation, referring to labour market restructuring, is of greater explanatory value than notions of residualisation that are grounded in a narrower housing perspective. It is certainly true that a focus on the economic marginalisation of many council tenants helps to explain the vulnerablity of council housing to further reductions in size and quality. Given that local authority housing accommodates a lot of unemployed and unskilled workers, and that the housing needs of the skilled, productive working class are increasingly met through owner occupation there is little economic or political pressure to improve the public sector. However, while an emphasis on poverty and marginality is useful in understanding the current vulnerablity of council housing, it does little to explain the processes which brought about the concentration of the least well off in this tenure. The important questions are to do with factors which determine where the marginalised population is housed at different times. To understand that, it is necessary to refer to historic processes of tenure restructuring which are to a considerable extent driven by housing market forces, and to past affluence rather than current poverty – it was rising living standards and full employment in the 1950s and early 1960s which fuelled the growth of home ownership and began to undermine council housing. The residualisation of council housing is not dependent upon the growth of the marginalised poor; on the contrary it reflects a long-standing supply-side preference for private market provision, specifically individual home ownership in the post-1945 period, and growing consumer preference for owner occupation, heavily influenced by housing policy.

Returning to the question of policy, it is necessary to refer to the residualisation of housing policy, or the reshaping of policy in ways designed to bring about a residual council sector. This means policies designed to make private housing more attractive and accessible to better-off households, whilst making council housing less attractive and less accessible to them. It also involves measures to open council housing to the least well off, e.g. through means-tested assistance with rents. A variety of measures have been introduced at different times which have given housing policy a residual appearance. For instance, in the 1930s and late 1950s local authorities were required to concentrate on slum clearance rehousing, leaving to the private sector the role of building for 'general' housing needs. It is important to acknowledge here the distinction between the shape and direction of policy at any one time and the role that public housing fulfils at that time.[75] Whereas policy was residualised in the 1930s and late 1950s, it was not the case that council housing as a whole was residualised in those periods. However, an important feature of the contemporary situation is that an increasingly residualist set of policies exist alongside an increasingly residualised council sector.

It is, of course, arguable that some parts of the council sector have always been residualised, and that in some places, such as Scotland, it is inappropriate to describe a tenure embracing half the population as residual.[76] It is necessary, therefore, to acknowledge the extent and significance of local variations in terms of both policy implementation and outcomes. In this context it is appropriate to mention the link between the pursuit of residualist housing policy and the increasing central government assertiveness in relation to local housing action. The pressure to residualise council housing can be seen as setting up and exacerbating tensions between central and local government. Central and local government have different aims, objectives, and preoccupations in relation to housing. Whereas the centre is concerned with overall economic regulation and maintenance of profitable conditions for private capital, local government is more concerned with local political pressures, the management of the housing stock, and costs falling on local residents in the form of rents and rates. A number of significant policy developments affecting council rents, rebates, sales, investment, and homelessness, all involving reductions in local autonomy can be explained against this background. From the point of view of central government the expansion of home ownership and the residualisation of council housing may appear to be a highly attractive and necessary development. But from the point of view of local councillors, a residual public sector is not necessarily so appealing, offering little political advantage though at the same time carrying political risks.

To sum up this discussion, there are three key elements to be borne in mind in relation to residualisation: the nature of the housing stock, the social composition of the tenants and the content of policies affecting housing. Residualisation is a complex phenomenon, which requires consideration of developments in all tenures, the actions of central and local government, and changes occurring over a prolonged period of time. The title of this chapter posed the question of whether Britain is moving towards a residual public housing sector. The evidence presented above has demonstrated that this is in fact the case, and the following chapter provides a historical overview which shows how deeply rooted are the residualising forces.

References

1 *House of Commons Debates*, vol. 414, October 1945, col. 1222.
2 William Waldegrave, speech in Bristol, 28 August 1987, Conservative Central Office, London.
3 P. Dunleavy, *The Politics of Mass Housing in Britain 1945–75*, Clarendon Press, London, 1981.
4 *Housing and Construction Statistics, 1976–1986*, HMSO, 1987, Table 9.3.
5 CIPFA (Chartered Institute of Public Finance and Accountancy), *Housing Statistics, Part 1, Rents, Rebates and Allowances at April 1976, and Housing Rents Statistics, 1986*.

6 R. Forrest and A. Murie, *Selling the Welfare State: The Privatisation of Public Housing*, Routledge, London, 1988, p.121.

7 ibid., p.157.

8 CIPFA, op. cit.

9 T. Cantle, 'The deterioration of public sector housing', in P. Malpass (ed.), *The Housing Crisis*, Croom Helm, London, 1986.

10 Department of the Environment, *An Inquiry into the Condition of the Local Authority Housing Stock in England*, 1985.

11 Audit Commission, *Improving Council House Maintenance*, HMSO, London, 1986, p.2.

12 'Housing – room for a new view', *Guardian*, 30 January 1987.

13 W. Waldegrave, op. cit., p.8.

14 Conservative Central Office, 19 May, 1987.

15 W. Waldegrave, *Address to the Institute of Housing Conference*, Brighton, 19 June 1987.

16 S. Duncan and M Goodwin, *The Local State and Uneven Development: Behind the Local Government Crisis*, Polity Press, Cambridge, 1988.

17 *Roof*, January–February 1987, p.24.

18 Audit Commission, *Managing the Crisis in Council Housing*, HMSO, 1986

19 *Improving Council House Maintenance*, op.cit.

20 A. Power, *Property Before People, the Management of Twentieth Century Council Housing*, Allen & Unwin, London, 1987.

21 A. Power, *The Crisis in Council Housing: Is Public Housing Manageable?* Discussion Paper no. 21, Welfare State Programme, LSE, London, September 1987, p.7.

22 A. Coleman, *Utopia on Trial*, Hilary Shipman, London, 1985.

23 N Teymur, T Markus, and T Woolley (eds), *Rehumanising Housing*, Butterworth, London, 1988.

24 A. Coleman, op.cit., pp.102–3.

25 P. Minford, M. Peel, and P. Ashton, *The Housing Morass: Regulation, Immobility and Unemployment*, Institute of Economic Affairs, London, 1987.

26 R. Pahl, foreword in M. Harloe, R. Issacharoff, and R. Minns, *The Organisation of Housing*, Heinemann, London, 1974. p.x.

27 P. Minford *et al.*, op. cit. p.118.

28 For a fuller account of housing policy in the 1980s see P. Malpass and A. Murie, *Housing Policy and Practice*, Macmillan, Basingstoke, 2nd edition, 1987, Chapter 5.

29 *Housing*, September 1979, p.26.

30 See Heseltine's evidence in *First Report of the Environment Committee, Session 1979–80*, HMSO, 1980, HC 714.

31 *Housing: The Government's Proposals*, HMSO, 1987, Cm. 214.

32 Forrest and Murie, op.cit.

33 D. Usher, *Council Estate Sales*, Working Paper 74, SAUS, University of Bristol, 1988.

34 They are in Sandwell, Leeds, Sunderland, Tower Hamlets, Lambeth, and Southwark. *Inside Housing*, 15 July 1988.

35 S. Platt, 'Goodbye council housing?', *New Society*, 26 February 1988.

36 P. Leather, 'Housing (Dis?)Investment Programmes', *Policy and Politics*, vol. 11, no. 2, 1983, pp.215–27.

37 Forrest and Murie, op.cit., p.10.

38 *Capital Expenditure and Finance: A Consultation Paper* DoE/Welsh Office, July 1988, p.2.

39 ibid., p.2.
40 *The Government's Expenditure Plans, 1988–89 to 1990–91*, Cm. 288, HMSO, 1988, p.154.
41 D. Stafford, 'Speed Up Council House Sales', *Economic Affairs*, January 1984, pp. 25–8.
42 Cm. 288, op. cit., p. 112–13.
43 ibid., p.97.
44 R. Forrest and A. Murie, 'Marginalisation and Subsidised Individualism', *International Journal of Urban and Regional Research*, vol. 10, no. 1, January 1986, pp. 46–65.
45 J. Brookes, 'St Mellons Joint Finance Scheme', *Housing Review*, vol. 36, no. 3, May–June 1987.
46 *Housing Tenure*, Building Societies' Association, London, 1983, and *Housing and Savings 1986*, BMRB, London, 1986.
47 F. Gray, Chapter 8 in S. Merrett, *State Housing in Britain*, Routledge & Kegan Paul, London, 1979, p 201.
48 ibid., p. 201.
49 R. Robinson and A. O'Sullivan, 'Housing Tenure Polarisation, Some Empirical Evidence', *Housing Review*, July–August 1983.
50 G. Bentham, 'Socio-tenurial Polarisation in the United Kingdom, 1953–1983: the income evidence', *Urban Studies*, vol. 23, no. 2, 1986, pp.157–62.
51 *Family Expenditure Survey 1986*, Department of Employment, HMSO, 1987, Tables 4 & 22.
52 C. Hamnett, 'Housing the Two Nations: Socio-Tenurial Polarisation in England and Wales, 1961–81', *Urban Studies*, vol. 21, no. 4, 1984, pp. 389–405.
53 Forrest and Murie, op. cit., 1988, p. 69.
54 DoE evidence submitted to the Duke of Edinburgh's *Inquiry into British Housing: The Evidence*, NFHA, London, 1985, p. xiv.
55 D. Pickup, *When We Build Again: Partnership*, unpublished paper presented at the conference, 'When We Build Again', SAUS, University of Bristol, September 1986.
56 Forrest and Murie op. cit., p. 68.
57 ibid., pp.67–9.
58 *Council Tenants in London*, London Research Centre, 1988, Tables 1 & 2.
59 ibid., Table 4.
60 M. Ball, *Housing Policy and Economic Power*, Methuen, London, 1983, Chapter 1; 'Coming to Terms with Owner Occupation', *Capital and Class*, no. 24, 1985, pp. 15–44; 'Housing Analysis: Time for a Theoretical Refocus?', *Housing Studies*, vol. 1, no. 3, 1986, pp. 147–65. See also M. Ball, M. Harloe, and M. Martens, *Housing and Social Change in Europe and the USA*, Routledge, London, 1988, Chapter 1.
61 P. Marcuse, 'Determinants of state housing policies: West Germany and the United States', in N. and S. Fainstein (eds.), *Urban Policy Under Capitalism*, Urban Affairs Annual Reviews, vol. 22, 1984, p. 84.
62 M. Harloe, 'The recommodification of housing', in M. Harloe and E. Lebas (eds), *City, Class and Capital*, Edward Arnold, London, 1981, pp.19–20.
63 A. Murie and R. Forrest, 'Wealth, inheritance and housing policy', *Policy and Politics*, vol 8, no. 1, 1980, pp. 1–19.
64 R. Forrest and A. Murie, 1988, op. cit.
65 P. Willmott and A. Murie, *Polarisation and Social Housing*, Policy Studies Institute, London, 1988.
66 C. Hamnett, op. cit.

67 P. Somerville, 'Housing tenure polarisation', *Housing Review*, vol. 35, no. 6. 1986, pp. 190–3.
68 R. Forrest and P. Williams, 'Commodification and housing: emerging issues and contradictions', *Environment and Planning A*, vol. 16, 1984, pp. 1163–80. See also M. Harloe, in Harloe and Lebas, 1981, op.cit.
69 R. M. Titmuss, *Social Policy: An Introduction*, Allen & Unwin, London, 1974, pp.30–1.
70 M. Harloe, 'The green paper on housing policy', in M. Brown and S. Baldwin (eds), *The Yearbook of Social Policy in Britain 1977*, Routledge & Kegan Paul, London, 1978.
71 P. Malpass and A. Murie, *Housing Policy and Practice*, Macmillan, London, 1982 and 1987; J. English, 'Must council housing become welfare housing?', *Housing Review*, September–October, 1982; D. Clapham and D. Maclennan, 'Residualisation of public housing: a non-issue', *Housing Review*, Jananuary–February 1983; P. Malpass, 'Residualisation and the restructuring of housing tenure', *Housing Review*, March–April 1983; R. Forrest and A. Murie, 'Residualisation and council housing: aspects of the changing social relations of housing tenure', *Journal of Social Policy*, vol 12, no. 1, 1983, pp. 453–68; N. Williams, J. Sewel, and F. Twine, 'Council house sales and residualisation', *Journal of Social Policy*, vol 15, no. 3, 1986, pp. 273–92; R. Forrest and A. Murie, 1988, op. cit.
72 J. English, op. cit., p. 154.
73 P. Malpass 1983, op. cit., p. 44.
74 R. Forrest and A. Murie 1983, op. cit.
75 ibid.
76 D. Clapham and D. Maclennan, op. cit.

Chapter two

The development of public housing in Britain: an overview

Before we turn in subsequent chapters to the more detailed analysis of rents and subsidies policies since 1945, it is appropriate to consider the overall restructuring of housing provision in the twentieth century and the wider historical background to contemporary housing debates and issues. More extended general accounts are available elsewhere in the literature,[1] and the intention here is not to provide merely an abbreviated historical narrative, but to stand back from the detail, to identify the overall shape of developments over a long period, and to highlight the themes of residualisation, continuity, and local autonomy, in relation to different aspects of policy over time.

The modernisation of housing provision

The most frequently discussed indicator of the dynamic nature of housing provision in Britain is the changing pattern of tenure, summarised in Table 2.1. Accounts of tenure growth and decline tend to treat each one in isolation, minimising opportunities to perceive the restructuring of housing provision as a whole.

Table 2.1 Housing tenure in England and Wales

	Owner-occupied	Rented from local authorities and new towns	Rented from private landlords	Rented from housing associations
	%	%	%	%
1914	10	negligible	90	
1951	31	17	52	
1971	52	29	19	
1986	65	24	8	2.6

In Scotland the pattern of change has been significantly different, and by

1986 owner occupation stood at only 42 per cent whilst local authorities still owned 49.4 per cent of the stock.

The purpose of this section is to put forward a perspective on change in housing provision which links the main tenures, emphasising the need to interpret developments in any one tenure in relation to events and trends elsewhere. In particular, it is argued that changes affecting council housing have to be seen in terms of the restructuring of the private housing market. From the vantage point of the late 1980s it is clear that over the last seventy years or so owner occupation has gradually replaced private renting as the main tenure and that local authority provision has played an important, but changing, role which has to be understood in relation to changing conditions in the housing market. The decline of private renting is often rather simplistically attributed to the imposition of rent controls, while the growth of owner occupation is usually explained by a one-sided emphasis on consumer demand. However, it is necessary to take into account other factors affecting the organisation of the supply of housing. The transition from private renting to individual home ownership represents the modernisation of the housing market, in which a form of provision that was increasingly obsolete, in social, political and economic terms, was superseded by a form that was more appropriate to contemporary circumstances.

Private renting can be seen as a mode of provision which emerged in the nineteenth century as an appropriate form for that early phase of capitalist economic and urban development. At a time when the new urban working class on the whole earned low wages and had little scope for saving, renting enabled people to obtain access to an essential commodity which they could not afford to buy. Private renting also allowed investors and builders to realise profits from housing, even though most people could not afford to buy outright. The decline of this system reflects its growing obsolescence in the twentieth century.

Private landlords were typical and successful representatives of the local capitalism of the last century, but they have become victims of change in the transition to a more national and international phase of capitalist development.[2] Thus private renting can be seen as giving way to individual ownership as a form of provision that is more appropriate to the capitalism of the twentieth century. As Harloe has suggested,[3] owner occupation represents the modern form of the private housing market, which is the most effective form from the point of view of capital. It is in this sense that it is useful to conceive the restructuring of housing tenure since the First World War as a process of the modernisation of the housing market. This process necessarily took many years since it required the growth and development of new mechanisms and institutions; in particular its pace was contingent upon a substantial and sustained growth in the real incomes of consumers. There was therefore a long transitional period during which time it was not always clear or inevitable that individual home ownership would emerge as the dominant tenure. It was also a period when the role and purpose of local authority provision was subject to important changes of emphasis which were not just the result of changes of government.

The development of alternatives to private renting, and the relative importance of these alternatives within the overall provision of housing, was a matter to be determined politically. Housing has long been an issue around which political conflicts have revolved, and it is significant that historically the demands of organised labour were for the control of the private landlord and for the provision of municipal housing, not for individual home ownership. Important gains were made on these demands during and just after the First World War when the disruption of the housing market and a shift in the balance of class forces in favour of the working class led the state first to introduce rent control and then to undertake a major programme of subsidised municipal housing construction. The war diverted resources away from house building, reducing still further the level of investment which had already been in decline for several years before 1914. The war also created conditions which meant that with the return to peace in 1918, it was both politically necessary to build houses and effectively impossible for the unaided private sector to produce the required dwellings at affordable rents. It was in this situation that large-scale subsidised municipal house building began.

Throughout the 1920s local authorities built houses in order to reduce the overall shortage of accommodation. This so-called general needs housing was of a high standard compared to typical pre-1914 working-class housing, and the quality of the accommodation was reflected in the rents charged, despite the impact of subsidy. The local authorities were in effect taking over or supplementing the role of private builders in providing new accommodation for that section of the working class which could afford the rents of new dwellings. These were the very people who had been best placed in the pre-war housing market. It is essential to remember that the high quality and relatively high rents of 1920s general-needs housing meant that the main beneficiaries were the better-off skilled workers rather than the poor, and that this was no accident or economic inevitability. In this respect, state housing was more a response to a political problem than a housing problem, reflecting the political power and economic importance of organised skilled labour. As Byrne and Damer have argued:

> For the state the housing problem at the level of physical reproduction was the housing conditions of those who were worst housed. The political problem in terms of articulated political pressure came from the better housed in the working class who wanted cheap high quality council housing.[4]

Council housing, then, did not emerge as housing for the poor but as a response to the demands of the rather better off. However, there were always those who argued that the proper role of local authorities was to clear the slums and to provide only for the least well off, those who, even in 'normal' economic conditions could not secure a socially acceptable standard of accommodation in the private market. After 1930 these voices become more influential as circumstances changed: organised labour had suffered a series of setbacks in the 1920s, made worse by the very high unemployment of the early 1930s, and conditions began to favour an expansion of private house building. In this context the local authorities were pegged back to a more restricted role, clearing the slums and rehousing the needy, whilst the better off were attracted into the rapidly growing market for home ownership. The abandonment of general-needs housing construction by local authorities for a time in the 1930s was specifically to remove competition with the private sector and to enable the market to recolonise an area of demand from which it had withdrawn before the First World War.

The private housing boom of the 1930s was ended by the outbreak of the Second World War which again seriously disrupted the market, worsened the housing shortage, and created political conditions in which it was necessary to build houses in large numbers in response to working-class demands. After 1945 there was a decade in which housing policy concentrated on the production of local authority housing, of a high standard, before a reassertion of private sector interests once more led to the local authorities being confined to a more specialist role, complementary to the market rather than in competition with it.

In the political struggle to determine how housing needs should be met in the twentieth century, private sector interests have generally been predominant, with local authority housing achieving only a temporary ascendancy after the two world wars. Variations in the quality, quantity, and form of local authority output and in the prevailing policies on rents and allocations can be related to what was happening in the private market at the time, and should not be seen simply in terms of shifts between Conservative and Labour governments. The development of council housing has reflected a focus on different sections of the working class at different times, according to the balance between working-class strength and the state of the housing market. The important point to be established here is that council housing did not develop primarily as housing for the least well off. In analysing housing policy in the twentieth century, the differentiation within the working class is of great significance. The distinction can be made between the better off, mainly skilled workers, whose productive skills made them centrally important to the working of the economy, and the less well off, less skilled workers who were more peripheral to the economy and who therefore had less political and economic power.[5] During the first four decades of the modernisation of the private housing market, council housing played a crucial role in meeting the demands of the better off for decent accommodation at times when the market could not deliver. For the rest there was still a huge stock of less adequate but generally cheap (or cheaper) private rented housing, although, of course, some did find their way into the public sector, principally through slum clearance.

Over the years the position changed. On the one hand, the growth of owner occupation (fuelled by the long period of post-war economic growth and prosperity, full employment, and thirteen years of Conservative government, 1951–64) drew in more and more working-class purchasers. The continued growth of this modernised form of private housing provision came to depend upon the maintenance of demand from a widening range of working-class consumers. This in turn implied the adoption of policies to favour home ownership and to discourage demand for council housing (by poorer standards, higher rents, and other devices). On the other hand, the contraction of the private rented sector, which greatly broadened the social base of owner occupation, nevertheless increasingly meant that the least well off had no alternative but to seek council accommodation. And to facilitate their entry to council housing a different set of policies were required, to give them priority in allocation procedures and to enable them to afford the rent.

This way of conceiving the restructuring of housing tenure represents an attempt to integrate developments in each tenure. Council housing is seen as emerging as a political response to the tensions in the early phases of the modernisation of the housing market, which were exacerbated by the effects of warfare. In retrospect it is clear that council housing has never been allowed to develop as a threat to the dominance of market-based provision. On the contrary it has played a supportive, complementary role, underpinning the private sector. Having originated and grown mainly as housing for the rather better off within the working class, council housing has become subject to gathering pressures to transform it into a residual tenure for the least well off. Thus residualisation is an important sub-plot within the wider modernisation process.

Looking at tenure restructuring in this way not only produces an integrated explanation, but it also indicates how the residualisation of the public sector has been in progress for many years, and how the forces behind it are quite fundamental and not just the product of the rightwards swing of the political pendulum in the 1980s. At the same time, however, the policies of the Conservative government in the late 1980s are a reminder that the housing system remains dynamic, and that it is a mistake to assume that the long transitional period since the First World War is going to settle into a stable future, based on a two-tenure model in which the owner occupied sector is complemented by substantial local authority provision.

Council housing between the wars

The First World War was a major watershed in the development of housing policy in Britain. It marked the beginning of a much more interventionist approach by the state, in which measures that had been resisted for many years before the war were at last introduced, and subsequently became enduring features of the housing system. First, rent control was introduced in 1915, fixing rents (and mortgage interest rates) at their August 1914 levels. This was of central importance for the second break with past policy, namely the introduction of Exchequer housing subsidies in 1919.[6] Rent control helped to ensure that subsidies would be made available at the end of the war because it was clear that, if private builders were to respond to the severe housing shortage, they could do so only if rents were raised significantly. It was the lack of profitability in working-class housing which had contributed to the pre-war decline in investment, and the higher rents were a prerequisite of a profitable revival of private building. But war-time rent controls, coupled with establishment fears of post-war social unrest and even revolution, meant that 'Increases in rents staved off in deference to public opinion during the war could scarcely be regarded as an appropriate form of peace celebration.'[7]

If houses were to be built after the armistice, and a substantial housing programme was widely understood to be politically inescapable, then subsidies were inevitable, and so, in practice, was local authority participation in the programme. This was partly because municipal provision was what leaders of working-class opinion demanded, but also because in the immediate aftermath of the war it was the only way to ensure that houses were built. It was expected that there would be a period of price inflation as the economy adjusted to the return of peace, and in such conditions prudent investors and builders would hold off until prices returned to a more stable level. Those who built at high prices would subsequently be disadvantaged in competition with the lower rents that could be set for cheaper dwellings built later on.[8]

The total stock of council housing in Britain in 1914 was only 24,000 but by 1922 local authorities were able to build 86,500 dwellings in a single year, and by 1939 a total of more than 1,300,000 dwellings had been completed. In a very short period local authorities became established providers of rented housing, sometimes on a large scale. The London County Council, for instance, was very active and soon acquired a substantial housing stock, including the Becontree estate in Essex where some 27,000 dwellings were constructed in less than twenty years. A number of other large urban authorities, such as Leeds, Manchester, Birmingham, and Sheffield, rapidly built up their housing stocks, but it is important to remember that responses varied widely and that the rate of investment was effectively a matter to be determined at the local level, taking into account local needs and market conditions as well as local political factors.[9] It is not surprising that some authorities continued to be most reluctant to build, even with the assistance of Exchequer subsidy. Jennings records that 30 per cent of all authorities in England and Wales built no houses at all under the terms of the 1919 Housing and Town Planning Act.[10]

Local autonomy was an important influence on the uneven pattern of development of council housing, both geographically and over time, but authorities were nevertheless subject to attempts by the centre to steer their decisions in directions consistent with changing circumstances and government priorities. The strength of the local authorities' position was reflected in the kinds of mechanisms used by the centre to influence their behaviour. Rather than becoming closely and directly involved in controlling implementation, successive governments relied mainly on financial inducements through the housing subsidy system. The form of subsidy adopted in the 1919 Act was particularly generous to the local authorities, reflecting their powerful bargaining position during the wartime planning of the housing programme. In the face of a shortage conservatively estimated to be at least 610,000 dwellings, at a time when prices were expected to rise, and in a political situation in which a positive response was recognised to be essential, central government planned to build 500,000 houses in the three years after the end of the war. To approach this level of building in very difficult economic circumstances, local authority co-operation was necessary and a high price had to be paid to obtain it.

Subsidy was required to bridge the gap between the cost of providing a house and the level of rent that could be obtained. The 1919 Act limited local authority liability to the product of a penny rate, with the Exchequer paying the balance. This open-ended subsidy commitment gave central government a very close interest in the level of costs incurred by local authorities, and a series of eleven regional commissioners were appointed to monitor local policy and practice. An important part of the commissioners' work was to negotiate on standards, costs and rents, to ensure value for money and that rents were not set at levels regarded by the Exchequer as unreasonably low. However, the regional commissioners' offices were abolished when the 1919 Act programme was curtailed in July 1921, ostensibly on economic grounds amidst allegations of profligacy by spendthrift local authorities. Thereafter the Ministry of Health (which had responsibility for housing) maintained a position of standing back from direct involvement in the details of local implementation of housing policy. This stance led Bowley to conclude:

> The experience of [1923–1939] showed, in short that the local authorities have been given powers which they are only partially willing to exercise, and duties many of which they are in fact unwilling to perform. In the absence of any effective central control, the local authorities can flout

policies approved by Parliament, and the local councils can, and do, in practice, relegislate as to the extent to which they will carry out, or accept, a national policy.[11]

The 1919 Act housing programme was in practice limited to 174,635 local-authority dwellings, and it was not until 1929 that the total number of council houses built since the war reached 500,000. The 1919 Act was followed by the 1923 Housing Act which was primarily intended to provide a stimulus to private house building through the offer of subsidy, although local authorities could build with subsidy if they could show that private enterprise was failing to meet local needs. The short-lived Labour Government of 1924, however, revived local authority building programmes by introducing a more generous subsidy and a long-term plan for housing construction. Under the 1924 Housing Act (known as the Wheatley Act) a total of 505,000 dwellings were built, making it in numerical terms the most significant of the inter-war Housing Acts.

The Wheatley Act subsidy established a pattern which endured for thirty years: the Exchequer contribution was a fixed amount per dwelling for forty years and there was a statutory rate-fund contribution, which could be supplemented by discretionary local subsidy, depending upon local costs and political priorities. This framework was much more satisfactory from the point of view of central government, since it left the onus on the local authority to secure value for money and to decide the overall balance between rent and subsidy. Increases in costs would not be reflected in lower subsidies.

House-building costs were spectacularly high immediately after the war, compared with both the years before 1914 and the remainder of the period up to 1939. Completion costs in 1920 were running at £1,000–£1,200 per dwelling, compared with less than £300 in 1933–5.[12] Costs were, however, falling by April 1921, even before the curtailment of the 1919 Act programme, and there was a consistent downward trend in local authority construction costs from 1926–34. In 1926 the government announced its intention to reduce subsidy in twelve months' time; this accounts for the high level of output in 1927 as local authorities rushed to complete houses before the deadline of 30 September. A further cut scheduled for 1929 was prevented by the return of a Labour Government in May of that year, but in 1933 the Wheatley Act subsidy was abolished altogether.

In their different ways the Acts of 1919, 1923 and 1924 were designed to promote the construction of housing to reduce the overall shortage. New building for the replacement of the cleared slum housing was negligible during the 1920s, as local authorities became established as providers of housing for general needs. However, in 1930 central government attempted to steer local authorities in a new direction by means of an additional subsidy which was introduced with the intention of launching a national programme of slum clearance and rehousing. A new, higher level of subsidy became available in relation to houses built specifically for rehousing families from slum clearance areas. Unfortunately local authorities showed little enthusiasm for slum clearance and the national campaign had to be relaunched in 1933, at the same time that the general-needs subsidy was withdrawn. This gave councils the clearest possible indication of where central government expected them to concentrate their efforts. The confinement of local authority activity in this way has to be seen in the context of the boom in private house building during the mid-1930s. The government was responding to pressure from the builders to remove subsidised competition with their activities at the cheaper end of the private market. Total annual private sector output in England and Wales rose from 109,000 in 1930 to 260,000 in 1934, and remained above 250,000 for the next four years. Against this background the scale of slum clearance rehousing looks distinctly half-hearted: in the whole of the period 1930–9 only 262,000 dwellings were built in association with slum clearance in England and Wales.

The switch from general needs to slum clearance rehousing reflects a change in policy about the *distribution* as well as the production of council housing, and it is important to consider other ways in which central government sought to influence distribution. The centre could influence the level of output by altering the flow of subsidy,[13] but access to council housing was partly a function of the relationship between costs, standards, subsidies and rents. It is necessary to understand that, in the period of highest costs, immediately after the First World War, when standards were high, so too were subsidies, but not sufficiently so to bring rents down to a level that was within reach of the least well off. At a time of acute shortage and high costs it is significant that the government deliberately set standards at a high level rather than adopting a policy of maximising output by low standards. Rents inevitably reflected this approach, and it is arguable that, subsidies notwithstanding, central government was operating a high rent policy in the early 1920s. Average net rents for 1919 Act houses remained around 9s.5d. throughout the inter-war period,[14] but in London the top of the range reached 21s.6d. in 1924.[15] Rates generally added around 40–50 per cent to the net rent. Bowley suggests that during the inter-war period 10s. was generally considered to be the maximum gross rent, including rates, affordable by unskilled and semi-skilled labourers.[16]

Official statistics on the levels of rents in different authorities over time are incomplete, reflecting the view that, 1919-Act houses apart, it was the responsibility of the local authorities to set their own rents. Ministers maintained a position of non-intervention, and backed this up by not gathering information about local rents. However, it was understood at the time that in most cases the rents of houses built before the late 1920s were beyond the reach of the lower-paid workers. For instance, the Ministry of

Health acknowledged in 1931 that in relation to the 1924 Act, 'Rents were originally so high as to require a careful selection on financial grounds of the possible tenants, which in some cases led to the acceptance, as tenants of subsidised houses of persons of substantial financial capacity.'[17] Contemporary observers such as Jarmain and Bowley also reported that rents were high in relation to the incomes of the poor:

> There is really no doubt about how rent policy worked out in practice. The market for local authority houses was largely confined to a limited range of income groups, that is, in practice, the better-off semi-skilled workers with small families, and fairly safe jobs. Right up to the economy campaign of 1932, and even later, it was these families who absorbed most of the houses.[18]

Swenarton has referred to the London County Council's (LCC) income bar which operated in the early 1920s; far from channelling housing to the poor the LCC required prospective tenants to show that their weekly income was at least five times the sum of the rent, rates, and fares to work, and that they had a good record of rent payment.[19]

However, as costs continued to fall in the late 1920s a great change took place in the terms of the housing debate. When costs were high, there was no real question of houses being occupied by people who did not need the assistance of subsidy, but, as costs fell, it began to be argued that it was wrong for relatively affluent tenants to continue to receive subsidy, while the less well off remained largely excluded from the benefits of council housing. From the late 1920s a number of policy mechanisms were developed to redirect council housing towards lower-paid workers. It is important to appreciate the contrast with earlier years; when costs were high governments refused to raise subsidies or reduce standards in order to ensure that the less well off had access to the new council houses, but when costs fell subsidies also fell (including both Exchequer assistance and local rate fund contributions). The main route towards housing for the lower paid was reduced standards.

The annual reports of the Ministry of Health in the early 1930s provide a clear record of encouragement to local authorities to build smaller, cheaper houses, aimed at the lower paid, in order to leave private enterprise to provide for the better off. It was not just dwellings built to rehouse families from slum clearance that were built to lower specifications. General needs housing, built under the 1924 Act, was also subject to government constraints, and authorities were restricted to three-bedroomed non-parlour houses of no more than 760 square feet (or 650 square feet for two-bedroomed houses). According to the *Annual Report* for 1934 this provided 'adequate accommodation and amenities for average working class families,'[20] but it was a maximum which compared badly with the average of more than 860 square feet for the 1919 Act houses built 1920-1.[21]

Another way of channelling council housing to the less well off was to treat new, cheaper estates separately from older, more expensive, estates for accounting purposes, thereby enabling the rents of newer houses fully to reflect reductions in costs. Authorities were encouraged to adopt this approach from the late 1920s, but many were apparently reluctant to do so.[22] A different approach, tried in some areas, was to put pressure on households that had been rehoused in the early post-war years to vacate their subsidised houses in favour of people in greater need. In a move which stood in stark contrast to its earlier policy on incomes the LCC wrote to 300 tenants on two of its estates suggesting that they should move out on the grounds that incomes or family circumstances made continued occupation of subsidised housing inappropriate.[23]

What emerges from this is that general needs council housing was subject to a residualising tendency within government policy, initially under the Conservative government in the late 1920s and then under the Conservative-dominated National government from 1931 onwards. The cessation of subsidised general needs construction after 1934 and the revival of slum clearance represents a further residualisation of policy.

At this point it is appropriate to refer to an aspect of rents policy that was introduced as part of the 1930 Housing Act which launched the slum clearance programme. Throughout the 1920s subsidies had been applied in the form of general assistance, producing lower rents for all tenants, but by the end of the decade it was being argued that subsidy should be given only to those tenants who actually needed it, and only for so long as they needed it. The 1930 Act introduced the freedom for authorities to channel subsidy to specific tenants in the form of rent rebates or differential rents schemes. In view of the later significance of income-related assistance it is important to establish that the principle of rent rebates was not at all central to government policy at the time of the 1930 Act. Indeed, the power for authorities to operate rebate schemes was introduced into the bill at a late stage in response to a campaign by two back-bench MPs, Eleanor Rathbone and Sir Ernest Simon, and the government's position was unenthusiastic and confused. The Labour government at that time obviously did not want to be seen to support the 'waste' of taxpayers' money in the form of subsidies to people who were able to pay the full rent, but equally it could not be associated with support for means testing. Somewhat more surprisingly the Conservative-dominated governments after 1931 also displayed a reluctance to embrace and promote rent rebates. Instead they preferred to encourage lower rents through lower standards.

All governments after 1930 left the issue of rent rebates to be decided at the local level, but very few authorities in England and Wales adopted rebate schemes. Precise figures for the spread of rebate schemes are not available. A semi-official report in 1939 referred to schemes operated by only 80 councils out of over 1,400 local authorities in England and Wales.[24] In Scotland, however, the Scottish Office was more enthusiastic than the Ministry of Health in the south and rebating became more widely used. The issue of rebates was unpopular with local authorities and tenants alike. The local authorities tended to display a preference for the better-off tenants and were not keen to create easier access for the poor. In addition, rebating was administratively much more complicated to establish and operate, requiring regularly updated information about tenants' incomes. Until 1936 it was necessary for authorities to maintain separate accounts for houses built under each Housing Act, adding to the administrative difficulty of rebating. In any case, it was not clear until a test case in 1935 that authorities were entitled to apply rebate schemes to houses built under Acts other then the 1930 Act.

The slow spread of rebate schemes may also reflect the resistance of tenants, especially the better-off existing tenants whose rents would inevitably rise in order to redistribute assistance to less well-off tenants. In Leeds an ambitious attempt to introduce a comprehensive rebate scheme was bitterly opposed by tenants and was held to be a major factor in the outcome of the local council elections in 1935.[25] And in Birmingham in 1939 a rebate scheme designed to remove the better off from council housing stimulated a prolonged rent strike by 6,000–8,000 tenants.[26]

To conclude this discussion of council housing between the wars there are one or two points to be made. Throughout the period 1919–39 housing subsidies did very little to help the poor. It was falling costs and lower standards of provision which did most to bring council housing within their reach. It is important to remember that the quality of public sector housing output varied over time in ways that were closely related to the groups who were intended to become the tenants of the new dwellings. The poor were largely excluded from council housing for a decade, and then, when they were drawn in in larger numbers, they found that what was on offer was a distinctly inferior product.

The switch to slum clearance in the 1930s should also be seen in relation to its implications for the less well off. There is an important difference between a housing programme framed around the needs of low-income people and one based on the removal of unfit housing. By abolishing the Wheatley Act subsidy in 1933 the government turned away from a housing policy that could be interpreted as embracing all households in need. Instead it was concentrating on an activity, slum clearance, which was necessary on public health grounds but unprofitable for the private sector. In other words, the state was clearly acting in the interests of house-building capital rather than working-class consumers, or in Bowley's phrase, 'the Government had gone as near to rejecting responsibility for working class housing as it could.'[27]

Finally, on the question of residualisation, it is clear that *policy* was subject to residualising changes of direction, but that, partly because of the extent of local automony and the attitudes of local authorities, council housing as a whole was not converted into a residual sector. It is also worth pointing to the contrast between policy in the 1930s and at the present time. The concentration on slum clearance was about poor housing, not poor people as such; in the 1980s policy de-emphasises slum clearance but pays more attention to local authorities as providers for households in greatest need, reflecting changes in the quantitative supply of privately rented housing.

Council housing since the Second World War

By 1938 local authorities owned just 10 per cent of the total housing stock, and, given the boom conditions prevailing in the private sector, it might have appeared that councils were set to continue on the residual course established in the previous four years. However, the outbreak of the Second World War in September 1939 again disrupted the housing market. Comprehensive rent control was imposed and resources were rapidly diverted away from housing production and repair. During the next six years very few new houses were completed, maintenance was neglected, some 450,000 dwellings were destroyed by bombing (many more were damaged to a lesser degree), and the population grew by a million. This meant that, as in 1918, there was a severe housing shortage after the war, and a political climate in which social reconstruction was a major priority for the Labour government elected in July 1945.

In certain important respects the course of housing policy in the twenty years after 1945 bears considerable resemblance to the twenty years between the wars, although there are also major difference. After both wars there was roughly a decade in which policy was directed to reducing the overall housing shortage, and only then did the questions of replacement and distribution re-emerge, at which point the local authorities were edged out of general needs housing, leaving the field clear for the resurgent private sector. Another striking similarity is that in the years immediately after each war, when the shortage was most acute and the economy was most disrupted, the quality of new local authority housing was highest, and rents policies favoured the better off. In the 1950s, as in the 1930s, the quality of new public housing fell as policy shifted away from general needs towards slum clearance replacement.

The similarities reflected the similar underlying problems, of shortage, market disruption, and a politically unavoidable need to build houses. Nevertheless there were also significant differences in the economic and political context. Whereas in the early 1920s there was a brief spell of rapid inflation, followed by a long period of falling prices, after 1945 prices rose continuously, but relatively slowly until the 1970s, and housing policy developed in an inflationary setting which came to exert considerable influence on both local authority housing and the demand for home owner-ship. Full employment was another characteristic of the British economy for more than twenty years after 1945, whereas high levels of unemployment, albeit regionally concentrated, persisted throughout most of the inter-war period. Full employment, economic growth, and rising living standards undoubtly contributed to the wider popularity of mortgaged house purchase. Politically the post-1945 period was different to the extent that a Labour government remained in office for the first six years after the war, and that this government retained its commitment to council housing. The subsequent thirteen years of Conservative government provided an opportunity for consolidation of fundamental changes in housing policy.

The scale of the local authority housing programme was much greater after 1945 than during the period 1919–39. Annual production exceeded 100,000 only twice between the wars, but, having topped that figure in 1948, the number of completions never went below 100,000 until 1973. For almost twenty-five years after the war there was general agreement that there was a need for high levels of housing production in order to eliminate the accumulated shortage, to remove the slums, and to provide for a growing population. Estimates varied as to what was needed and also what was feasible, but the main political parties vied with each other to promise more and more new houses. Production targets and 'the numbers game' became a familiar part of the politics of housing in the 1950s and 1960s.

During the first ten years after the Second World War more than 1.6 million new local authority dwellings were built in Great Britain as a whole. This was substantially more than in the whole of the inter-war period, and more than in any subsequent decade. That the public sector should more than double in size in ten years was in large measure due to the commitment of the 1945–51 Labour government, which pursued a policy that was very different to that of the years just before the war. It was also a policy which differed from the approach of 1919 in that after 1945 wartime controls on private building activity and the supply of materials were maintained. In addition local authorities had access to low-interest loans via the Public Works Loans Board, in contrast to the high cost of borrowing in the unfettered market of the the early 1920s. In the aftermath of the Second World War the housing programme was developed in an atmosphere where central direction and planning were characteristic of government thinking on a range of policy areas. Aneurin Bevan, Minister of Health, 1945–51, summed up the case for concentrating on local authority building by saying, 'If we are to plan, we have to plan with plannable instruments, and the speculative builder, by his very nature, is not a plannable instrument.'[28] During the six years of the Labour government overall output was in line with the policy of four council houses for every one private house.

Bevan, however, was also a staunch defender of standards, arguing that 'While we shall be judged for a year or two by the *number* of houses we build, we shall be judged in ten years' time by the *type* of houses we build.'[29] Local authorities in the the late 1940s concentrated on the production of three-bedroomed *houses* (very few flats were built at this time), and these houses remain the most spacious council houses ever built, averaging more than 1000 square feet (compared with the upper limit of 760 square feet in the early 1930s). Both the quality and the quantity of council houses built in the early years after the Second World War indicate the commitment of the Labour government to council housing as the main response to the housing problem. In view of the subsequent changes of direction in housing policy, and current criticism of council housing as such, it is important to remember that forty years ago a model of housing provision was being developed which could have led to very different outcomes.

The development of high-quality council housing in the 1940s took place in a context where on the one hand there was a serious housing shortage and on the other hand a series of economic crises which after 1948 led first to a containment of production and then to reductions in standards. The most important cuts in housing standards, however, came after the return of a Conservative government in the general election of October 1951. By this stage the worst effects of the war were over and economic prospects were improving.[30] The new government took office on the promise of 300,000 dwellings per year, representing an increase of almost 50 per cent on the achievements of 1950–1. Within the government there was disagreement about the desirability of a rapid expansion of house building, with critics of the policy arguing that resources should be devoted first to rebuilding Britain's exporting industries. The argument was partially resolved by a compromise in which an increase in the number of houses to be built was facilitated by a marked decrease in quality of new local authority dwellings. As had happened between the wars, the reduction in quality began during the phase of general needs construction, before the revival of slum clearance.

In order to achieve 300,000 house per year in the shortest time, it was necessary to rely on local authorities, since they were in a better position than private builders to expand their programmes to the desired level. Initially, therefore, the Conservative government promoted record levels of building by local authorities: in 1953 local authority completions in Great Britain topped 229,000 dwellings, followed by nearly 224,000 in 1954. However, once the election promise had been fulfilled, important changes were put into effect.

The mid-1950s can now be seen a a period of major restructuring of housing policy. During the first decade after the war both Labour and Conservative governments had concentrated on tackling the housing shortage through public sector construction, with very little replacement activity. But in the period 1954–7 a series of changes was introduced, charting a course for housing policy as a whole which successive governments have continued to pursue. The general strategy was to stimulate the private market for both home ownership and renting, and to confine local authorities to the supportive roles of carrying out slum clearance, with associated rehousing, and providing for other 'special needs', e.g. the poor elderly, squeezed out of the private sector. In addition, local authority housing was to be made simultaneously more expensive for the better-off existing tenants (giving them an incentive to move into the private sector), and more affordable for the less well off. Donnison and Ungerson have aptly summarised this strategy in the following terms:

> For a while it looked as if the government was extricating itself from its extensive, though never comprehensively planned, involvement in the housing market and reverting to a residual role. The local authorities would clear the slums – still regarded as a finite, public health problem for which a final solution would soon be found. Thereafter they would administer their inheritance of some three and a half million houses as a form of social service, adding a few to bring about the expansion of selected towns and to meet the special needs of selected groups in the population. The 'free market' would meet all normal requirements.[31]

A White Paper in November 1953 set the tone by stating that 'One object of future housing policy will be to continue to promote, by all possible means, the building of houses for owner occupation. Of all forms of saving, this is one of the best. Of all forms of ownership this is one of the most satisfying to the individual and the most beneficial to the nation.'[32] The revival of private sector construction from the very low levels of 1945–51 was encouraged by the gradual relaxation of licensing restrictions, which were finally removed in November 1954. Output expanded rapidly, but did not overtake the declining public sector programme until 1959.

The endorsement and promotion of home ownership were accompanied by a package of measures dealing with the rented sector. Legislation in 1954, the Housing Repairs and Rents Act, was concerned with the problems of neglected and sub-standard privately rented housing. Strict rent control had been continued after the war, but now provision for rent increases was introduced, on condition that landlords had first brought dwellings into a satisfactory state of repair. As a relaxation of rent regulation this was a very minor concession, unlikely to have much impact. However, the Act also required local authorities to draw up plans to deal with slums remaining in their areas, and this did have a much more widespread effect.[33] Again comparison with the early 1930s is interesting; slum clearance was relaunched alongside a continuing programme of general needs housing, but then the general needs subsidy was withdrawn. In 1956 the Housing

Subsidies Act confined the provision of subsidy to two types of accommodation: slum clearance rehousing and one-bedroomed flats (for the elderly). At the same time the structure of subsidies was altered to encourage high-rise development by the provision of financial assistance which increased according to the number of storeys in the block. In the early 1950s flats in blocks of over five storeys had constituted less than 7 per cent of all new public sector dwellings, but by 1966 the proportion rose to 25.7 per cent of dwellings in approved tenders, before tailing off rapidly by the early 1970s.[34]

Local authority housing output fell by over 50 per cent between 1954 and 1961, reaching a low point of 105,529 dwellings. At the same time the slum clearance programme was expanding from just under 30,000 houses demolished in 1955, to 67,256 in 1961, implying that at least two-thirds of local authority output was being absorbed by households rehoused from clearance areas. As production fell, so too did space standards: by 1959 the average size of new three-bedroomed houses had fallen to 897 square feet, but it is relevant to note that in 1959 three-bedroomed houses constituted a much smaller proportion of total output than in earlier years, and therefore that most new council dwellings were in fact much smaller. It is also worth noting that the reduction in house-building activity by local authorities was achieved in the absence of direct central government controls over capital spending; manipulation via the subsidy system continued to produce the outcomes sought by the government.

Another key component of the mid-1950s restructuring of housing policy concerned local authority rents policies, and here too the centre was able to exert pressure on councils without resort to direct intervention. This development is discussed in detail in Chapters 3 and 5, and here it is sufficient to note that, although there was no legislation on rents, there was nevertheless a major policy change in 1955, when the Minister of Housing stated that in future local authorities would be expected to pool rents across the whole of their stock, and to make greater use of rent rebate assistance for the less well off. It will be shown below that this represented *the* major turning point in the post-war development of council house rents policies. Since that time there has been a gathering tendency for the policies of successive governments, Conservative and Labour, to move away from general subsidy towards greater reliance on income-related assistance. For the moment, however, it is intended only to locate the rents policy change of the mid 1950s in the context of the more visible and better known legislative measures of that period.

The final element to be put in place was the Rent Act, 1957, which was designed to deregulate the private rented sector. There were two parts to the deregulation process. Rents of dwellings with rateable values above a specified level were decontrolled as from a named date, and rents of dwellings with lower rateable values became decontrolled at the next change of tenant. Deregulation, together with the removal of subsidy for local authority, general needs housing, was intended to create conditions where consumer demand and investment yield would lead to a revival of the private rented sector.

This grand strategy was not wholly successful. Private sector construction continued to expand almost uninterruptedly from the early 1950s until the mid-1960s, but investment went into owner occupation, not private renting. Indeed the private rented sector continued to decline at an even faster rate after the 1957 Act, since it gave landlords easier access to vacant possession, allowing them to sell at the highest price, and by reducing security of tenure it gave sitting tenants an incentive to buy. In 1961 the government restored the general needs subsidy for local authority building, in response to the continuing shortage of rented accommodation, thereby implicitly admitting the failure of at least part of the strategy which had been put together less than five yeas previously.

Local authority housing received another boost when thirteen years of Conservative rule were ended by a Labour victory in the 1964 general election. However, there was to be no return to the policy of the 1940s, and the extent to which Labour housing policy had changed was revealed in the 1965 White Paper:

Once the country has overcome its huge social problem of slumdom and obsolescence and met the need of the great cities for more houses to let at moderate rents, the programme of subsidised council housing should decrease. The expansion of the public programme now proposed is to meet exceptional needs: it is born partly of a short term necessity, partly of the conditions inherent in modern urban life. The expansion of building for owner occupation on the other hand is normal; it reflects a long term social advance which should gradually pervade every region.[35]

The Labour governments of the 1960s had none of the confidence in, and commitment to, council housing that had been such a feature of the early post-war years. The 1965 White Paper proposed only that the public sector would provide up to half of the annual output of 500,000 dwellings per year that was the target by 1970. The increase in local authority building was excused in terms of the severity of the contemporary housing problem, rather than being advocated as a desirable development in itself. In this respect Labour's policy was similar to that of the Conservatives in the early 1950s.

For a period total output did expand, exceeding 400,000 in both 1967 and 1968. Subsidies were increased in 1967, but, interestingly, the increase was accompanied by exhortations to local authorities to extend their provision of rent rebates, using some of the new financial assistance for this purpose. In this respect, too, Labour was converging on positions previously associated with the Conservative Party. Wider economic problems led the government to cut back the building programme as part of the package of public expenditure reductions following the devaluation crisis of November 1967. Public sector completions fell away sharply from the 1967 peak of 181,000 to just 88,000 in 1973. The White Paper of 1968, *Old Houses into New Homes*, marked the end of the policy commitment to high levels of housing production. This commitment, variously interpreted and applied, had been shared by governments since 1945, but since the late 1960s other considerations have come to dominate policy debates.

The retreat from high levels of house building was accompanied by a shift from slum clearance to improvement of existing dwellings. This was not just about levels of investment and public expenditure but also about ownership and tenure. Public experience and perception of redevelopment in the 1950s and 1960s were that municipal rehousing, particularly in the new-style tower blocks and industrialised system-built estates, was not always a guaranteed improvement on the old housing. As redevelopment programmes progressed during the 1960s they inevitably moved into areas of rather better quality, or less unsatisfactory, housing where levels of home ownership were higher. In these circumstances there was the likelihood of intense resentment of and resistance to comprehensive redevelopment.[36] Rehabilitation thus became a politically more attractive policy, helping to promote home ownership amongst the working class.

During the 1970s, issues of finance came to replace production in dominating the politics of housing. The main reason for this was the impact of inflation and rising interest rates on government assistance with housing costs in both the public and owner occupied sectors. The level of subsidy on new council houses had been raised in 1967, and in the owner occupied sector assistance in the form of tax relief on mortgage interest tended to rise as a result of growing numbers of mortgagors. But, in particular, public attention was focused on the cost of tax relief by the unprecedented rise in house prices in 1972–3, and by the increase in the mortgage interest rate from 8 per cent in 1971 to 11 per cent in 1973. In the period 1967–8 to 1976–7 total relief to mortgagors rose by 146 per cent in real terms, and on the same basis subsidies in the public sector rose by 107 per cent.[37] These increases, which took place against the background of falling completions of new houses, not surprisingly raised questions about the wisdom of the Exchequer's paying out larger and larger sums on what was seen as unproductive expenditure.

The main housing policy legislation carried through by the Conservative government of 1970–4 was the Housing Finance Act, 1972, which concentrated on reforming the rented sectors, leaving the issues of finance for owner occupation untouched. The Act aimed to create a standard, market-related pricing system for all unfurnished rented housing, whether it was owned by a private landlord, a local authority, or a housing association.

Underpinning the so-called 'fair rent' scheme was a standard, mandatory system of income-related assistance, providing, for the first time, for tenants in the private sector as well as in council housing. This highly controversial and important Act requires detailed discussion in subsequent chapters since it relates to all three of the themes of residualisation, central–local relations, and policy continuity: it was intended to hasten the residualisation of council housing by raising rents and increasing reliance on rebates; it removed local autonomy in rent setting; and it stands as a major landmark in the long-term development of rents and subsidies policy.

The Housing Finance Act, 1972, proved to be too controversial to survive the return of a Labour government in February 1974, but the theme of the reform of housing finance continued in the form of a review carried out by the Department of the Environment. This exercise was launched in late 1974, apparently with a view to bringing forward proposals for the fundamental, all-tenure, reform of housing finance. However, a decision to broaden it into a review of wider issues in housing policy led to delay, and by the time of publication of the Green Paper in the middle of 1977 the possibility of fundamental reform had been lost. The outcome of more than two years' work was widely regarded as an insipid document,[38] reflecting perhaps the weakness of the government's parliamentary position at the time. No major changes were proposed for the private sector, but a new subsidy system for local authority housing was outlined. This later appeared in the Housing Bill which fell with the Labour government in May 1979.

If the 1970s was a decade when financial issues were prominent in housing debates, the 1980s has become a decade when questions of tenure and ownership have dominated policy. The Conservative governments under the leadership of Margaret Thatcher since 1979 have given priority to boosting home ownership and private renting, using council housing as a resource to fuel the growth of the private market sectors. The Labour Party initially opposed the introduction of a statutory right for council tenants to buy their houses, but by 1987 the principle of sales had lost its earlier controversial edge, and indeed council housing as a whole had lost much of the support that it had received from the Labour Party since the beginning of the century. At the same time the critics and detractors of council housing have been in the ascendant since 1979, as the previous chapter showed. In a sense 1980 marked a major turning point in the history of council housing, being the year that sales began to exceed new building and the stock began to decline in size for the first time. Since the Conservatives took office, council housing has existed in a hostile climate, in which ideological opposition to local authority services in general has been allied to economic policies which identified housing as an area where major public-expenditure savings could be achieved. A series of acts and other measures, discussed in Chapter 1, have been characterised by preference for private market solutions to housing problems, a disregard for traditional preoccupations with housing shortage, housing need, or living conditions, and an increasing enthusiasm for the break-up of municipal housing stocks. In short, privatisation has been a major theme of housing policy in the 1980s, reinforcing the trend towards residualisation.

Conclusion

Housing has never been far from the centre of attention of Britain politics during the twentieth century, and a stream of legislation has flowed from successive governments over many years. This has led some commentators to emphasise the changes of policy from one government to the next. Donnison and Ungerson, for instance, have referred to housing policy swinging drunkenly back and forth,[39] while Yates has employed the analogy of the political football in relation to housing.[40] However, it is more useful to acknowledge that some level of change is almost bound to occur over time, and to look for the common themes and continuities, rather than being distracted and misled by apparent differences. The modernisation thesis outlined in the first part of this chapter provides a framework for under-standing the interlinked developments in public and private sectors over the century as a whole. Subsequent sections focusing on the inter-war and post-war years have identified the main contours of policy at different times, referring to both similarities and differences. Despite the differences it can be argued that the important underlying factor in the periods following both wars was the shifting balance of class forces, tilting first towards working-class demands in the immediate aftermath of war, and then tilting firmly towards capital as favourable market conditions were re-established.

On this view the housing policy restructuring of the mid-1950s becomes visible as the main turning-point in the post-war period, since it set the course of policy in favour of home ownership, giving council housing an increasingly residual role. Between the wars *policy* was residualised, but in a context where local authorities retained considerable autonomy, and for only a few years before the renewed outbreak of hostilities. Council housing as a whole, therefore, continued to play a largely non-residual role in the housing system. Following the restructuring of the 1950s there was only a brief, and not altogether convincing, attempt by the Labour govern-ment in the mid-1960s to revive the idea of council housing as a genuine alternative to home ownership. Apart from this, however, there has been a continuation of policies whose effects have been to residualise council housing, and central government has been increasingly assertive in seeking to impose its views on local authorities.

Following chapters trace the course of polices on rents and subsidies in a way which demonstrates in more detail the 1950s origins of residualisation and the degree of continuity in policy since that time.

References

1 S. Merrett, *State Housing in Britain*, Routledge & Kegan Paul, London, 1979; A. Holmans, *Housing Policy in Britain*, Croom Helm, London. 1987; P. Malpass and A. Murie, *Housing Policy and Practice*, Macmillan, Basingstoke, 2nd edition, 1987.

2 D. V. Donnison, *The Government of Housing*, Penguin Books, Harmondsworth, 1967, p.228.

3 M. Harloe, *Private Rented Housing in the United States and Europe*, Croom Helm, London, 1985, p. xxiii

4 D. Byrne and S. Damer, 'The state, the balance of class forces and early working class housing legislation', in *Housing, Construction and the State*, Political Economy of Housing Workshop, London, 1980, p. 68.

5 D. Byrne and D. Parson, 'The state and the reserve army : the management of class relations in space', in J. Anderson, S. Duncan and R. Hudson, (eds), *Redundant Spaces in Cities and Regions?*, Academic Press, London, 1983.

6 See L. Orbach, *Homes for Heroes*, Heinemann, London, 1981.

7 M. Bowley, *Housing and the State*, Allen & Unwin, London, 1945, p. 9.

8 A. Holmans, op. cit., p. 295.

9 M. Daunton (ed.), *Councillors and Tenants: Local Authority Housing in English Cities, 1919–39*, Leicester University Press, Leicester, 1984: J Melling (ed.), *Housing, Social Policy and the State*, Croom Helm, London, 1980; P. Dickens, S. Duncan, M. Goodwin and F. Gray, *Housing States and Localities*, Methuen, London, 1985.

10 J. H. Jennings, 'Geographical implications of the municipal housing programme in England and Wales 1919–39, *Urban Studies*, June 1971, pp. 121–38.

11 M. Bowley, op. cit., p. 258.

12 J. R. Jarmain, *Housing Subsidies and Rents*, Stevens, London, 1948, p. 273; *Report of the Departmental Committee on the High Cost of Building Working Class Dwellings*, Ministry of Health, Cmd. 1447, 1921, p. 44; M. Swenarton, op. cit., p.22.

13 S. Merrett, op. cit., p.44.

14 *Ministry of Health Annual Reports*, various years.

15 Parliamentary answer, *House of Commons Debates*, vol. 171, col. 445, 1924.

16 M. Bowley, op. cit., p. 96–7.

17 *Annual Report of the Ministry of Health, 1930–31*, Cmd. 3937, 1931, p. 97.

18 M. Bowley, op.cit., p.129.

19 M. Swenarton, op. cit., p. 174.

20 *Annual Report of the Ministry of Health 1933–4*, Cmd. 4663, 1934, p. 153.

21 S. Merrett, op. cit., p. 332.

22 M. Bowley, op. cit., p.127.

23 *Annual Report of the Ministry of Health 1933–4*, op. cit., p. 160.

24 *The Management of Municipal Housing Estates*, First Report of the Housing Management and Housing Estates Sub-Committee of the Central Housing Advisory Committee, 1939, p. 33.

25 A. Ravetz, *Model Estate: Planned Housing at Quarry Hill, Leeds*, Croom Helm, London, 1974; R. Finnegan, 'Housing policy in Leeds between the wars', in J. Melling, op. cit., 1980.

26 S. Schifferes, 'Council tenants and housing policy in the 1930s', in *Housing and Class in Britain*, Political Economy of Housing Workshop, London, 1976.

27 M. Bowley, op. cit., p. 140.

28 House of Commons Debates, vol. 420, March 1946, col. 451.

29 M. Foot, *Aneurin Bevan, Vol. 2 1945–60*, Davis Poynter, London, 1973, p. 82.
30 S. Pollard, *The Development of the British Economy 1914–1980*, Edward Arnold, London, 3rd edition, 1983, p.235.
31 D. Donnison and C. Ungerson, *Housing Policy*, Penguin Books, Harmondsworth, 1982, p. 149.
32 *Houses, the Next Step*, Cmd. 8996, MoHLG, HMSO, 1953.
33 For details see J. English, R. Madigan, and P. Norman, *Slum Clearance: The Social and Administrative Context in England and Wales*, Croom Helm, London, 1976, Chapters 1 and 2.
34 E. Gittus, *Flats, Families and the Under Fives*, Routledge & Kegan Paul, London, 1976, p.132.
35 *The Housing Programme 1965–70*, Cmd. 2838, HMSO, 1965, para. 15.
36 N. Dennis, *People and Planning*, Faber, London, 1970, and *Public Participation and Planners' Blight*, Faber, London, 1972.
37 S. Lansley, *Housing and Public Policy*, Croom Helm, London, 1979, p. 144. Figures based on the green paper, *Housing Policy*, Cmd. 6851, HMSO, 1977.
38 M. Harloe, Ch. 1 in M. Brown and S. Baldwin, *The Year Book of Social Policy in Britain 1977*, Routledge & Kegan Paul, London, 1978; S Lansley, op. cit., p. 218.
39 D. Donnison and C. Ungerson, op. cit., p. 285.
40 D. Yates, 'The English housing experience: an overview', *Urban Law and Policy*, vol. 5, 1982, pp. 203–33.

Chapter three

Rents and subsidies: a policy approach

The first two chapters have dealt with developments in council housing as a whole, and here the focus is narrowed down to questions of finance, introducing the issues to be discussed, and the approach to be used, in the later historical account of rents and subsidies policies since 1945. Some writers take the view that, 'Trying to understand a British housing subsidy system [is] as pointless as running for a bus on Oxford Street – there will always be another one along in a minute.'[1] Statements of this sort unfortunately reinforce the widely held belief that housing finance is a complex and difficult subject for non-specialists to engage in and understand. Such statements also help to perpetuate a view of history as just one thing after another, a series of unconnected events which is unlikely to yield any insight into what might happen next. Housing finance is an area which has been effectively colonised by economics, and debate is largely conducted in terms of the language, assumptions and models of that discipline. However, other methods of analysis have a contribution to make, and a policy approach provides an alternative perspective which may also be more accessible to a wider audience.

What then is meant by a policy approach in this context? In general a policy approach is concerned with political and administrative processes. It embraces: first, the formulation of political priorities and the ways in which conflicts amongst different objectives are resolved (or not); second, the translation of broad policy objectives into action; and third, the impact and outcomes of policy action. In other words, a policy approach is concerned with issues of political ideology, policy making, and implementation. In relation to housing finance it is an approach which proceeds from the observation that housing finance arrangements in Britain seem to owe more to political processes and the historically grounded transformation of housing provision, than to economic theory. In the case of rents and subsidies the particular approach adopted here specifies three main areas of interest, reflecting the main themes of the book as a whole:

1 It is important to consider the wider context of housing policy and

indeed government policy as a whole. Rents and subsidies arrangements have to be seen in relation to other aspects of policy, and in particular the long-standing preoccupation with the expansion of home ownership has exerted considerable influence on subsidies, rents, and the residualisation of council housing.

2 Recognition of the continuing, long-term commitment to the growth of home ownership leads to an interest in the continuities in rents and subsidies policies. The argument here is that, while at one level it is possible to point to the frequency of legislation on subsidies and to identify the detailed difference between successive systems of subsidy, it is more informative to recognise and proceed from an understanding of the underlying coherence and continuity of policy in this area.

3 Within the wider context and long-term trends it is necessary to consider the functional division of responsibility between central and local government and the tensions generated by that division. The role of local government in the interpretation and implementation of rents and subsidies policy is of considerable importance for an understanding of both the way legislation is adapted and its eventual impact at local level.

In 1974 Anthony Crosland, then Secretary of State for the Environment, referred to housing finance arrangements in Britain as 'a dog's breakfast' and 'whimsical in the extreme'. Since that time there has been considerable change in housing finance, reflecting developments affecting market institutions and processes, as well as state housing policy, but no government has been prepared to undertake the fundamental rationalisation that is widely regard as highly desirable. The failure of successive governments to effect thoroughgoing reform reflects not their inability to understand the prescriptions of economic theory, but their pursuit of objectives other then theoretical rectitude. In practice British governments have shown little interest in notions such as tenure neutrality, and they have been immune to arguments about the distortions produced by subsidies. On the contrary, they have been prepared to tolerate and even exacerbate these distortions in pursuit of the goal of more widespread home ownership and a reduced role for council housing. A striking feature of housing policy over the years has been the tolerance of a growing burden of assistance given to home owners through the tax system, while there have been several acts designed to alter the financial arrangements in the rented sectors.

Commitment to tenure restructuring tends to over-ride interest in notions of economy, efficiency, equity, and theoretical elegance in housing finance. The continuity represented by the long-term commitment to home ownership has been accompanied by a consistency in policy on rents and subsidies, in the sense that over the period since the mid-1950s there has been a gradual shift towards greater reliance on individual means-tested forms of assistance. It is also true, however, that within this consistent trend there is an important element of short-term expediency, reflecting problems of reconciling a variety of political objectives and issues of administrative feasibility. The details of policy at any given time reflect the outcome of negotiations between central government departments and central government's view of what can be achieved in practice, given the role of local authorities in housing provision and the implementation of policy. Thus a policy approach to rents and subsidies embraces both a longer-term perspective which recognises the continuities in policy, relating them to processes of housing market modernisation, and an awareness that individual acts are influenced by a variety of factors operating at a particular time. In particular, it is necessary to consider relations between the central-government departments responsible for housing, social security, and finance, but the main focus has to be the central–local relationship. This is essential to understanding developments in rents and subsidies policies. The fact that council houses are built, owned, and managed by local authorities, yet substantially subsidised (one way or another) by central government, establishes a relationship in which the centre clearly has an interest in decisions made at local level. Local automony and central government responses to it represent key factors in the formulation and implementation of policies on rents and subsidies, overshadowing questions of principle.

In general terms the provision of social rented housing on a non-commercial, non-profit (or limited-profit) basis, at rents which are below market clearing levels,[2] means that there has to be some alternative to the market mechanism for determining rents. This in turn raises the issue of who is to decide, and how any revenue deficit is to be measured and dealt with. In the British case local authorities have been the major developers and providers of rented housing, and historically they enjoyed considerable autonomy in rent setting. Rather than deriving from principled commitment to the freedom of local government, this autonomy can be explained by reference to the way in which Exchequer subsidy was administered, which was in turn related to the wider housing policy concern with production levels. When central government provided a fixed subsidy for every house that was built by local authorities, rent decisions at the local level had no impact on Exchequer spending and could therefore be more or less ignored by the centre. However, as housing policy moved away from high levels of council house building towards a focus on individuals and consumption issues, so the relationship between central and local government changed, raising problems of and for local autonomy.

Later sections of this chapter map out the main features of the changing landscape of rents and subsidies policies since 1945, but first it is necessary to introduce some basic concepts and terminology.

Concepts in housing finance

General introductions to housing finance are available elsewhere, for instance in the works by Aughton[3] and Garnett, Reid, and Riley.[4] Here the intention is just to identify and discuss a number of ideas and distinctions which are important for the analysis of rents and subsidies policies.

The first point to make is that housing finance can be divided into two parts, development finance and consumption finance. Rents and subsidies are part of the consumption side of housing finance, reflecting the fact that housing is both an essential item of consumption and yet inherently expensive, too expensive for most people, especially at the start of their housing careers, to buy outright from income or savings. Various mechanisms have therefore been devised to permit people to consume what they cannot purchase outright. Renting, whether public or private, and mortgaged house purchase represent different responses to the problem. In general the consumption side of housing finance embraces all the ways in which households spread the costs of housing over time, and it includes all the various forms of direct and indirect subsidy provided to assist in meeting housing costs.

The development side of housing finance, on the other hand, refers mainly to the ways in which money is raised to pay for the initial construction of dwellings, although it also covers subsequent major works. In order to build houses, particularly on a large scale, it is necessary to raise substantial sums of money to purchase land and materials and to hire labour. This is conventionally done through borrowing, with loan repayments over time representing an important component of the housing consumption expenditure of most households.

The second point to make is that public sector housing finance should not be seen as entirely separated from market forces. The need to see council housing as existing within the capitalist economic framework has been argued by, for instance, Ginsburg[5] and Harloe,[6] and it is a point which bears a little elaboration. Although council housing developed on the basis of non-market approaches to rent setting and also to dwelling allocation and management, it nevertheless remained very closely linked to private markets in land, building, and loan finance. In other words, the consumption aspects of housing were socialised, but the production aspects were not. In effect local authorities took over the roles of developer and landlord in order to ensure continued production of working-class dwellings, to satisfy consumption demands, but at the same time they did so in a way which supported the privately owned construction industry and ensured continued profitability for the various capitalist interests involved in the production process.

Although tenants on the whole do not pay market rents, the total cost to be borne by rents and subsidies reflects the fact that local authorities have to buy land at market prices, they have to borrow money at market rates of interest, and the great majority of council houses have been built under contract by private builders, whose prices are in turn influenced by the market prices for labour and materials, and by their own need to make a profit. (This is something of an over-simplification because in the early post-Second-World-War period local authorities did have easy access to cheap loans and until 1959 they did not have to pay the full market price for the land.)

Reliance on the private market has had major implications for council housing. In financial terms it has meant that costs have been maximised, and the debt burden borne by councils has historically accounted for a very large proportion of annual expenditure. It has been suggested that ultimately the debt burden 'represents the overriding control exercised by the capitalist market over council housing'.[7] It can also be argued that rent averaging (or pooling), which is a definitive feature of council housing finance, is a way of making tenants bear the burden of debt imposed on local authority housing by its location deeply embedded in the capital finance market.[8] Despite these interactions with the market system council housing in Britain has been, and even now remains, characterised by non-market-based approaches to pricing.

Pricing systems can be conveniently divided into those based on cost (expenditure) and those based on value. The latter represent market or market-related approaches, while the former constitute an alternative to the hegemony of market ideas. The term 'historic-cost pricing' is often used to indicate that rents are related to original cost of production (or purchase), but rents also include an element for management and maintenance. Current-value pricing, on the other hand, reflects what the dwelling is worth on the open market, which, of course, need have very little relation to its original production cost. In the British experience historic-cost pricing has normally been associated with pooled or collective methods of accounting. Thus the rents of individual council houses have not been closely related to their own historic costs, but total rental income in each local authority has been related to the aggregate costs of its housing stock. This approach has posed as a separate issue the problem of setting rents for individual dwellings, and a variety of methods have been devised by local authorities up and down the country.

Whereas pooled historic-cost pricing starts from the aggregate rental income and works down to the individual rent, current-value pricing tends to be conceived the other way up: the starting-point is the rents of individual dwellings and the aggregate rental income is merely the sum of all the individual rents. This distinction between the two approaches assumes considerable importance in terms of relations between central and local government. In the British experience pooled historic-cost pricing in the past meant that central government specified only that in each local area total income from rents and subsidies must equal total expenditure. This gave local authorities considerable autonomy in determining both the level of any subsidy funded by local ratepayers and the method of differentiating individual rents across the housing stock. Current-value pricing on the other hand, in the form that was introduced in Britain in 1972 (and abandoned in 1974), involved central government in setting the criteria for the determination of individual rents, removing the need for a separate locally controlled rent structure. However, it is theoretically possible to devise forms of current-value pricing which preserve an element of local autonomy. For instance, if the centre were content to confine its involvement to the setting of aggregates, in the form of an overall target rate of return, then the local authorities would retain some autonomy in the setting of individual rents.[9] This indicates that although in practice current-value pricing is normally associated with individual dwellings, it need not be so. Equally, historic-cost pricing is not inevitably collective and in theory rents could be closely related to individual historic costs (albeit resulting in some very wide differences in rents which would not reflect current demand, popularity, or utility).

In turning to the issue of subsidy, there are some definitional problems to be acknowledged. One approach is to measure subsidy in terms of money actually paid to reduce the price paid by consumers. However, some economists reject this cash-flow definition, arguing instead that the correct measure of subsidy is the difference between the actual price and the price that would be paid in a free market. Thus, if council tenants in total paid rents which matched the cost of debt repayment, management, and maintenance, without any financial assistance from taxpayers or ratepayers, according to the economic definition there would still be a subsidy, to the extent that rents were below market-clearing levels.[10]

In this book the term subsidy is used to refer to cash flows, and the major distinction to be drawn is between general and income-related forms of subsidy (although it can be convincingly argued that income-related assistance with housing costs should be seen as a form of income maintenance or social security, rather than a housing subsidy). General subsidy in this context refers to cash sums provided to bridge the gap between housing expenditure and rental income (plus any other relevant income). General subsidy is indiscriminate in the sense that it results in prices at less than average costs irrespective of the means of individual consumers. Individual means-tested assistance, however, seeks to relate assistance to the consumer's ability to pay, thus permitting the basic rent to be set at an unsubsidised level.[11]

It is important to remember that general subsidy can exist alongside income-related assistance, and that both can be associated with different pricing policies. Thus current-value pricing could involve an element of general subsidy, in the form of a socially defined rate of return somewhat below market levels, and this could be combined with a system of income-related assistance, or it could operate with either form of subsidy in isolation.

In addition it is necessary to refer to the sources of general assistance and to distinguish different methods of calculating subsidy. Throughout the period since the First World War there have been three main sources of income from which councils have covered their housing expenditure: rents, Exchequer subsidy, and rate-fund contributions. The relative significance of these components has changed over time and varied from place to place. During most of the period local authorities have been *required* to make a contribution from their general rate fund, and they have had the *freedom* to make discretionary payments in addition to mandatory contributions, but from 1990 the concept of ring-fencing will isolate housing from local authorities' general income (see Chapter 8 for a full discussion).

Despite the large number of acts specifying different subsidy systems over the years, it is appropriate to see a distinction between just two broad approaches. From 1923 to 1972 all subsidies were related to construction costs and subsequent loan charges; the level of Exchequer assistance was calculated on a per house basis and fixed at the point of construction. This reflected both the policy of encouraging local authorities to build houses and the recognition that debt charges were a major expenditure for authorities. In other words, it was a production-centred approach to subsidy which, as mentioned earlier, had the advantage of giving central government a fixed financial liability whilst giving local authorities both an incentive to build and control of rents policy.

However, inflation has a distorting effect on rents when subsidies are fixed, and the alternative approach, which has found favour with governments since 1972, is referred to as deficit subsidy. Under this approach the focus is the current situation rather than historic costs, and the level of subsidy is calculated by reference to the gap between expenditure and income (from rents and other sources). It should also be recognised that deficit subsidy is really a transitional arrangement which should be seen as part of the process of shifting away from general subsidy altogether. This has the advantage of permitting direct subsidy of management and maintenance costs, as well as debt charges, but it has serious implications for rent fixing and local autonomy, as later chapters will describe in more detail.

The final point to make before looking at the historical frameworks for analysing rents and subsidies, concerns the way in which local authorities organise their housing accounts. There are really two related points here, the first concerning the capital–revenue distinction, and the second referring to the separation of housing revenue from other local authority accounts. The distinction between capital and revenue is of fundamental importance for any understanding of housing finance. However, it is a distinction which is to some extent arbitrary and difficult to pin down.[12] In simple terms, there is a close link with the development–consumption distinction drawn earlier in this chapter. Capital expenditure refers to the provision of durable assets, whereas revenue expenditure covers a range of recurring costs associated with the use of assets. In accounting terms the convention adopted by the government is that items are counted as capital expenditure if the main benefits accruing from the expenditure are spread over a number of accounting periods (i.e. years), whereas items are counted as revenue if the benefits fall wholly within a single accounting period.[13]

In relation to council housing the capital–revenue distinction is important because of the way construction costs (capital expenditure) in any one year lead to loan repayments (revenue expenditure) over many years. Unlike services such as health and education where staff and running costs are the main categories of expenditure, in housing it is the capital programme and its revenue consequences which are most significant.

In terms of local authority accounting the capital–revenue distinction is also of great relevance for understanding housing finance. Local authorities borrow money on a regular basis for a variety of budgetary reasons and they normally operate a single account, the consolidated loans fund, from which individual capital projects are financed. This means that, although housing capital costs are conventionally repaid over sixty years, the actual borrowing can be organised quite differently, according to changing circumstances. The money for each housing project may be borrowed *from* the consolidated fund over a sixty-year period, but the borrowing *by* that fund from external sources may be over much shorter periods. This illustrates how housing capital is in a sense indistinguishable from and integrated with other local authority programmes. However, housing revenue expenditure is kept quite separate, in a statutory housing revenue account (HRA). Since 1936 all housing authorities have had to keep a separate HRA covering all their housing stock. Into the account is paid income from rents, subsidies from the Exchequer, and the authority's general rate fund, and any other income arising from charges or interest. The main expenditure items are loan charges, management, and maintenance. Over the years the pattern of income and expenditure items has changed quite significantly, and further changes are planned for the 1990s, but for present purposes it is sufficient to note the separation of the HRA from the general rate fund.

Having looked at these basic concepts and ideas we can now turn to the historically grounded analysis of rents and subsidies policies.

The old system of housing finance

Although successive post-war governments regularly altered the levels of subsidy to council housing and narrowed or widened the scope of subsidies, there were no attempts at thoroughgoing reform until the Conservatives'

Housing Finance Act of 1972. Despite the appearance of regular change, the system of public sector housing finance was based on four principles which had remained unaltered since the 1930s. These principles were:

1 *The inviolability of existing subsidies* Changes in subsidy levels affected only new houses built in the future, not existing commitments under earlier legislation in respect of dwellings already in use. It was accepted that no government could interfere with payments pledged by its predecessors.

2 *Housing subsidies were not related to the incomes of individual tenants* Subsidies were always expressed as so many pounds per house per year, for so many years, irrespective of the needs of the tenants actually occupying the houses.

3 *Rent fixing was a local authority responsibility* The principle of local autonomy in matters of rent policy was cherished by councillors and elaborately respected by ministers (who nevertheless made it very clear to local authorities what they were expected to do about rents).

4 *There was a 'no profit' rule applied to local authority housing revenue accounts* It was a basic tenet that council housing was not to be run for profit; nor was the account to be allowed to fall into deficit – any shortfall in the annual account had to be made up from either an increase in rents or a rate-fund contribution.

Within this framework there was considerable scope for changes in policy and practice in response to changing conditions. The two key factors which lay behind modifications in rent policy were the pervasive inflation in prices and wages throughout the post-war period, and the transition of the private rented sector from low controlled rents to much higher fair rents. Over a period of almost twenty years changes were made within the flexibility contained in the four basic principles, but eventually the capacity of the system to adapt to policy developments became exhausted and then its rigidity became a problem for policy implementation, requiring a break-out to a new conceptual framework.

There were two main types of change in rents policy in the period from 1955 to 1972: the development of rent pooling and rent rebates. Until 1955 subsidies for new houses were fixed periodically by reference to the gap between the costs of provision and the rent that it was reasonable to expect tenants as a whole to pay *at that time*. Inflation put this approach under great strain. Houses built for £300 or £400 in the 1930s still attracted subsidy twenty years later, even though wages had risen considerably, to levels where almost anyone in work could afford the full unsubsidised rent on such houses. At the same time, however, new houses were being built for about five times the cost of 1930s houses. To subsidise these new houses to the level required to produce a reasonable rent in relation to current incomes imposed a growing burden on the Exchequer and still left a significant gap between the rents of old and new houses.

Rent pooling was the method of getting round this problem from 1955 onwards. Basically, rent pooling meant that councils were encouraged to charge rents for all their houses which were reasonable in relation to current levels of income, irrespective of the actual costs of providing particular houses. Rent pooling was a means of spreading the cost of housing provision more evenly across the stock, and in so doing it broke the link between the cost of providing an individual house and the rent charged for it. The point is that, although in terms of the basic principles identified above subsidies were paid in relation to specific houses, the system was flexible enough to permit subsidy income to be transferred to other houses. Rent pooling was a way of withdrawing subsidy from older houses and using it to lower the rents of more expensive newer houses. A further point here is that, although governments never cancelled subsidies committed by their predecessors, they did take into account (albeit in a very imprecise way) the value of these subsidies when calculating levels of subsidy for new houses. After 1955 subsidies were explicitly reduced to encourage transference of existing subsidies from older to newer houses. In other words, the old subsidies were not directly withdrawn, but a similar effect was achieved by reducing the level of current subsidies.

Rent pooling was a useful device by which central government was able to persuade local authorities to charge higher rents for older houses and to increase the total rental income obtained. It proved to be very effective for some years as a way round the impact of inflation. It enabled central government to appropriate the beneficial effects of historic costs arising in an inflationary environment and it enabled the government to transfer from the Exchequer to the tenants of older houses part of the cost of subsidising new construction.

The idea of rent pooling was that total subsidy income, along with any surplus rental income from older houses, was to be seen as a fund which could be used to reduce the rents of new high-cost houses. Another use to which this fund could be put was rent rebates. Rent pooling and rent rebates went together to the extent that pooling raised the rents of older houses and thereby made them less accessible to low-income families. The extension of rent rebates, therefore, was a logical parallel development, providing extra help to needy tenants wherever they were found in the stock. Local authorities had complete freedom about whether to provide rebates or not, and what type of scheme to adopt. But from the mid-1950s onwards they were subject to growing moral pressure from central government to adopt some sort of rebate scheme. The Labour Party had never been enthusiastic about rebating but by the mid-1960s the Labour government was fully supportive of the principle and actually published a model scheme for authorities to adopt. The response of local authorities to the pressure from central government is best measured in terms of two variables. First, the number of authorities operating rebate schemes grew considerably, from under 10 per cent in 1950 to around 60 per cent in the early 1970s. On the other hand, there was a general reluctance to use a high proportion of subsidy income for the payment of rebates; only about 10 per cent of subsidy was used for rebate purposes.

The idea underpinning rebating is to relate assistance to the needs of individual tenants by use of a means test. The point here is that local authorities were increasingly encouraged to use their subsidy income for the benefit of the less well-off tenants and to distribute it on the basis of income qualifications, even though the total sum paid by the Exchequer to each authority was calculated on a completely different basis. This then is an indication of the flexibility of the system: subsidies calculated on a bricks and mortar basis were to be used for income-related assistance.

The pre-1972 public-sector housing finance system was flexible in other ways too. Local authority autonomy over rent levels and rent rebates meant that there was room for manoeuvre at local level. It was, for instance, possible to resist rent pooling, or to reduce its impact, by increasing rate-fund contributions, and a number of authorities chose this policy. Some authorities (often the same ones) also refused to operate rebate schemes. Thus, while the flexibility in the system enabled it to adapt to developments in government policy, at the same time different aspects of that flexibility enabled local authorities to resist the imposition of these new policies. From central government's point of view, therefore, flexibility had its disadvantages.

As a means of raising rents, rent pooling had limitations, which became increasingly apparent as time passed. Of particular significance in high-lighting the issue were developments in private sector rents policy. For many years rent control had kept the rents of private housing for the working class below the levels charged in the public sector. The 1957 Rent Act which began the process of removing rent control and restoring rents to current market levels was followed by the introduction of fair rents under the 1965 Rent Act. The impact of these two acts was to invert the relation-ship between public and private sector rents.

The transition to fair rents began to push private sector rents to levels considerably above the average in the public sector. When council rents were higher it had mattered little that they were below market levels, but when private rents became higher questions began to be asked about the wisdom of indiscriminate subsidies to the public sector, especially given that there was no subsidy in the private sector. It was clear that a government wishing to revive the private market in rented housing would have to do something about removing the differential between private and public sector rents. From the point of view of the Conservative Party, therefore, the gradual removal of rent control and the emergence of fair rents in the private sector provided both an incentive to reform council rents and a model on which to base that reform. Even before losing office in 1964 the Conservatives were planning to overhaul the subsidy system on the basis of generally higher rents, with a mandatory rebate system for the less well off.

Labour's private sector reforms provided a set of criteria which could be used to set rents in the public sector too, although the Wilson government of 1964–70 balked at this step. However, Labour was by now clearly in favour of subsidy channelling and the wider use of means-testing in council housing. That is, while not going as far as accepting fair rents in the public sector, Labour did support rent pooling and rebating.

Both parties were broadly in agreement on the policy of letting basic rents rise in real terms and concentrating assistance on those in greatest need through the use of rebates. There was a degree of convergence, but the parties were pulled apart by the Conservatives' espousal of fair rents for everyone. This was a move which was consistent with, though a development from, earlier policies. The adoption of fair rents in the public sector implied a turn of several notches on the ratchet of council rent levels, but it was not the great break with past policy that is sometimes assumed. The broad policy objectives remained consistent, but the radicalism of the Housing Finance Act lay in the changes in the legal framework of basic principles which were required to achieve fair rents.

The old system, based on the four principles outlined above, was reaching the end of its potential and utility: it could not deliver the rent increases necessary to achieve fair rents. On the one hand the flexibility of local autonomy was in conflict with the idea that rents should be set in accordance with a standard principle which was linked to the state of the market. On the other hand certain aspects of rigidity of the system also barred the way forward. Most obvious in this respect were the inviolability of subsidies and the no-profit rule.

The problem, from the point of view of a government wishing to move to a fair rent system was that rent pooling had greatest impact on authorities with substantial programmes of new building and steadily rising costs, but it had much less impact where new building was minimal, or even non-existent, and where as a result costs were rising much less quickly. Low-cost authorities were virtually immune from central government leverage on rents via the rent pooling mechanism. However, even if such authorities wanted to move to fair rents, and some of them did, they were likely to be prevented from doing so by the no-profit rule. The inviolability of subsidies committed by earlier acts meant that low-cost authorities which raised rents to fair-rent levels would soon move into surplus on their housing revenue accounts (unless they could find ways to spend the additional income). What was required in these cases was the power to remove existing subsidies and, ultimately, to sanction surpluses on the housing revenue account.

At the other end of the spectrum were high-cost authorities with a continuing need to maintain a substantial new building programme. In these cases attempts to drive up rents by reducing the proportion of rising costs borne by subsidy might be countered by either, or both, increased rate fund contributions or less new building. Under existing arrangements fair rents could not be guaranteed. What was required here was a means of ensuring fair rents without unacceptable reductions in new building in areas of shortage. It was clear that for reasons which differed in low- and high-cost authorities the old principles of public-sector housing finance would have to be replaced if a fair rents policy was to be implemented.

Towards a new system of housing finance

By the early 1970s the case for reform of public-sector housing finance was being argued on the basis of four main points: (i) that the gradual spread of fair rents in the private sector was beginning to invert the longstanding relationship between public and private rents, giving renewed strength to claims that council rents were 'too low'; (ii) that, the previous point notwithstanding, council rents varied considerably from one authority to another in a way which bore little or no relation to variations in the quality or popularity of the dwellings in different places; (iii) that subsidies were inequitably distributed amongst local authorities, with some receiving more than they needed in order to charge rents which were reasonable in relation to current wages and prices, while others received too little; (iv) that subsidy was inequitably distributed amongst tenants – that the use of subsidy to provide general rent reductions meant that some rather well-off tenants received help that they did not need, while others who were less well off received inadequate assistance.

The Housing Finance Act of 1972 represents a major watershed in the development of public-sector housing finance in Britain, not just because it was an attempt to deal with these four points, but also because in doing so it breached all four of the basic principles on which the old system had been built.

It was argued that existing methods of rent fixing were upside down. In effect, local authorities derived the total amount to be raised in rents (R) from the relationship between expenditure (E) and Exchequer subsidy (S), plus any discretionary rate fund contribution (RFC):

$$E - (S + RFC) = R$$

The alternative was to fix rents first, in accordance with current values and wages, and to derive subsidy, if any, from the relationship between rents and expenditure. The simplest reformulation of the above equation would be:

$$E - R = (S + RFC)$$

In this case RFC is not a discretionary amount but a prescribed proportion of the deficit. The problem here is to determine the value of E, and, if it is to be the actual expenditure incurred by the local authority, then the incorporation of a mandatory RFC as a significant proportion of the deficit subsidy would act as a brake on spending. The alternative would be to take a more interventionist position on reckonable expenditure, but to permit additional unsubsidised expenditure to be funded by discretionary RFC.

Another way of reformulating the equation would be:

$$E - (R + RFC) = S$$

Here central government would take a view on reckonable expenditure and notional rental income, covering the notional deficit by Exchequer subsidy, but allowing the authority to determine the actual values of E and R, and to make discretionary RFCs in support of either higher expenditure or lower rents.

The first reformulation ($E - R = (S + RFC)$) provided the basis for the Housing Finance Act 1972, while the second ($E - (R + RFC) = S$) underpinned the Housing Act 1980. The new financial regime for the 1990s takes RFC out of the equation altogether. All these approaches are effectively about raising the real value of rents and removing general subsidy, relying instead on income related assistance for the least well off. In order to move forward from the situation which existed in 1970 it was necessary to abandon all four of the principles on which rents and subsidies policy had been based for more than a generation. In the period since the early 1970s a degree of political consensus has been established around three basic principles:

1 *That rents should be set in relation to the current value of money, reflecting current wages and prices generally* Implicit in this is some kind of index linking, whether it be to rents related to the retail price index or the state of the housing market.
2 *That general subsidies should be calculated on a deficit basis* reflecting any shortfall in HRA income as a whole, after rents have been fixed in accordance with the first principle.
3 *That means tested assistance should be available on a standard basis in all areas.*

The key practical and political problems arising from these principles are precisely what criteria to use in order to relate rents to current values, how to measure reckonable expenditure for purposes of identifying any deficit, and who should make the decisions. The political consensus around the principles exists more at the level of national debate but does not extend to the local level. This is because if Exchequer subsidy derives from the relationship between rents and expenditure, then clearly central government has an enhanced interest in how both these amounts are determined, and this inevitably draws the centre into areas previously regarded as the domain of local authority decision-makers. It also opens up the whole question of local variation in need, potentially embroiling the centre in complex disputes about local expenditure levels.

The first attempt to resolve the issue was to invoke the notion of 'fair rents', but this was rejected by the Labour government of 1974–9 and has not been revived since. Instead attention has focused on the level of rent increase rather than the rent itself. The deficit subsidy system devised under the Labour government in the late 1970s, and operated with certain changes by the Conservatives since 1981, took the existing pattern of rents, subsidies, and rate fund contributions in each area as given, and provided a mechanism for achieving rent increases year by year. This proved to be a very potent means of raising rents and reducing general subsidy, but after two or three years the new subsidy system began to lose its leverage on rents in many areas, thereby raising new questions about what was an appropriate level of rent, and how to achieve it.

It is reasonable to interpret the approach since 1979 as not so much a rents policy, but more a strategy for eliminating general subsidy and replacing it with income-related assistance. The transition from a system based on general subsidies to one which emphasises income-related assistance is an important feature of housing finance since 1972. However, the failure to establish a clear criterion for fixing overall rent levels, as distinct from rent increases, suggests that a stable and coherent new system of public-sector housing finance has yet to be achieved.

There are two points remaining to be made about what has been achieved so far. First, the adoption of the deficit subsidy principle involved a departure from the idea that rent fixing was a local matter, and gave central government a much more direct interest in rent fixing. Since 1972, there has been a much firmer stance taken by the centre in relation to local-authority rents than in earlier times (although the degree of assertiveness and nature of enforcement have varied). In general terms, if central government is responsible for funding all or part of any HRA deficit, then it obviously requires some limitation on its liability, by reference to the local authority's income and expenditure which determine the size of the deficit.

The second point is that the transition to a system of assistance with housing costs based on means-tested benefits represents the residualisation of rents policy. This means that rents policy has moved away from a universalistic distribution of assistance to council tenants as a whole. Now subsidy is effectively targeted on those with the lowest incomes on the basis of a means test. This represents a policy change of the utmost significance for council housing because on the one hand it increases housing costs for the better-off tenants, making home ownership more attractive, while on the other hand it enables the least well off to afford council housing. The residualisation of rents policy is an important factor in the overall residualisation of council housing itself.

Conclusion

Before turning to the detailed analysis of post-war developments in rent and subsidy policies, a number of points need to be made. First, it has been suggested above that the 1972 Housing Finance Act represents a major watershed in the development of rents policy, and that it should be seen as marking the end of what has been called here the old system of housing finance. However, it is also important to add that, although the 1972 Act breached the basic principles of the old system, it did so because these principles were becoming a barrier to the achievement of the objectives of rent policy which were broadly accepted by both main parties, i.e. that rents should in some way reflect current incomes and prices, and that subsidies should be increasingly income related. In this sense, therefore, it is appropriate to point to the *continuity* of policy across the 1972 watershed, and to see the Act as an attempt to provide a new framework to pursue broadly similar objectives.

Second, now that it has been argued that a radical and controversial measure should be understood in terms of continuity with the past, it is also necessary to draw attention to the changes in policy which occurred *without* recourse to similarly contentious legislation in the two decades before 1972. This is really a methodological point, suggesting that a focus on policy change through legislation would, in the case of rents policy in the post-war period, miss out some very important developments. In this connection, too, it is relevant to draw attention to the way in which, although rent pooling was introduced in 1935 as a device to simplify local authority housing accounts, it had very little impact on rent levels over the following twenty years and only in the mid-1950s was it picked up as a policy tool to be used by central government as a lever on local authority rents.

Third, the point was made earlier in this chapter that council housing represented only a partial removal of housing from the market, a process which can be labelled the decommodification of housing consumption, leaving production and loan finance firmly in the private sector. As a way of understanding the general thrust of rents and subsidy policy over the last thirty years it is important to recognise the underlying consistency of movement towards the removal of that partial decommodification. In other words, the long-term process of raising basic rents, reducing general subsidy, and concentrating on means-tested assistance for the least well off represents a penetration of market principles into council housing. This represents more than the assertion that the 'proper' role of council housing is to accommodate the least well off. It includes the idea that, in doing so, council housing should be made more like private housing.

Finally, there is a point to be made about the methodology and presentation of the historical analysis in subsequent chapters. Following on from the previous observation about the overall shape and direction of policy, it is appropriate to point out here that rents and subsidy policy has been carried forward mainly by Conservative governments and that Labour governments have tended to go in the same general direction albeit rather more slowly and perhaps more reluctantly. As a reflection of this differential enthusiasm for the development of rents and subsidy policy, the analysis and description in the following chapters deliberately devotes more attention to periods of Conservative administration.

References

1 J. Hills, *Twenty-First Century Housing Subsidies: Durable Rent-Fixing and Subsidy Arrangements for Social Rented Housing*, WSP 33, London School of Economics, 1988, p.10.
2 M. Ball, M. Harloe, and M. Martens, *Housing and Social Change in Europe and the USA*, Routledge, London, 1988, p. 42.
3 H. Aughton, *Housing Finance: A Basic Guide*, Shelter, London, 2nd revised edition, 1986.
4 D. Garnett, B. Reid and H. Riley, *Introduction to Housing Finance*, Longman, London, 1989.
5 N. Ginsburg, *Class, Capital and Social Policy*, Macmillan, London, 1979, p. 139.
6 M. Harloe, in Ball, Harloe and Martens, op. cit., p. 42.
7 Community Development Project, *Profits Against Houses*, CDP Information and Intelligence Unit, London, 1976, p. 34.
8 M. Ball, 'British housing policy and the house building industry', *Capital and Class*, no. 4. 1978.
9 M. A. King and A. B. Atkinson, 'Housing policy, taxation and reform', *Midland Bank Review*, March 1980.
10 A. J. Merrett and A. Sykes, *Housing Finance and Development*, Longman, London, 1965; S. Goss and S. Lansley, *What Price Housing?*, SHAC, London, 1981; A. O'Sullivan, 'Misconceptions in current subsidy debate', *Policy and Politics*, vol. 12, no. 2, April 1984, pp. 119–44.
11 Goss and Lansley, op cit.; Association of Metropolitan Authorities, *A New Deal for Home Owners and Tenants: Proposals for a Housing Allowance Scheme*, London, 1987.
12 N. Hepworth, *The Finance of Local Government*, Allen & Unwin, London, 7th edition, 1984, pp. 9–11.
13 *Capital Expenditure and Finance: A Consultation Paper*, Department of the Environment, London, 1988, p. 19.

Chapter four

Rents and subsidies in a 'welfare state'

The decade after 1945 was a period of reconstruction, in social, economic, and physical terms. The period from 1944 to 1948 saw a series of major Acts of Parliament which laid down the framework within which reconstruction took place. Important reforms in education, health, social security, and child care established the basis of the 'welfare state'. In the case of housing, there was no equivalent to the epoch-making legislation in these other areas of provision, but the housing policies of the late 1940s, and to a lesser extent the early 1950s, were consistent with the principles of the welfare state. The emphasis was on breaking down the barriers and distinctions between groups in society, opening up public services to all on the basis of need, without investigation of ability to pay. This was reflected in council housing allocations and rents policies.

In a sense there was no need for reforming legislation in housing because the events during and just after the First World War had established the principles and frameworks for the provision of public housing. In addition the post-1945 government had the advantage of hindsight and was able to learn from the experiences of 1919–22. The key measures taken to regenerate housing production were, first, to retain the wartime controls on the supply of materials and private-sector development, and second, to increase the value of local authority housing subsidies to take account of higher standards and costs. It is appropriate to mention here that the government also retained rent control in the private sector, in line with the report of the Ridley Committee in 1945.[1]

In a speech in the House of Commons in October 1945 the Minister of Health, Aneurin Bevan, set out Labour's housing policy, noting that before the war the speculative builders had had a very successful period building for owner occupation. Labour's policy would be quite different:

We propose to lay the main emphasis of our housing programme ... upon building houses to let. That means that we shall ask the local authorities to be the main instruments for the housing programme.... It is ... a principle of the first importance that the local authorities must be looked to as the organisations and source for the building of the main bulk of the housing programme. The local authorities are admirably suited for this purpose.[2]

The Housing Act, 1946

The financial provisions for the support of the housing programme were established in the Housing (Financial and Miscellaneous Provisions) Act, 1946. The government's approach was outlined in the opening speech on the second-reading debate in the Commons in March 1946, by the Parliamentary Secretary to the Ministry of Health, Mr Key. He began by identifying three issues to be addressed by the bill: the refusal of working people to tolerate 'the cribbed and cabined quarters of the past', the need for housing at rents which people could afford to pay, and the need to overcome what he saw as the temporary problem of high costs. 'High costs must not prevent us from building now, but costs must not be allowed to remain so high as to frustrate the fulfilment of our task: the building of better homes at reasonable rents for the poorest of our people.'[3] The Bill provided for an annual review of subsidy levels, starting in December 1946, so that if costs fell, then subsidy could be reduced accordingly. If costs rose, however, then higher subsidy would require new legislation.

The basic Exchequer subsidy was set at £16.10s. per house per year, plus a minimum of £5.10s. from the local rates (this latter amount could be supplemented at the local authority's own discretion). There were six variations on the basic subsidy, dealing with the special needs of agricultural areas and flats on expensive sites. Mr Key explained in his second-reading speech that the subsidy had been calculated on the assumption of an average rent of 10s. per week (net), which on current building costs was assumed to leave an annual deficit of £22[4] (taking into account a contribution for repairs, though this was not stated). Different rents were assumed in agricultural areas (7s. 6d.) and for flats (12s.). This set of assumed rents was not to be taken as any more than a guide to local authorities who retained the freedom to set actual rents. These assumed rents were 'regarded as a reasonable average to charge for the higher standard of accommodation that is to be provided.'[5] The standard target rent of 10s. per week represented a victory over the Treasury, which had aimed for a figure of 12s.[6]

In the context of 1946, 10s. per week net rent represented less than 8 per cent of average income and was probably well within the grasp of the great majority of households. Certainly in real terms it was less than many council tenants had been paying in the years before the war. It has been estimated that council house rents averaged 7s. per week in 1936 and 9s. in 1946; on this basis the rents of pre-war council houses fell by 23 per cent in real terms over this period.[7] According to the same source money wages almost doubled between 1936 and 1946, giving an average wage of £6.6s.7d. in 1946, and average rent fell from about 11 per cent to about 7 per cent. This, of course, refers to rents of *pre-war* houses and gives no indication as to the actual level or impact of the rents of the post-war houses. However, it does show that in attempting to hold the rents of new, higher-quality houses broadly in line with pre-war houses, the government was aiming at a reduction in real terms compared with the rents paid before the war. It may be concluded, therefore, that in so far as rents were in practice held at 10s. per week, council housing could be opened up to a wider range of low-income households. According to the first report of the Girdwood committee[8] on the cost of house building, there had been a rise in the standard of living during the war – wages increased by 49 per cent and the cost of living by 31 per cent – but against that it must be remembered that in the post-war period levels of taxation were higher.

The success of the policy depended on what happened to costs. If costs rose then, as Barbara Castle pointed out in one of the few speeches to address the rents issue in the debates on the 1946 Bill, the local authorities were going to be rather exposed. It is worth quoting in full the relevant passage from the speech:

> I suggest to the Minister that he is leaving the local authorities rather single-handed to fight this battle of building costs – one of the most serious battles which face us in the housing field. Is the deficit on these houses going to be £22, as the Minister visualises, or is it going to be £30 which the local authorities visualise? If the Minister is wrong and the local authorities are right then we are faced with this situation: local authorities will have to take the rap. They will be left with the decision as to whether they should put an extra burden, in addition to their statutory rate contributions, on the rates, or let these houses at more than 10s. a week rent: and that will mean in many cases that with rates included – these houses will let at something nearer a gross rent of £1 a week... are we always going to deny to the low income groups a share in our progress in housing development, because the rents have moved beyond their range?[9]

This proved to be a remarkably prescient comment, as the following sections show.

Standards and costs

The standards to be adopted in post-war housing were set out in the Dudley Report in 1944,[10] and later incorporated in Ministry of Health advice to local authorities. During the 1930s most local authority houses were less than 800 square feet. The Dudley Report recommended a minimum of 900 square feet for a three-bedroomed house, plus a further 70–100 square feet of external storage. Although the committee's recommendations were broadly accepted at the time, it was not until November 1945 (i.e. after the election of the Labour government) that the 900 square feet standard was made the minimum acceptable standard, with clear encouragement to local authorities to build in the range 900–950 square feet, plus outbuildings. Table 4.1 shows the way in which local authorities responded to the freedom to build larger houses.

Table 4.1 Average floor area (inclusive) of three-bedroomed houses in tenders approved by local authorities in England and Wales, 1945–51 (square feet)

1945	1946	1947	1948	1949	1950	1951
979.5	1,026.8	1,046	1,052	1,054.8	1,051.6	1,032

Source: Transposed from Merrett's interpretation of graphs in the Reports of the Girdwood Committee, 1948 and 1952

The overall size of houses is only one indicator of quality, and it should be added that during the 1940s there was a very heavy emphasis on the construction of three-bedroomed houses rather than two, and on the building of houses rather than flats. In the period 1945–8 'well over 80 per cent' of new council houses had three bedrooms, but from 1948 there was a growth in the number of two-bedroomed dwellings.[11]

The construction of higher-quality houses added significantly to their cost, and it was calculated in 1948 that 'the additional cost of the larger size and improved amenities of the post-war house amounts to more than a quarter of the total building cost and is itself equivalent at the present rate of interest to a weekly rent of over 4s.6d.'[12] In addition, inflation since before the war had an even greater impact on prices. Inflation in the building industry had been much greater than in the economy as a whole, with the effect that in mid-1946 the average *tender* price for a three-bedroomed house was £1170, compared with a *total* cost of £380 in 1938–9. And prices continued to rise, as Table 4.2 shows.

Table 4.2 Average tender price for three-bedroomed local authority houses in England and Wales, 1945–51

1945	1946	1947	1948	1949	1950	1951
£1,045	£1,163	£1,230	£1,281	£1,294	£1,320	£1,361

Source: as for Table 4.1

Tender prices actually understate the total cost of house building and so give a misleading impression of the relationship between costs, subsidy, and rent. The total cost, including roads, sewers, and professional fees, was considerably above the tender price, with consequential implications for rent, as the Girdwood Committee clearly showed in their second report:

	House of 1,029 sq. ft. completed in Oct. 1947		House of 1,050 sq. ft. completed in Oct. 1949	
	Cost	Weekly rent equivalent	Cost	Weekly rent equivalent
	£	s d	£	s d
Building	1,242	17 3	1,321	18 4
Land, roads & sewers	122	1 8	158	2 2
Fees for architect & QS	36	6	36	6
	1,400	19 5	1,515	21 0
	per annum		*per annum*	
Repairs, management, etc.	10	35 10	10	35 10
Economic weekly rent		23 3		24 10
Subsidies	22	8 5	22	8 5
Subsidised rent		14 10		18 10

Source: *The Cost of House-Building*, 2nd Report of the Girdwood Committee, HMSO 1950 p. 23.

This report therefore showed that on average the subsidised rent of a new council house completed in October 1947 was no less than 48.3 per cent higher than the guideline set in the debate on the 1946 Housing Act only eighteen months earlier. Two years later, in October 1948, the average subsidised rent was 64.1 per cent above the guideline. These figures, of course, do not represent averages calculated from the rents actually charged by local authorities, merely what they would have had to charge if their costs were average, and if there had been no voluntary rate fund contribution. In fact there was a very wide variation in building costs. According to a survey in 1950 the range of capital costs for three-bedroomed houses built in 1949–50 was from £1107 to £2320.[13]

It seems that in 1946 the Ministry took building costs of £1100 as the basis for calculating the subsidy necessary to leave a rent of 10s. per week.[14] At that time Bevan reported that the average tender price in the period up to 31 January 1946 was £980, plus land and services.[15] However, by the time the Bill was passed the figure of £1100 was below even tender price. On the other hand, there was a cut in interest rates in June 1946 which was used to justify not increasing the subsidy to compensate for rising costs.

To conclude this section, is it possible to say that during the war the rents of pre–war houses had fallen in real terms, and that the cost of building had gone up more than the index of wages or prices generally. Despite the relatively very high level of building costs, the Labour government embarked on a plan to build houses to a higher standard, thus incurring extra costs, and to let them at rents not much above the deflated levels charged for inferior pre-war houses. This appeared to be a highly redistributive policy, based on improved standards, even in a period of high costs and rents which were lower in real terms than the average rent paid in the 1930s. Adherence to this policy would surely have meant that good-quality council housing became accessible to the poorest families, and the price barrier would have been substantially removed. However, as has been shown, there were powerful forces at work tending to drive up council house rents. In the face of this upward pressure on rents the government failed to increase subsidy levels throughout the period 1946–51. In other words, there was a fall in the real value of subsidies, relative to the level set in 1946, throughout the remainder of the period of the Labour government. As Barbara Castle had predicted, this left the local authorities with some difficult political decisions to make.

The rents of council houses

Information on actual rent levels during the years before 1949–50 is hard to come by because no systematic records were kept by central government. What evidence there is suggests that on average net rents of new houses exceeded the target of 1946, often by substantial amounts. For instance, the Girdwood Committee believed that in 1950 net rents of 18s. were by no means uncommon.

The first systematic studies of rent levels were carried out in 1949 and 1950. In 1949 a survey of 162 authorities in England and Wales was carried out by the Institute of Municipal Treasurers and Accountants (IMTA) and reported in a Political and Economic Planning (PEP) broadsheet.[16] This limited study revealed that the average gross rent (including rates) for pre-war houses was 15s. per week and for post-war houses the figure was 21s. Just over half (51 per cent) of authorities in the sample charged gross rents averaging more than £1 per week for post-war houses. There was wide variation in the rents of post-war houses, but 47 per cent were in the range 15s. to 20s. The authors of the report drew attention to the contrast between north and south, with rents tending to be lower in the north, and for high-rent authorities to be concentrated in the south.

A slightly later PEP report, dated April 1950,[17] stated that gross rents were generally in the range 21s.6d. to 25s., but it also gave a higher figure for the average male industrial wage, £7.2s.8d. This report also observed that the average working-class family before the war spent about 12 per cent of income on rent (other sources suggest pre-war rents may have averaged out at 15 per cent of working-class incomes[18]) but by 1950 the average was only 8 or 9 per cent.[19] The main factors here were, of course, the rise in money wages on the one hand and the pegging of private sector rents at 1939 levels on the other hand. Nevertheless it is clear that new council houses represented an expensive option when compared with existing rented accommodation. It should also be noted that, in taking one-sixth, or 16.6 per cent as a reasonable proportion of income to be paid in rent, PEP was setting a norm which was not only well above the post-war average but above the pre-war average as well. On this basis it was argued that at the prevailing level of subsidy the average new council house could be afforded by families earning £6.9s. per week, if they paid one-sixth in rent, or as little as £5.7s.6d. if they paid one-fifth.[20] In other words, families on below-average earnings could obtain new council houses only if they were prepared to devote a higher-than-average proportion of their incomes to rent. But, of course, it is precisely people on lower incomes who are least able to allocate high proportions of income to rent, which led the PEP report to observe that:

As far as the tenants and prospective tenants are concerned, there is evidence of some resistance to the level of rents for new houses. This may be caused in part by traditional attitudes concerning reasonable rents, but much of it is undoubtedly the result of genuine hardship.[21]

In March 1951 the Institute of Municipal Treasurers and Accountants (IMTA) published the first of their series of *Housing Statistics*, relating to 1949–50.[22] The data, based on returns from local authorities, were extensive but incomplete. Rather than presenting overall averages the summary table emphasised the range of costs and rents. Thus for three-bedroomed pre-war houses the lowest average new rent (i.e. average within one authority) was 5s.10d. and the highest was 22s.5d. For three-bedroomed post-war houses the averages ranged from 8s.2d. to 29s.3d. The highest net rent for post-war three-bedroomed houses was 41s. in Bristol. This very high figure reflected the city council's policy of building some houses to be let at full economic, unsubsidised rents. By 1951 over 1000 dwellings had been built under this scheme.[23] At the opposite end of the scale Widnes was able to let some of its new three-bedroomed houses for as little as 5s.7d.

Amongst the biggest housing authorities, the county boroughs, only Dewsbury out of the total of 83 charged an average rent of under 10s. for its post-1945 three-bedroomed houses. A third (27) had average net rents of 15s. or more, and in over half (44) the latest rents fixed were 15s. or more. Nevertheless 59 per cent (49) of these authorities were making voluntary additional payments from the rates in support of the housing revenue account. Amongst the non-county boroughs almost half had rents of 15s. or more, but the proportion making a voluntary rate fund contribution (RFC) was markedly lower at 42 per cent. It is fairly clear then that, in 1949–50 at least, the pressure on rents arising from standards and costs was resulting in both high rents and widespread extra subsidies from the rates.

In addition to the higher costs of new houses local authorities had to meet the higher costs of maintaining the pre-war stock which had been widely neglected during the war itself. By charging higher rents for older houses the authorities could both cover the extra maintenance costs and defray some of the burden imposed by new building. The IMTA Housing Statistics for 1950–1 indicate the last date of comprehensive rent review, and it is clear that an overwhelmingly large proportion of authorities had reviewed rents generally since the war.

Amongst county boroughs only 4 had not reviewed rents since 1946 (7 did not respond), and only 3 out of 199 responding non-county boroughs had carried out no review since 1946. In Bristol, for example, rents of pre-war and temporary dwellings were increased in 1948 by an average of 3s.9d. per week, bringing them up to levels comparable with post-war houses (which were generally of superior quality).[24] It is important to remember that higher costs affected all parts of the stock and were reflected in higher rents all round. This tended to reduce the capacity of authorities to use their pre-war stock as a source of low-rent houses for the least well-off. The Girdwood Committee reported in 1953 that in overall terms the cost of repairs in that year was three times as much as in 1939,[25] and that despite higher rents local authorities had 'generally had to adopt lower standards of general maintenance'.[26]

The retreat from the high-quality low-rent policy

From 1947 onwards the Ministry of Health acted increasingly to contain house building rather than to raise levels of output.[27] At the same time the continued escalation in building costs was exerting pressure on rents, but subsidy was not increased in response. In the period when costs and standards were both rising, the increased burden was loaded entirely on to rents and/or rates. In an interesting speech in the House of Commons in 1952, Harold Macmillan, then Minister of Housing, set out the progression of assumed rent levels.[28] He explained that subsidy was calculated on the basis of three sets of assumptions, covering capital costs, maintenance costs, and rents. He stated that in 1946 the 10s. assumed rent had been linked with capital costs of £1100 and maintenance costs of £7.8s. per year. According to his version of cost increases, the capital cost of a three-bedroomed house was £1350 in 1949, £1500 in 1951, and £1575 in 1952. By 1952 the assumed level of repairs expenditure was £12. On this basis he argued that Labour's failure to raise the subsidy after 1946 must have been due to acceptance of higher rents, because it was 'inconceivable' that all the extra burden should have been deemed to rest on the rates. Macmillan went on to say that Bevan appeared to have accepted notional net rents of 13s. to 14s. in 1949, and in 1950 14s.3d. was accepted, and was referred to as 10 per cent of average wages. By November 1950 14–15s. was accepted and, he said, in the review carried out in May 1951, 'the only basis upon which a refusal to raise the subsidy could possibly have been justified would have been to accept a notional rent for this purpose of 16s.' Macmillan judged this to be fair and on the same basis he himself now assumed 18s. In his defence Bevan replied that the increased notional rents were designed to be in proportion to increased wages.[29] He did not challenge Macmillan's figures.

From 1950 the average size of new three-bedroomed council houses began to fall, and the proportion of two-bedroomed houses began to increase. Bevan was a staunch supporter of high standards but, when he left the Ministry of Health in January 1951, his housing responsibilities were taken over by Hugh Dalton in the newly formed Ministry of Local Government and Planning (renamed the Ministry of Housing and Local Government by the Conservatives in October 1951). In April 1951 the new ministry issued a circular to local authorities headed *Housing Standards* (circular 38/51) and dealing with the issue of costs and standards. The ministry's objective was to find ways of reducing the cost of new houses 'without prejudice to essential standards'. The argument was put that skilled designers had shown how to make savings in cost by reducing the *overall* size of houses without reducing room sizes. Local authorities were given the freedom to build three-bedroomed houses of less than 900 square feet, provided that room size and total 'living space' did not fall below the present standard, and to omit the second w.c. from houses, as a further cost-saving measure.

For the sake of historical accuracy it is necessary to establish that the decline in standards was heralded by this Labour circular, although the process was carried forward with greater vigour and enthusiasm under the Conservatives after October 1951.

The Conservatives took office having promised the electorate 300,000 houses per year, which was a 50 per cent increase over the production achieved in 1951. In order to reach this target in the shortest time it was necessary to rely on the local authority sector, and output increased from 162,500 in 1951 to 229,300 in 1953, despite balance of payments problems. Output declined thereafter as private sector production expanded. Lower standards helped to maximise the number of dwellings that could be produced for a given outlay, and helped to contain the growth in the share of capital investment devoted to housing. At the same time lower standards helped to contain the overall level of subsidy expenditure, which was bound to grow anyway as output rose. Lower standards also helped to reduce the case for higher subsidy per dwelling.

In fact the Conservatives did raise the level of subsidy per dwelling, in money terms, in the 1952 Housing Act. The standard Exchequer subsidy rose from £16.10s. to £26.14s., with corresponding increases in RFC from £5.10s. to £8.18s. Meanwhile, however, the long-term interest rate charged by the Public Works Loans Board rose from 3 per cent to 3.75 per cent in November 1951 and then to 4.25 per cent in February 1952. Thus, although the subsidy was raised by £13.12s., loan charges were also raised, as a deliberate act of policy, by £19.13s.6d. (a capital cost of £1575 in 1952 is assumed). In other words, the fall in the real value of subsidies was continued, indeed hastened, by the Conservatives in 1952, indicating the retreat from a low rent policy.

Ministers said little about rents until rather later in the 1950s, but within a month of the Conservatives' taking office in 1951 a circular (70/51) was issued to local authorities, emphasising the need to obtain more houses from the available resources of materials, labour, and money. An appendix to this circular listed a number of different house types of different sizes, all well below the 900 square feet minimum (plus storage) which had been proposed in the Dudley Report of 1944. The smallest three-bedroomed house referred to was a mere 737 square feet or less than the lowest levels of the 1930s. The exhortation to lower standards was continued in supplements to the 1949 *Housing Manual* issued in 1952 and 1953, although the case was presented in terms of obtaining more houses *without* loss of standards or amenity. In fact the so-called 'People's House' did involve a reduction in standards which Merrett has described as brutal.[30] The decline continued steadily until 1959, by which time the average size of a new three-bedroomed council house was down to 897 square feet (*including* external storage).

Rent rebates in eclipse

In retrospect, the years 1945–54 appear as a period marked by a widespread lack of interest in rent rebate schemes. The very modest advances made by the advocates of the principle of rebating during the 1930s were partly reversed in the decade after the war, in a period when universal rather than selective approaches to social policy enjoyed majority support. This was perhaps the time when public hostility to means testing had most influence on policy and a report of a survey by the Society of Housing Managers, published in 1950, referred to rebating as a 'limited experiment', limited in terms of both the number of authorities running rebate schemes and the proportion of their housing stock which they included in such schemes.[31] The report quoted Wilson's estimate of 112 authorities with rent-rebate schemes in 1939 and set against this the finding that only 78 authorities (8.2 per cent of 941 responding authorities) were operating schemes in 1950. Some 55 authorities, virtually half according to Wilson's estimate, which had schemes in 1939 had actually abandoned them, although some others had begun rebating. A report from the Central Housing Advisory Committee (CHAC) three years later confirmed this view:

The up-to-date evidence which we have obtained of the position in 1953 goes to confirm that rebate schemes have lost, at any rate for the time being, much of their former importance for even where they are still operating the percentage of tenants qualifying for rebate is, in these days of full employment, very small.[32]

It seems, then, that after the Second World War rent rebate schemes underwent a period of decline. The number of schemes, the number of recipients, and the value of rebates and their overall cost were all down on pre-war levels. Several factors combined to reduce the importance of rent rebates, even from the low priority given them before the war. The Society of Housing Managers' report summed up the situation by suggesting that, 'the former problem of helping the poorest families in a time of fairly normal housing cost has become that of helping families within the lower wage groups during a time of exceptionally high housing cost.[33] Whilst it is possible to dispute the accuracy of this statement it does have the value of indicating contemporary perceptions of the problem of rents and subsidies.

On the demand side, the ability of tenants as a whole to pay council house rents had been improved by the elimination of mass unemployment, the rise in the real value of wages, the provision of family allowances, and the availability of help from the newly created National Assistance Board for those who depended upon state benefits. These factors contributed to the belief that poverty had been virtually eliminated in post-war Britain, and that therefore special arrangements to help tenants with their rent were no longer needed. The role of family allowances in this context is particularly interesting and deserves a word of comment. It must be remembered that the campaign for rent rebates in the 1930s was led by the Family Endowment Society, (FES), which existed primarily to promote the idea of family allowances (see chapter 2 above). It has been argued that it was the presence of children in a family that made it especially difficult for low-wage earners to afford decent housing, and therefore a system of child rent rebates had been proposed. With the achievement of family allowances in 1945, and the death of Eleanor Rathbone, the FES soon ceased to operate and the main pro-rebate pressure group was silenced. However, there is some contemporary evidence that the provision of family allowances was seen to remove the need for rent rebates.[34]

On the supply side, for those who remained unable to afford the rents of new council houses there was the stock of cheaply built lower rent pre-war houses. The availability of this source of lower rent houses distinguished the pre- and post-war periods: houses, many of which had been relatively expensive to rent in 1939, had been transformed into relatively cheap dwellings by 1945. To the extent that pre-war houses continued to be let at rents below those set for new houses, then they constituted an alternative to rent rebates (albeit at the cost of a degree of social segregation within the public sector, a not insignificant factor in view of later developments such as council house sales).

Nevertheless, it is necessary to point out that the case for rent rebates was not entirely neglected. In April 1950 PEP produced a broadsheet which was unequivocally in favour of rebates: 'it seems reasonable to conclude that subsidies should no longer be attached directly to the houses, but to those families who could not otherwise afford them.[35] The method outlined by PEP bore a remarkable resemblance to the scheme later incorporated in the Housing Finance Act of 1972.

In 1953 two more reports endorsed this general strategy. The CHAC report, *Transfers, Exchanges and Rents*, distinguished rent rebates from differential rent schemes. Whereas the former involved rebates from standard rents for low income tenants, the latter involved rent payments calculated on the tenant's ability pay – the more the income the greater the rent, subject to a maximum figure. The CHAC sub-committee considered rebates to be obsolete but commended differential rent schemes as one type of 'modern experiments in rent fixing'. The others considered were additional earner charges and rent surcharges, imposed when the tenant's income exceeds a certain figure. Although no general recommendation was made (in grounds of varying local circumstances), local authorities were urged to consider these schemes, *not*, it appears, to help the poorest families to enter council housing, but to raise the amount of revenue received in total by the local authority.[36]

The other report to consider rebating in 1953 was published by the Institute of Housing and drawn up by the Senior Officers' Discussion Group of the Institute's London branch.[37] One of the most striking characteristics of the report, considering that unlike the CHAC document it was written by housing professionals rather than party politicians, was its commitment to the sort of policies shortly to be pursued by the Conservative government. The report made four recommendations: that the structure of subsidies should be reviewed, bearing in mind the increasing costs to national and local funds (in fact the cost of subsidies was very low in relation to total public expenditure, and probably falling as a proportion at this time); that the Rent Restriction Acts should be amended at the earliest opportunity; that local authorities should aim to reduce discretionary rate fund contributions to the housing revenue account; and that subsidies should be given only to tenants who were unable to pay the full economic rent – grading of estates and rent rebates were recommended as a means of achieving this last objective. In fact the scheme proposed by this committee was a differential rent scheme, based on one seventh of earnings.

Conclusion

The first point to draw out of this discussion of the first post-war decade is that, in keeping with the wider approach to social policy in the new welfare state, housing policy was strongly non-residual. Emphasis was placed on the quality and quantity of new building to reduce the overall shortage which affected all sections of the population. Policy concentrated on production rather than distribution, and there were no specific measures to target new housing on the least well off. Even after the retreat from the highest standards of the late 1940s, the objective was to achieve maximum output within the constraints on resources, rather than to channel new housing to particular groups.

Second, the Labour government set out in 1945 with a low rent policy, but in practice the commitment to high quality was given greater priority in the environment of continually rising costs and macro-economic problems. In terms of rents policy the failure to raise the level of subsidy in response to rising prices was of the greatest significance. As had happened in the early 1920s, high-quality council housing became associated with relatively high rents, and in the widespread absence of rent rebate schemes the least well off were again faced with a significant price barrier. In this sense, therefore, rents policy took on an appearance of being the *opposite* of a residual approach: general subsidy and high quality made council housing attractive and accessible to the rather better off, but squeezed out the least well off.

The effect of this policy was to channel new housing towards skilled and semi-skilled workers, those groups on whom Britain's economic recovery depended to a large extent. The poorest, with least political and economic power, were the losers in this situation. However, in terms of party politics, allegations of indiscriminate distribution of subsidy fuelled the Conservatives' attacks on the achievements of the Labour government of 1945–51. A flavour of right-wing criticism is obtained from the following statement by Ernest Marples in the House of Commons in 1952:

> I still maintain the view that a large number of people are living in council houses and are receiving subsidy when, in fact, they could well afford to pay the full rent ... What I cannot stomach is a man earning £3,000 per year and receiving a subsidy from the taxpayers and rate-payers.[38]

(In 1952 the average *household* income amongst council tenants was £528 per year.[39])

The Labour government's policy of concentrating resources for new building in the public sector had the effect of at first dictating terms to the new Conservative administration after October 1951. However, having achieved their output target of 300,000 dwellings per year, the Conservatives were poised to launch a major restructuring of housing policy, and one of the targets of their strategy was the rents and subsidies regime inherited from Labour.

References

1 *Report of the Inter-Departmental Committee on Rent Control*, Cmd. 6621, HMSO, April 1945, p. 9. This Report envisaged continuation of rent control for ten years.
2 *House of Commons Debates*, vol. 414, October 1945, col. 1222.
3 *House of Commons Debates*, vol. 420, March 1946, col. 341–2.
4 ibid., col. 344.
5 ibid., col. 344.
6 K.O. Morgan, *Labour in Power 1945–51*, Clarendon Press, Oxford, 1984, p. 14.
7 *Housing Policy Technical Volume*, Part 1, p. 43, Table 1.27, HMSO, 1977.
8 *The Cost of House Building*, Ministry of Health, HMSO, 1948, para. 27.
9 *House of Commons Debates*, vol. 420, March 1946, cols 397–8.
10 *Design of Dwellings*, Report of the Design of Dwellings Sub-Committee of Central Housing Advisory Committee, HMSO, 1944.
11 *Report of the Ministry of Housing and Local Government 1950–51 to 1954*, Cmd. 9559, HMSO, 1955, p. 9.
12 *The Cost of House-Building*, op. cit., p. 30.
13 *Housing Statistics*, Institute of Municipal Treasurers and Accountants, London, 1951, p. 5.
14 *House of Commons Debates*, vol. 420, 1946, col. 230.
15 *House of Commons Debates*, vol. 420, 1946, col. 60, written answers.
16 PEP, 'The economics of the council house', *Planning*, vol. XIV, no. 308, 23 January 1950.
17 PEP, 'A new policy for housing subsidies', *Planning*, no. 312, 24 April 1950.
18 Institute of Statistics, Oxford University, *Bulletin*, no. 7, 1945, p. 91.
19 PEP, *Planning*, no. 312. 1950, op. cit., p. 262.
20 ibid., p. 262–3.
21 ibid., p. 263.
22 *Housing Statistics 1949–50*, IMTA, London, 1951.
23 J.B. Abbey, 'Bristol and its housing problems', *Housing*, vol. XIII, no. 1, June 1951.
24 ibid.
25 *The Cost of House Maintenance*, Report of the Girdwood Committee, Ministry of Housing and Local Government, HMSO, 1953, p. 18.
26 ibid.
27 M. Foot, *Aneurin Bevan, Volume 2*, 1945–60, Davis Poynter, London, 1973, p. 95.
28 *House of Commons Debates*, vol. 499, April 1952, cols 230–5.
29 ibid., col. 258.
30 S. Merrett, *State Housing in Britain*, Routledge & Kegan Paul, London, 1979, p. 246.
31 *Rent Rebates: A Review*, Society of Housing Managers, London, 1950, p. 4.
32 *Transfers, Exchanges and Rents*, 4th Report of the Housing Management Sub-Committee of Central Housing Advisory Committee, HMSO, London, 1953 (reprinted 1965), p. 17.
33 *Rent Rebates: A Review*, op. cit., p. 6.
34 *Looking Ahead: a policy for housing in England and Wales*, Report of the Conservative Housing Sub-Committee, January 1945, p. 40.
35 PEP, *A New Policy for Housing Subsidies*, op. cit., p. 264.
36 *Transfers, Exchanges and Rents*, op. cit., p. 23.
37 *Rent Rebates*, Institute of Housing, London, June 1953.

38 *House of Commons Debates*, vol. 499, April 1952.
39 'Household income, rent and rates', Oxford Institute of Statistics, *Bulletin*, vol. 16, no. 4, April 1954, p. 106.

Chapter five

Restructuring rents policy: the rise of rent pooling

This chapter deals with a period which began in 1955 with a major change in rents policy, and ended in 1970 with the election of a government committed to radical reform of housing finance. It was shown in chapter 2 that the mid-1950s was a period of restructuring in housing policy as a whole, and here it will be argued that, as far as rents and subsidies are concerned, the policy changes introduced in 1955 represent the key turning-point in post-war policy development, establishing the origins of a line of continuity running through to the new 'regime' for the 1990s.

The policy established in the mid-1950s was essentially about bringing the rents of houses of all ages more into line with the current level of earnings, whilst at the same time providing targeted assistance for those on the lowest incomes. Rent pooling provided central government with a convenient means of implementing this policy, without resorting to legislation, and without precipitating conflict with local authorities. The importance of rent pooling as a policy instrument goes far beyond issues of local-government financial accounting. It was a political choice, motivated by a desire to put pressure on local authorities to raise rents, and it is essential to establish that, whereas rent pooling is now seen as a source of low rents, it was then an efficient device for raising them. For the Conservative government in the 1950s, whose objectives were to diminish public housing, to reduce public expenditure on housing, and to revive private renting, rent pooling was a very important aspect of policy.

A new policy for rents and subsidies

Harold Macmillan had promised that a Conservative government would build 300,000 houses per year, and in the face of some criticism from within his own party he was prepared to accept a temporarily high level of council house building. Whereas some of his colleagues preferred an early assault on private sector rent control, Macmillan took the view that 'The houses must go up before the rents.'[1] Once the 300,000 bench-mark had been achieved and the worst of the post-war shortage was beginning to ease, it was possible to turn to the question of rents, which meant increases all round. In the public sector there were four main components of the policy for raising rents: lower subsidies, rent pooling, higher interest rates, and removal of the requirement on local authorities to contribute to housing from the rates. The first to begin to take effect was higher interest rates.

There were two aspects to the increase in interest rates. The first to begin to be implemented was that the rate charged by the Public Works Loans Board (PWLB) was raised in November 1951 to 3.75 per cent from 3 per cent, which had been the rate since 1948. This was followed by a rise of a further 0.50 per cent in February 1952. The rate fell back to 4 per cent in October 1953, and then to 3.75 per cent in June 1954. But in September 1955 there was a steep rise to 5 per cent and by October 1956 the rate was up to 5.75 per cent. Higher interest rates only applied to new loans, but in the context of the massive building programmes of 1952–5 their impact was particularly marked, dragging up the average interest rate on total debt.

The second means of increasing interest rates was foreshadowed in January 1953 when local authorities were given the freedom to borrow on the open market directly, rather than through the PWLB. Such borrowing was likely to be more expensive because the government, in the form of the PWLB, was considered to be a more secure borrower. Merrett records that the first council to raise money on its own behalf, Birmingham, had to pay almost 1 per cent above the PWLB rate.[2] In 1955 the policy was taken a stage further when local authorities were not merely permitted to borrow on the open market but were *required* to do so, unless they could show that they could not raise the necessary funds in this way. Those authorities who were allowed to borrow from the PWLB would be charged a rate based on that paid by local authorities of good standing in the market, rather than the lower rate obtainable by the Board itself. The result of this important policy change was that, whereas in 1951–2 85 per cent of local authority borrowing had been from the PWLB, by 1959–60 it was down by 8 per cent.[3] And the result of this was that local authorities paid considerably more in interest on the loans raised to build council houses.

The second major component in the plan to raise rents was the reduction of subsidies, which was closely related to the third component, the encouragement of rent pooling. The erosion of the real value of subsidy was a continuous process, given that costs were rising, but there were certain offsetting factors, such as the temporary fall in interest rates in 1953–4. However, this fall in interest rates was used to justify a reduction in the money value of subsidy in October 1954. In that month the Minister (Duncan Sandys) brought to Parliament the Housing (Review of Contributions) Order 1954,[4] the first time that the procedure built into the 1946 Act had been used to reduce subsidies. Subsidy was reduced from £26.14s. (plus £8.18s. RFC) to £22.1s. (plus £7.7s.) for dwellings completed after 1st

April 1955.[5] Similar reductions were made in respect of flats on expensive sites.

A year later Sandys made a statement in the House during which he admitted that, since the new subsidy levels had been set, interest rates had risen appreciably, and that, if the government was to follow what he called previous practice and raise subsidy accordingly, then the new level of assistance would have to go to 'well over' £30.[6] However, the government thought that this was neither necessary nor desirable. The minister announced that subsidy would continue at its present level, but only in relation to houses built to rehouse families from slum clearance. The government had decided to abolish altogether the general needs subsidy within a 'year or so' and in the meantime a reduced subsidy of £10 would be payable.[7]

In November 1955, a month after his statement to the House, Sandys returned with a Bill to implement the subsidy changes.[8] This Bill, which was to become the Housing Subsidies Act, 1956, introduced the £10 subsidy and retained the £22 subsidy for slum clearance rehousing as an incentive to local authorities to press ahead with redevelopment. The second-reading debate was the first major debate on the fundamental principles of housing since 1945.[9] It is therefore worth looking quite closely at what the Minister said in his contribution, because it does clearly reveal the new approach of the government. Early in his speech Sandys referred to the differential subsidy arrangements and explained that, whilst the government could have chosen a higher slum clearance subsidy rather than a lower general needs rate, they did not do so because:

we were satisfied that the total amount of subsidy which the Exchequer is now paying out in respect of existing houses is larger than is really necessary and provides a margin which can properly be used for financing some part of the future housing programme. I think it is worth remembering that housing subsidies are granted with one object only, namely, to ensure that nobody, through lack of means, shall be prevented from having a decent, healthy home...we on this side of the House do not agree that it is in the general interest to keep the cost of housing artificially low for all council tenants regardless of their incomes. The justification for housing subsidies is need and, in our opinion, need alone.[10]

And he went on to say. 'There is no doubt that the rents of a large number of council houses are at present being subsidised to a greater extent than the financial circumstances of the individual tenants require.[11]

It is interesting that the better-off tenants were singled out for attention and the thrust of the argument was concerned with what Sandys had earlier called the 'misuse of public money'.[12] The justification for changes in subsidy arrangements was primarily that rents were too low, or 'still surprisingly low and quite out of line with the current level of earnings.'[13]

The Bill seemed to be motivated by a desire to *withdraw* subsidy from the better-off who had been drawn into public housing since the war, rather than to ensure that subsidy actually went to people in need.

The lower real value of subsidies was, then, conceived as a way of levering up rent levels across the whole stock. Local authorities were encouraged to make good the shortfall in subsidy in relation to new houses by raising rents for existing tenants, i.e. by extending rent pooling. This policy was carried further forward during 1956 and there was thus a three-stage process of subsidy elimination: the lowering of subsidies in 1954 took effect on houses completed after 1 April 1955; the 1956 Act applied to houses in tenders approved after 3 November 1955, and then SI 1956 No. 2051 abolished the general needs subsidy altogether for houses in tenders approved after 2 November 1956. So from 1956 there was no subsidy for general-needs housing, apart from one-bedroomed dwellings for the elderly and a subsidy for slum clearance rehousing and overspill, the value of which was seriously eroded by rising costs, especially higher interest rates.

A further incentive to local authorities to charge higher rents was contained in Clause 8 of the Housing Subsidies Bill. This clause removed the requirement on authorities to make a rate-fund contribution (RFC) to the housing revenue account, and was quite explicitly introduced with the intention of raising rents, and was linked with rent rebates. Announcing the intention to abolish mandatory RFCs, Sandys said:

> Unless local authorities will exercise more discrimination in giving rent relief to their tenants, there is bound to be a continued misuse of public money. At present, councils are discouraged from introducing differential rent schemes by reason of the fact that, no matter how much they increase their revenue from rents, they still have a statuary obligation to pay into the housing revenue account a fixed contribution from the rates. We therefore propose to abolish this obligation. This will allow local authorities, if they so desire, to use any savings they make to reduce the rate burden, and will give them for the first time an incentive to adopt realistic rent policies.[14]

The removal of mandatory RFCs shows the government's enthusiasm for redistributing the costs of council housing, away from taxpayers and rate-payers, on to tenants themselves. The point needs to be made here that in addition to attacking the so-called waste of money on subsidies for well-off tenants, there was concern about the aggregate cost of subsidies. As Sandys said, 'We feel...that the time has come to restore some measure of fairness to our housing finances and to put some reasonable brake upon the continuous growth of subsidy burden, which bears so heavily upon taxpayers and ratepayers alike.'[15] In fact in 1956 total Exchequer subsidy expenditure on council housing was £50m per year, and growing at about £3m per year.[16] This represented less than 25 per cent of HRA income (for county boroughs in 1956–7 Exchequer subsidy averaged 23.7 per cent). Even less was being paid from the rates to subsidise council housing; about 10 per cent of HRA income came from the rates, although in some individual authorities the level was much higher.[17] In terms of public expenditure as a whole, subsidies to council tenants were very low. Total public spending on housing was 8.2 per cent of all public spending in 1950, and housing was one of the three slowest growing programmes in the 1950s.[18] Nevertheless, the public expenditure argument was used to support cuts in subsidy and RFC.

Finally there is the issue of rent rebate schemes. The point to establish is that encouragement for rebate schemes was based on the wish both to withdraw assistance from the better-off *and* to raise the total amount of revenue collected by the local authority. The decision to remove mandatory RFCs was clearly not simply concerned with the *redistribution* of total subsidy, away from the better-off tenants and towards the less well-off. The intention was that local authorities should redistribute and reduce the total amount. So, on the one hand the government argued that local authorities should pool rents, and that if they did so then they would require 'appreciably less Exchequer assistance,'[19] while on the other hand councils were given the incentive to reduce, even eliminate, their own support for housing.

The notion of rent rebates was implicit in the policy contained in the 1956 Housing Subsidies Act, but nothing in the Act *required* local authorities to devise such schemes, and the whole topic was generally treated very elliptically in the parliamentary debates. Most speakers did not address themselves to the issue at all. Sandys expressed his support for differential rents, saying that he favoured the rent rebate type of scheme.[20] Bevan, on the other hand, condemned the whole idea as divisive and retrogressive,[21] arguing that means testing would set tenant against tenant, and would lead the better-off tenants to leave council estates, making them into second-class neighbourhoods.

Sandys was very careful to say that it was up to local authorities themselves to decide whether to operate rebate schemes, and he recognised that there might be circumstances where rebating was inappropriate.[22] A ministerial circular, 29/56, issued in May 1956, scrupulously avoided direct encouragement of rebating, confining itself to a discussion of the principles involved and outlining examples of existing schemes, but local authorities were left in no doubt that the government strongly supported the spread of rebate schemes. The essential point to establish here is that rebate schemes were not just intended to redistribute subsidy: their main function was to reduce the overall level of subsidy. The government's position was that 'indiscriminate' subsidy kept rents too low, and that, if authorities set 'realistic' rents, giving assistance only to those who needed it, then there would be a saving to the ratepayers. It is of the upmost importance for understanding the gathering passion for rent rebates that such schemes were intended to raise average rents.[23]

Before we look at the impact of the new policy, it is necessary to refer to the way it was modified by the reintroduction of a general needs subsidy in the Housing Act, 1961.

The Housing Act 1961

In February 1961 the government published a White Paper, *Housing in England and Wales*,[24] in which were set out, amongst other things, the government's view of the role of public housing and proposals for a new form of subsidy. The residual role of public housing was clearly stated:

> The government's aim is to secure that there will be houses for rent in sufficient numbers to keep pace with the rising demand of a prosperous society. As real incomes go up, more and more of this need, both for sale and to rent, should be met by private enterprise. For those who can neither afford to buy their own homes nor to pay economic rents there will be the 3½ million publicly owned houses – increasing in number as local authorities continue to build for the needs which only they can meet. The taxpayer already subsidises the houses to the extent of some £61 million a year, but at present, many council houses and flats which ought to be available to those who really need them are still occupied by people who, whatever their situation when they first became local authority tenants, have since become well able to make their own arrangements without need of subsidy. Increasingly, however, such tenants are making their own arrangements as councils adopt more realistic rent policies.[25]

This suggests that government policy was still preoccupied by the spectre of wealthy yet subsidised council tenants, and motivated by the desire to drive them into the private sector.

The government proposed what it called radical changes in the subsidy system to remedy the situation. Authorities that satisfied a test of need would in future qualify for the higher rate of subsidy, £24 per house per year, and other authorities would receive only £8. (In addition there would continue to be extra subsidy for flats in tall blocks, for dwellings on very expensive sites, and for certain special cases.) The test of financial need was to be based on the relationship between actual HRA expenditure and twice the gross value of all dwellings in the HRA. Where expenditure exceeded twice the gross value, then the £24 subsidy would be paid. Where expenditure was less than twice the gross value, the lower rate of £8 was to be paid, with the intention that the unsubsidised cost of new houses should be spread across the existing stock in the form of higher rents.

The new subsidy system was intended to achieve two linked objectives:

to deliver subsidy where need was greatest and to encourage low-cost authorities to raise rents. As the White Paper said:

> The government are entitled to assume that councils will pursue reasonable rent policies, and that changes now to be made in the subsidy arrangements will encourage them to do so. The assumed income for purposes of the test (twice the 1956 gross value of all the houses in the authority's account) is based on the conviction that local authorities can, if they so wish, adopt rent policies which would assure them of total rent income of that order, while still enabling them to adjust rents to the needs of their tenants.[26]

In this connection the White Paper announced another significant innovation: it argued that it was wrong to commit the Exchequer to subsidy payments for sixty years when experience showed that the rent-paying capacity of tenants could change to a considerable extent. The government therefore proposed to take powers to reduce payments on houses built with the new subsidy if, after a period of years (later set at ten), it appeared that payment at the original rate was no longer justified.[27]

It is very difficult to discover just which authorities benefited from the 1961 Act. The distribution of subsidy at the two levels amongst the authorities is not known for certain and is not readily calculable. However, Griffith, writing in the mid-1960s, stated that in 1962–3 there were 181 authorities receiving the £8 subsidy and 563 receiving the higher rate. In 1963–4 the corresponding figures were 'about' 169 and 676. He also asserted that in 1962–3 about one-fifth of new houses was entitled to the £8 subsidy, and that by 1964–5 it was only one-tenth.[28] It seems that the Act did not systematically favour rural as against urban authorities, nor, contrary to Short's view,[29] did it favour authorities charging the highest rents: high resource authorities with high rents received only the lower rate of subsidy. In terms of rent policy the Act was clearly intended to persuade authorities to exploit to the full opportunities for rent pooling and revenue raising. The 1961 Housing Act was an important forerunner of events to come and was a first step towards the goal of distributing subsidy in a more rational way.

The impact of the new rents policy

This section looks at the impact of the new rents policy in England and Wales in the period up to 1964, when the Conservatives lost control of Parliament. The main source of the data discussed here is the series of annual *Housing Statistics* produced by the Institute of Municipal Treasurers and Accountants (IMTA).

In terms of the overall average, the money value of rents doubled in the eleven years 1954–64, from 13s.6d. to £1.7s.[30] The steepest increases occurred in 1957–9. Rents also increased in real terms: according to Kilroy's calculations,[31] rents rose faster than prices generally in every year of the period, and Parker[32] notes that average male industrial wages rose by 62 per cent between 1957 and 1965, during which time rents, on average, rose by 66.6 per cent. However, an important feature of council rents is their variability, from place to place and within individual authorities. Table 5.1 illustrates the north–south split between county boroughs with the highest and lowest rents in both 1954 and 1964.

Table 5.1   County boroughs with highest and lowest rents 1954 and 1964

1954			1964			1954			1964		
	s	d		s	d		s	d		s	d
Newport	24	0	Croydon	47	7	Wakefield	12	1	Wakefield	21	6
Eastbourne	22	7	Bournemouth	47	7	Manchester	12	0	York	22	1
Burton	22	5	Portsmouth	47	4	Newcastle	12	5	Stoke	23	0
Croydon	22	1	Brighton	45	3	Rotherham	12	7	Grimsby	23	4
Birmingham	21	8	Oxford	44	6	Barnsley	13	0	Merthyr	23	5
Southampton	21	2	Coventry	43	3	Burnley	13	3	Norwich	23	8
Southend	21	2	Bath	42	0	Stoke	13	3	Hull	24	1
Wallasey	21	2	Newport	40	9	St Helens	13	8	Wigan	24	3
Coventry	21	0	Southend	40	10	Warrington	14	0	Oldham	24	6
Hastings	20	8	Southampton	40	6	Sheffield	14	1	Rochdale	24	10

Note: The rents quoted here refer to averages for post-war three-bedroomed houses

In both 1954 and 1964 the average rent in the highest rent authority was more than twice the average in the lowest rent authority. In 1954 the difference between the high- and low-rent authorities listed above was mainly due to the different costs arising from differences in the age structure of the housing stock in each authority. Low-rent authorities tended to have higher proportions of pre-1945 dwellings. By 1964, however, there was a different factor at work: the freedom to reduce rate fund contributions (under the 1956 Act) had resulted in marked variations in RFC. Low-rent authorities in that year were more likely to be making high RFCs than were high-rent authorities.

With regard to the patterns within authorities, there was a distinct narrowing of differences between pre- and post-war dwellings. In overall terms, the average net rent of pre-war three-bedroomed houses in county boroughs in 1954 was 11s.7d., compared with 16s.10d. for similar post-war houses. In 1964 the equivalent figures were 23s.10d. and 30s.6d. In other words, rents of pre-war houses had risen from 68.8 per cent to 78.3 per cent of the rents of similar post-war houses, and this was a trend which was apparent in each year during the period 1954–64. The narrowing gap between the rents for houses of different ages directly reflects the impact of the government's use of assumptions about rent pooling which were intended to have precisely this effect.

Another outcome of central government policy was that the proportion of housing revenue account income covered by subsidy and rate fund contributions fell during the period after the new policy was introduced. Thus, while ministers and other politicians referred to the growing burden of housing subsidies, the facts were that in each year the share of HRA income provided by the Exchequer was going down. Rates contributions, which were never very large (except in a few individual authorities), were also declining. Table 5.2 illustrates the trends, comparing county boroughs with rural districts.

Table 5.2 The structure of housing revenue account income in county boroughs and rural districts (percentages)

	County boroughs				Rural districts			
	Rents	ES	RFC	Other	Rents	ES	RFC	Other
1955–6	63.4	25.3	10.6	0.7	62.8	28.2	8.6	0.4
1956–7	65.6	23.7	10.0	0.7	69.0	26.0	4.3	0.7
1957–8	66.9	22.5	9.7	0.9	70.3	25.5	3.3	0.9
1958–9	68.8	21.9	8.5	0.8	71.6	24.8	3.0	0.6
1959–60	69.6	21.6	8.2	0.6	72.7	23.9	2.8	0.6
1960–1	70.1	21.1	8.0	0.8	73.2	23.5	2.6	0.7
1961–2	71.1	20.2	7.9	0.8	73.6	22.5	3.0	0.9
1962–3	73.9	19.4	6.1	0.1	75.1	21.5	2.5	0.9
1963–4	74.7	18.8	5.8	0.7	76.3	20.2	2.5	1.0

ES   Exchequer subsidy
RFC   Rate fund contribution

The most important observation on this table is that rising rents provided a growing proportion of HRA income. The trend is more pronounced in the rural districts where the decline in RFC over the period was particularly marked. It is especially notable that, as soon as authorities were given the freedom to reduce or withdraw RFC, the proportion of HRA income provided by ratepayers in rural districts fell by 50 per cent, and continued a downward trend. This reduction was accompanied by an increase of over 6 percentage points in the proportion provided by rents in 1956–57.

Amongst the county boroughs there was wide variation around the averages. For instance, in 1955–6 rents in West Ham provided only 46 per cent of total income, while 31 per cent came from the rates, whereas in Blackpool 75.5 per cent came from rents and only 2.1 per cent from the rates. By 1964–5 Salford derived only 48 per cent of its income from rents and 28.2 per cent from the rates, while places such as Eastbourne, Oxford, and Brighton drew over 87 per cent of income from rents. By 1963–4 a large number of authorities had responded to government policy and had reduced their rate fund contributions to zero. In that year all the London authorities still made rate fund contributions, most of them substantial, but outside London and the big cities the other authorities were not only likely to make low contributions, but also much more likely to pay nothing at all.

Table 5.3 Authorities making zero rate fund contributions in 1963–64

	Number	% of responding authorities
County boroughs	16	19.5
Non-county boroughs	104	40.5
Urban districts	160	41.8
Rural districts	176	53.0

On the question of the spread of rent rebates, there are three key variables to be examined: the number of authorities operating schemes, the number of tenants in receipt of help, and the value of rebates paid.

Table 5.4 Authorities operating rent rebate schemes (England and Wales)

	1949 No.	%*	1955–6 No.	%*	1957–8 No.	%*	1963–4 No.	%*
County boroughs	19	23.0	NA	23	35	42.0	46	55.0
Metropolitan authorities	2	6.6	NA	NA	13	43.0	18	62.0
Non-county boroughs	33	10.8	NA	17	99	35.7	120	46.1
Urban districts	8	1.4	NA	10	91	20.0	99	25.6
Rural districts	16	3.4	NA	10	111	35.0	141	41.0
Total	78	8.2		15	349	30	424	38.9

Sources: 1949, *Rent Rebates, A Review*, Society of Housing Managers
1955–6, R. A. Parker, *The Rents of Council Houses*, Table 11, p. 47
1957–8 and 1963–4, IMTA *Housing Statistics*
%* refers to the proportion of responding authorities only

In each class of authority there was a marked increase in the incidence of rent rebate schemes after authorities were freed from making RFCs in 1956. By 1964 all but two of the county boroughs in southern England had introduced rebate schemes (the exceptions were Ipswich and Plymouth). The authorities which held out against rebating were concentrated mainly in Yorkshire, Lancashire, and the north-east. It is worth remembering that, although there was a net increase in the total number of rebating authorities between 1956 and 1964, there were at all levels some authorities moving against the trend. For example, although the data are incomplete, it is clear that eight non-county boroughs and nine urban districts abandoned rebating during this period. In the case of one borough, Lancaster, which scrapped its rebate scheme in 1959, it is known that the reasoning was that most rebate claimants were also receiving National Assistance and therefore the HRA was considered to be bearing a charge which ought reasonably to be borne by the national authority.[33]

Despite the increasing numbers of authorities operating rent-rebate schemes, the numbers of tenants in receipt of rebates remained small in relation to the total. Amongst the county boroughs there was actually a *fall* in the proportion of tenants receiving rebates in the period 1958–64. In county-borough authorities *with rebate schemes* the proportion of tenants being helped declined from 32 per cent in 1958 to 17 per cent in 1964. If *all* authorities are taken together, including those with no rebate schemes, the proportion of tenants claiming rebates rose but by very little, as Table 5.5 shows.

Table 5.5   Proportions of tenants in receipt of rebates

	1958	1964
	%	%
County boroughs	9.2	10.8
Metropolitan boroughs and LCC	5.4	6.6
Non-county boroughs	10.3	9.1
Urban districts	5.6	4.6
Rural districts	11.0	11.0
All	8.3	9.0

In aggregate terms rebates comprised a very small proportion of total collectable rent. Of the 35 county boroughs with rebate schemes in 1958, only 10 awarded rebates totalling more than 10 per cent of collectable rents, and in 1964 the figure was 9 out of 46 authorities.

However, to think in terms of rent forgone and the cost of rebates is really to misrepresent their purpose. Rent rebate schemes in fact enabled local authorities to *increase* their total rent revenue. Perhaps the most significant statistic in this whole analysis is that, in both 1958 and 1964, average rents in rebating authorities, with rebates granted taken into account, were higher than in non-rebating authorities by a fifth.

Table 5.6   Average rents for post-war three-bedroomed houses in rebating and non-rebating county boroughs (in shillings)

	1958	1964
Rebating local authorities	24.23	33.43
Non-rebating local authorities	20.30	27.75

The difference was 19.5 per cent in 1958 and 20 per cent in 1964. Rent rebates can hardly be described as costing anything when their impact was to raise average rents. To take the point a stage further, it can also be shown quite clearly that rebate schemes were often associated with HRAs in which rents covered a higher proportion of expenditure. Parker calculated that in 1963–4 74 per cent of all authorities with rent-rebate schemes covered 75 per cent or more of total costs out of rent income, while only 47.8 per cent of authorities without rent rebates could raise as much as 75 per cent of expenditure from rents.[34]

He then went on to look at the relationship between rent-rebate schemes and RFCs, suggesting that the presence of a rebate scheme was likely to be associated with a low RFC and vice versa. 'The typical combination is a low rate contribution and a differential rent scheme or high rate contribution and no scheme.'[35] Amongst the 33 county boroughs which had rent rebate schemes in both 1958 and 1964, all but 7 continued to make some kind of RFC, but 21 made lower proportionate contributions.

The ratio of pre-war to post-war dwellings was the key factor. Authorities with high proportions of older houses were able to charge below-average rents and yet produce at least 75 per cent of HRA income from rents, thereby avoiding resort to very high RFCs. Five county boroughs in 1964 managed to combine above average proportions of rent income (over 75 per cent), nil RFC, no rebate scheme, and below-average rents. Authorities with low proportions of pre-war houses had a political choice to make between a low rent, no rebate, high RFC approach, or a high rent and rebate, low RFC approach, although a few authorities opted for high rents and no rebates. Authorities with higher proportions of pre-war houses were beyond the reach of government policy: they could continue with low rents, low RFC, and no rebate scheme. It would therefore be wrong to see the failure of rent rebate schemes to spread any faster during this period simply in terms of party politics, in particular Labour resistance to rebating. Certainly some Labour-controlled authorities did resist introducing a rebate scheme by resort to higher RFC. But other authorities, of whatever political composition, had no need to employ rebating because their financial circumstances were favourable.

To conclude this section there are a number of summary points to draw out, concerning:

the narrowing of the differences between the rents of pre-war and post-war houses, reflecting the spread of rent pooling;

the increasing proportion of HRA costs covered by rental income, and the corresponding decrease in the contributions from the Exchequer and the general rates fund (this is a valuable corrective to the widespread view that Exchequer subsidies followed a consistently upward curve over many years);

the role of rent rebate schemes in facilitating general increases in rents and net increases in the proportion of expenditure covered by rents;

the declining proportion of tenants in receipt of rebates, in rebating authorities, the continuing small proportion of recipients in total despite the spread of rebate schemes, and the consistently small proportions of subsidy income devoted to rebating;

the divergence in rents *amongst* local authorities, even though rents were becoming more uniform *within* authorities.

The government was successful in pursuing higher rents, lower subsidies, and greater use of rent rebates, but only up to a point. In general, authorities remained reluctant to devote more than a very small proportion of their subsidy income to provision of rent rebates, and some authorities, those with low costs, were less susceptible than others to central government pressures on rents and rebates. Given the very different financial positions of local authorities up and down the country, central government pressures were likely to amplify the variations in rents, thereby reinforcing local political factors.

The 1963 White Paper

An important pointer to the way policy would develop in the future was contained in the last White Paper on housing produced by the Conservatives before they left office in 1964. The document was mainly concerned with production issues and with encouraging the development of new-style housing associations under the aegis of a proposed Housing Corporation. These main items were enacted in the Housing Act, 1964. However, at the end of the White Paper there was a brief section on subsidies in which it was announced that the minister had invited representatives of local authorities in England and Wales to join with him in a complete overhaul of the existing system. The government's view was clearly stated at the outset of this overhaul:

The government adhere to their declared policy that while no one in genuine need of a house should be asked to pay more rent than he can reasonably afford, subsidies ought not to be given to those who do not need them. It follows that in considering what subsidy is required the government must assume that local authorities will charge rents properly related on the one hand to the cost of housing, on the other to the ability of tenants to pay. Hundreds of authorities have shown that rent rebate schemes can be worked fairly and without difficulty; and nothing is more unfair, whether to tax or rate-payer, than that he should be compelled to subsidise the rent of a tenant who does not need it – or to an extent that he does not need it – while himself often no better off and in many cases having to pay a higher rent or to meet mortgage payments. But given the assumption that proper rents are charged, subject to rebates for those who need them, the government will be prepared to see that local authorities receive whatever subsidy they need to carry through their housing responsibilities and to plan ahead with confidence.'[36]

The working party on subsidies met seven times and submitted its (un-published) report in September 1964, just before the General Election.[37] Complete and through-going reform of housing subsidies in the public sector was then delayed by the return of a Labour government with different housing priorities.

Labour's housing priorities

In the years from 1964 to 1970 the progress of housing policy in general, and rents policy in particular, along the paths mapped out in the preceding decade was affected by two main political and economic factors. First, on a political level the election of a Labour government in October 1964 brought to an end thirteen years of Conservative rule, and opened the way for a new approach. In certain important respects Labour's housing policy priorities over the ensuing six years differed quite substantially from those established in the previous ten years. Whereas public housing construction had been in steady decline, apart from a slight revival since 1962, Labour's policy was greatly to expand the building programme, for both general needs and the redevelopment of slum areas. Linked with the expansion of building was a reversal in the trend of subsidy policy, in the sense that the Labour government greatly increased general subsidies, both in total and per dwelling. Whereas the Conservatives had been planning a restructuring of housing subsidies, to reduce the aggregate amount and to increase chan-nelling towards the poorest tenants, Labour's priority was to expand the house building programme which produced a very different approach to subsidy policy. In addition the Labour Party in opposition had vigorously denounced the 1957 Rent Act, with its creeping decontrol leading to restoration of free market rents, and the new government was pledged to act on this issue.

However, it is important not to overstate the differences between Labour and Conservative housing policies. On the one hand, by the mid-1960s Labour accepted the growth of home ownership as a desirable element, while on the other hand Conservative thinking was beginning to accept the need for an accelerated building programme and more rapid progress with slum clearance.[38] According to Banting there was also agreement within the

Ministry of Housing that, whichever party won the 1964 general election, there was a need to restore a degree of rent control in the private sector.[39]

Action on private sector rents came in the Rent Act, 1965, which introduced the concept of 'fair rents'. The Act aimed to restore a measure of security of tenure, and to develop a system of rent regulation in which independent rent officers would set rents at levels regarded as fair to both landlord and tenant. Fair rents were to be moderated market rents and in the long run the fair rent system represented a means of allowing rents to rise more or less in line with wages and prices generally. In the shorter term the impact of the Act depended upon the rate at which landlords and tenants applied to have fair rents registered for their properties. In relation to council-house rents policy the unforeseen importance of the Act was that it would provide a model for rent setting which a future Conservative government would apply in all tenures.

In order to expand housing output in the public sector the Labour government raised the level of subsidy, in the Housing Subsidies Act, 1967. The Act was delayed by the general election of 1966 but it applied to dwellings for which local authorities had approved tenders after 25 November 1965. The new subsidy was based on the difference between loan charges calculated at 4 per cent and the actual rate of interest prevailing at the time of construction. (In fact, to simplify administration the ministry set a standard, or representative, interest rate each year.) The result was a dramatic increase in subsidy per dwelling. The minister explained that a dwelling then costing £3 000 to construct would attract subsidy of £67 per year, and a £5 000 dwelling would attract £112. These figures were indeed generous when compared with the existing subsidies of £8 or £24 under the 1961 Act. Once calculated, the subsidy remained fixed in money terms, with the result that subsequent general increases in interest rates might reduce its value. It was only new dwellings which were subsidised at the current rate of interest, and therefore the refinancing of old debt was at unsubsidised rates of interest.

One inevitable outcome of higher output and higher unit subsidies was a rise in total capital spending and Exchequer subsidies. Between 1964 and 1970 the average tender price of three-bedroomed council houses rose by just under 50 per cent, but the total local authority capital investment in housing doubled, and Exchequer subsidies rose by 83 per cent, from £68 million in 1963–4 to £124.6 million in 1969–70.[40]

Rents and counter-inflation policy

Rising costs of construction, higher levels of debt, and higher interest rates exerted pressure on rent levels, despite the more generous subsidies. However, unlike the previous Conservative government, Labour did not pursue a policy based on higher rents. After a decade of ministerial encouragement to local authorities to charge 'realistic' higher rents, Labour's attempts to hold down the rate of rent increases appeared to represent a markedly different approach. It is, however, necessary to see Labour's limitation of rent increases as primarily an aspect of its policy on prices and incomes rather than housing policy as such. Economic difficulties and inflationary pressures drew the government into measures to attempt to contain the situation. In July 1966 a White Paper, *Prices and Incomes Standstill*,[41] heralded a period of six months during which it was intended that both prices and incomes would remain unchanged, to be followed by a further six months of 'severe restraint'. The White Paper called on local authorities to give a lead in preventing or postponing increases, on the grounds that:

> Local authority rents are already on a non-profit making and unsubsidised basis. If increased costs are not met from rents they must be recouped from rates, which are also a charge on tenants....In the period of the prices standstill....the government expect local authorities to take such practical steps as are possible to prevent or postpone rent increases, including those already announced.[42]

In practice very few authorities raised their rents in this period: only 32 out of the 1600 housing authorities in great Britain went ahead with increases.[43] However, financial pressures were building up within many local authorities, and councils all across the country were becoming Conservative controlled in the municipal elections of 1967 and 1968. This meant first that there was a reduced readiness to avoid rent increases by drawing more heavily from the rate funds, and, second, a growing number of authorities began to consider adopting 'fair rents' policies. Most importantly, the Greater London Council, with a quarter of a million tenants, decided in December 1967 to move towards both fair rents and the complete elimination of its £4½-million rate fund contribution by 1970.[44]

Also in December 1967 the government referred the question of local authority rent increases to the National Board for Prices and Incomes (NBPI). The Board made several recommendations, concerning for instance long-term alterations in the principles underlying rent fixing in the public sector. Of short-term importance was their recommendation that rent increases should be made only once in a twelve-month period and that they should be limited to 7s.6d. per week on average, with no more than a 10s. increase on any individual dwelling.[45] In view of the rate at which rents had been increasing until the last year, this limit of 7s. 6d. seems like a plan for orderly growth of rents rather than a policy of restraint. ITMA statistics suggest that rents rose by under 7 per cent in the year to April 1967, but by nearly 17 per cent in the following twelve months.

Following the NBPI report powers were taken to limit local authority rent increases (and private sector increases) in the Prices and Incomes Act of 1968. Opening the second-reading debate Barbara Castle (Secretary of State for Employment and Productivity) said that because some authorities had failed to comply with earlier exhortations to keep rents down, the government were having to take powers to implement the NBPI recommendations.[46] In a revealing passage in her speech Mrs Castle stated that 'by far the biggest element in the increases which has taken place in the retail price index since the middle of 1966 has been the cost of housing, which has risen by no less than 10 points during this period.'[47] Although, of course, not all of this rise was due to local-authority rent increases (there was a 12 per cent increase in the price of new houses over the same period[48]), there was a perceived need to strengthen counter-inflation policy in this respect. The Act made it illegal for councils to raise rents without ministerial consent, and they were told in Circular 37/68 that average increases of more than 7s. 6d. per week would not be approved, nor would individual increases of more than 10s. This policy, with the same limits, was continued under the terms of the 1969 Rent (Control of Increases) Act, until it was reversed by the new Conservative government which took office in June 1970. Despite counter-inflationary measures the evidence shows that during 1964–70 local authority rents on average rose faster than pre-tax earnings and much faster than retail prices.[49]

The Labour government and rent rebates

The Labour Party had a long-standing principled opposition to rent rebate schemes, largely based on its more general rejection of means testing. However, there can be no doubt that by the mid-1960s the Labour government (as distinct from the Party) was firmly in favour of rent rebates, although it was equally firmly against legislation to make such schemes mandatory. The last time Labour had been in power, rent rebates had been in decline and as an issue were not on the political agenda. After thirteen years of Conservative government the incidence of rent rebates was much more widespread, and this growth continued so that by 1970 over 80 per cent of council tenants in England and Wales were renting from authorities which operated rent rebate schemes.[50]

The long-term restructuring of housing tenure no doubt had an influence on policy, but there were also more immediate political factors at work to draw out Labour support for rent rebates. First, government support for rent rebates was forthcoming as a means of justifying and defending the much higher subsidies made available by the 1967 Act.

Perhaps the clearest statement of the government's position was contained in the 1965 White Paper:

> Rent policies are....for local decision. But if the extra subsidies now to be provided are to be used, as they should be, to relieve those with greatest social need, these policies should reflect the fact that the financial circumstances of council tenants vary widely. This means that *subsidies should not be used wholly or even mainly to keep general rent levels low.* Help for those who most need it can be given only if the subsidies are in large part used to provide rebates for tenants whose means are small. A number of authorities have had the courage to adopt through going rent rebate schemes and have found that it does not entail raising general rent levels beyond the means of the majority of their tenants. The more generous subsidies now provided create an opportunity for all authorities to review their rent policies along these lines.[51] [Present author's italics.]

This message was reiterated in a ministerial circular [52] issued to all housing authorities in June 1967, in which advice was given on the sort of rebate scheme favoured by ministers, including a model scheme. Local authorities were left in no doubt, then, as to what kind of rent policy they were expected to pursue in distributing their annual subsidy income.

The second factor was the problem of rising costs during the period of restraint of rent increases as part of prices and incomes policy. In this case rent rebates were used to justify general rent increases. Thus the White Paper of July 1966 said:

> Where, in consultation with the Minister of Housing and Local government or the Secretary of State for Scotland, increases are deemed to be unavoidable, the government hope that local authorities will make provision for the protection of tenants of limited means through rent rebate schemes.[53]

The following White Paper, in November 1966, made exactly the same point, and under the 1968 Prices and Incomes Act, which made increases illegal unless approved by the minister, it emerged that the introduction or the extension of rebating arrangements would help to justify increases and to gain approval.[54]

The point made here is that irrespective of Labour's position on rebates as such, the government was drawn into encouraging rebate provision in association with its policies on housing subsidies and production, and prices and incomes. A final point to be made in this section is that, having introduced the notion of 'fair rents' in the private sector, Labour had opened the way to the argument that what was fair for private tenants must also be fair for council tenants. In addition, once it was accepted that subsidies should not be used wholly or mainly to keep general rent levels low, the obvious question was on what basis should rents be set? Fair rents seemed to be an equally obvious reply. In this way it can be seen that the Wilson governments helped, albeit largely unintentionally, to set up the conditions for fair rent legislation in the public sector.

Extra-parliamentary activity and the reform of housing finance

A notable feature of Labour policy on rent rebates was reluctance to legislate to make mandatory that which ministers were constantly urging on a voluntary basis. When challenged, as they frequently were, to make rebate provision mandatory on local housing authorities, ministers tended to shelter behind local autonomy and/or the existence of a working party considering the issue.[55] Deference to local autonomy is only partially convincing, and it may well be that a Labour government, representing the party historically associated with housing subsidies and the ideal of council housing, could not effect the changes in rents policy which were beginning to look logically irresistible to many housing specialists by the late 1960s. This was not, of course, because the Wilson government was committed to a Socialist housing policy, but because the party had not yet distanced itself from council tenants, nor from the legacy of association with council housing, to legislate for fundamental restructuring of public housing finance of which rent rebates were only a part.

As Merrett says,[56] there was in the mid to late 1960s a crescendo of advice, demands, and exhortations, all calling for rent rebates to be more widely available. However, there were two quite distinct messages being put across. On the one hand, the government, and some others, were calling for and discussing rebates within the framework of existing subsidies and reasonable rents, in direct line of descent from 1930. On the other hand, a growing number of writers, politicians, academics, and housing practitioners framed their demands for rent rebates within an entirely new approach to housing finance, in which rebates were linked to fair rents and deficit subsidies.

The case for a fundamental review and reform of subsidies and of rents policy gathered strength during the 1960s as a result of a number of factors. First, there was the continuing issue of the rising level of Exchequer assistance to local authority housing revenue accounts. As costs rose, so inevitably did the money value of the total subsidy bill, despite attempts to redistribute the cost burden towards tenants during the period up to 1964. It is important to remember that under the Conservatives, even though the total money value of subsidies rose, there was a definite trend towards subsidies meeting a smaller proportion of HRA income. Under Labour this trend was reversed, as a result of higher subsidies and counter-inflation policy.

Table 5.7 National housing revenue account composition (England and Wales)

	Rents	Exchequer subsidy	Rate-fund contributions	Other
	%	%	%	%
1964–5	74.1	18.7	6.2	1.0
1965–6	73.5	17.9	7.4	1.2
1966–7	73.4	17.7	7.7	1.2
1967–8	74.0	18.0	7.0	1.0
1968–9	73.0	19.0	8.0	—
1969–70	70.0	20.0	10.0	—

Source: IMTA *Housing Statistics*

Second, it is important to bear in mind the links between rents policies in the private and public sector. The decontrol of many private rents after 1957, as modified by rent regulation after 1965, resulted in pressure for higher public sector rents. Council rents had always tended to be higher, on average, than controlled private rents, but decontrol began the process of reversing that situation, and regulated rents were set to keep in line with changes in the value of money. If council rents fell behind private rents, then demand in the public sector would rise, and if it was met there would be a further increase in subsidy. As private rents became linked to the current value of money, so rent pooling on historic costs with existing subsidies became an inadequate basis for calculating council rents, because it yielded insufficient increase, especially in the long run.

Third, there were increasingly large anomalies in rent levels and in the distribution of subsidies both within and between local authorities. Some authorities were given more subsidy than they 'needed' in view of the age structure of their stock, while others received less than they 'needed'. The consequence was a wide variation of rent levels from place to place. At the same time authorities varied in their rebates policies, although most distributed only a small proportion of subsidy income as rebates. This meant that subsidy was not directed towards the tenants in greatest need. The whole subsidy system, it was becoming increasingly obvious, was incapable of delivering assistance in accordance with the needs of local authorities, and incapable of requiring authorities to use subsidies to help those tenants in greatest need. By the same token subsidy was being wasted on authorities and tenants who did not need it.

Table 5.8 illustrates the variation in local circumstances, showing the relationship between rents, debt charges, and the proportion of pre-1945 stock.

Table 5.8 County boroughs (CBs) with highest and lowest debt charges in 1969–70

	Average debt charge per dwelling per year	% HRA Income			Average rent per week	% pre war dwellings
		rents	subsidies	RFC		
	£ s				s d	
Portsmouth	159 12	82	17	0	63 9	14.7
Southampton	159 1	79	18	3	54 8	21.0
Luton	156 17	82	15	2	61 10	10.4
Oldham	156 10	53	23	24	43 10	24.1
Gateshead	146 17	53	25	22	41 11	20.1
Salford	144 16	50	29	21	35 4	36.9
Birmingham	144 15	69	22	8	50 9	46.1
Southend	144 8	76	15	7	65 3	15.8
Merthyr	143 0	51	19	30	41 8	19.4
Oxford	136 8	83	15	3	N.A.	N.A.
Average for all CBs	115 68	73	21	6	43 4	34.2
Rotherham	85 6	75	18	4	39 5	35.5
Northampton	82 15	80	18	0	39 6	45.0
Tynemouth	82 9	83	17	0	33 7	40.1
Warrington	81 16	77	18	3	30 8	38.8
Ipswich	80 12	83	17	0	33 1	36.4
Wakefield	80 7	80	19	0	29 2	48.2
York	78 12	80	16	4	32 8	43.1
Huddersfield	74 11	78	20	1	35 11	44.8
Carisle	62 10	84	16	0	34 1	45.0
Bury	56 10	82	15	2	26 1	55.0

HRA   Housing revenue account
RFC   Rate fund contribution

The case for reform was developed outside the government, and it was as early as 1963 that the Association of Municipal Corporations (AMC) put forward its view of what a new system might look like.[57] The AMC proposed that all existing fixed-rate subsidies should be superseded by a system in which subsidy (if any) would be paid on the basis of any deficiency in the housing revenue account after taking into account actual expenditure (on debt charges, repairs, and management) and notional income from rents and other sources of revenue. Consideration was given to the idea that there should be no general subsidy at all, and that the only assistance to tenants would be via means-tested rent rebates, but this was considered to be too radical to be put forward in the context of 1963. However, the idea of deficit subsidy took root in most proposals for the reform of local authority housing finance over the next few years. Deficit subsidy was linked to the view that council rents should be related to the current value of money and current wage levels, and that targeted assistance for the least well-off should be available as an essential part of the reform package.

A number of variations on this theme were put forward during the period 1965–70, without making any impact on government policy. In 1965 a joint working party on the question of fair rents was established by four professional bodies involved with residential property, and its two reports, in 1966 and 1967, both called for fair rents in all tenures.[58] In evidence to the Royal Commission on Local Government in England, the Institute of Housing (IoH) argued that larger authorities would be better placed to bring their rents into line with private-sector fair rents, and that in any case there was a need for firmer action by central government to influence local council rents policies.[59] Articles in professional journals, written by leading practitioners such as John Macey[60] (Director of Housing at the Greater London Council) and John Flemming[61] (Director of Housing at Bristol), carried the argument to a wider audience.

In 1968 the House of Commons Estimates Committee undertook a major investigation of housing subsidies, which provided an opportunity for a wide range of institutions to present their arguments for reform. Among those who took advantage of this situation were the IMTA, Royal Institution of Chartered Surveyors, GLC, IoH, AMC and National Union of Rate Payers' Associations.[62] After receiving so much evidence and hearing so many arguments in favour of fair rents, deficit subsidy, and mandatory rent rebates, the committee decided to recommend the further development of rebating, but held back from openly supporting fair rents in the public sector.[63]

Conclusion

The period 1955–70 is relatively discreet in terms of rents and subsidies policy, in the sense that it began with a new policy being devised and implemented, initially successfully, but latterly to the accompaniment of a chorus of criticism. The period ended with the election of a government which was prepared to respond to this criticism by legislating for thoroughgoing reform of rents and subsidies in all tenures. This was the period when rent pooling, which had been introduced in 1935, was at last picked up and used as a key instrument of policy. Whilst it was initially an effective device for raising the general level of rents, it was of declining potency by the late 1960s, and arguments were emerging for different tools to achieve the same objective.

In looking at the period in relation to the themes of continuity, central–local relations, and residualisation, it is interesting to note, first, that there were important continuities in policy either side of the 1964 general election. Although the incoming Labour government had different priorities in relation to production, it was able to pursue its objectives by altering the *level* of subsidy without changing the whole basis of rents and subsidy policy. Indeed, rents policy remained broadly consistent with earlier years, to the extent that local authorities were encouraged to make wider use of rebates, However, it can be argued that Labour's willingness to raise the level of subsidy in pursuit of higher output, whilst failing to tackle rents policy, ultimately heightened the tensions emerging in the system, thereby strengthening the case for reform.

Second, it is clear that the policy adopted in 1955 represented an erosion of local autonomy as central government took advantage of a device to exert leverage on council rents. Labour later took the unprecedented step of legally prohibiting rent increases and linking approval for increase to wider use of rebating as part of counter-inflation policy. Nevertheless, some authorities, notably those with low levels of expenditure per dwelling, were relatively immune to central government pressures, and overall there was a marked reluctance to comply with government policy on rebates: in 1969 only about 300,000 (less than 10 per cent) tenants received rebates, and in the financial year 1968–9 less than 15 per cent of total Exchequer subsidy was devoted to rebate provision.[64]

Finally, on residualisation, the conclusion must be that rents and subsidy policy was reorientated during this period but that in practice the outcome was not greatly to extend access for the least well-off. The objective of higher basic rents and greater reliance on means-tested subsidy implied conditions in which the better-off would prefer to buy or rent privately, whilst the least well off would find council housing increasingly affordable. However, this residualisation of council housing awaited a more effective set of policy instruments to push local authorities in that direction.

References

1 H. Macmillan, *Tides of Fortune 1945–1955*, Macmillan, London, 1969, p. 407.
2 S. Merrett, *State Housing in Britain*, Routledge & Kegan Paul, London, 1979, p. 155.
3 ibid., p. 156.
4 *House of Commons Debates*, vol. 531, July–October 1954.
5 SI 1954, no. 1407 (October).
6 *House of Commons Debates*, vol. 545, October–November 1955, cols 377–9.
7 ibid., col. 378.
8 *House of Commons Debates*, vol. 546, November–December, 1955.
9 ibid., col. 1061.
10 ibid., col. 793–4.
11 ibid., col. 794–5.
12 *House of Commons Debates*, vol. 545, col. 378.
13 *House of Commons Debates*, vol. 546, col. 807.
14 *House of Commons Debates*, vol. 545, col. 378.
15 *House of Commons Debates*, vol. 546, col. 795.
16 *Ministry of Housing and Local Government Annual Report*, Cmnd. 2688, HMSO, 1964.
17 *Housing Statistics 1956–57*, Institute of Municipal Treasurers and Accountants (IMTA), London, 1957, p. 5.

18 F. Gould and B. Roweth, 'Public spending and social policy: the United Kingdom 1950–1977', *Journal of Social Policy* vol. 9, no. 3, p. 357, 1980.

19 *House of Commons Debates*, vol. 545, col. 377.

20 ibid.

21 ibid., col. 1069.

22 ibid., col. 810.

23 J.B. Cullingworth, 'Public housing rent–income relationship established in many ways in England', *The Journal of Housing (US)*, June 1961, pp. 254–8; R.A. Parker, *The Rents of Council Houses*, Bell, London, 1967, p.47.

24 *Housing in England and Wales*, Cmnd. 1290, MoHLG, HMSO, 1961,

25 ibid., p. 3.

26 ibid., p. 8.

27 ibid., p. 9.

28 J.A.G. Griffith, *Central Departments and Local Authorities*, Allen & Unwin, London, 1965, p. 232–3. No source is given for these statistics.

29 J. Short, *Housing in Britain*, Methuen, London, 1982, p. 51.

30 S. Merrett, op. cit., table 7.3.

31 B. Kilroy, *Council House Sales – Financial and Economic Considerations*, evidence to the House of Commons Select Committee on the Environment, mimeo, 1981.

32 R. A. Parker, op. cit., p. 33.

33 J.B. Cullingworth, *Housing in Transition*, Heinemann, London, 1963, p. 184n.

34 R. A. Parker, op. cit., p. 47.

35 ibid., p. 48.

36 *Housing*, Cmnd. 2050, Ministry of Housing and Local Government (MoHLG), HMSO, May 1963, p. 16.

37 MoHLG, *Annual Report for 1964*, Cmnd. 2688, HMSO, 1964, p. 14.

38 Cmnd. 2050, op. cit.

39 K. Banting, *Poverty, Politics and Policy*, Macmillan,

Lo 1979, p. 30.

40 *Housing Statistics*, no. 21, May 1971, table XV.

41 Cmnd. 3073, HMSO, July 1966.

42 ibid., para. 12.

43 *Prices and Incomes Standstill: Period of Severe Restraint*, Cmnd. 3150, HMSO, November 1966, para. 20.

44 *Fourth Report of the Estimates Committee*, Session 1968–69, vol. II, pp. 123–8.

45 National Board for Prices and Incomes (NBPI), *Increases in Rents of Local Authority Housing*, Report no. 62, Cmnd. 3604, HMSO, 1968, col. 311.

46 *House of Commons Debates*, vol. 765, May 1968, col. 311.

47 ibid., col. 310.

48 *Housing Statistics* no. 23, November 1970, Table 50.

49 *Housing Policy, Technical Volume, Part I*, HMSO, London, 1977, pp. 186–7.

50 IMTA, *Housing Statistics*, Part I, February 1971.

51 *The Housing Programme 1965–70*, Cmnd 2838, HMSO, 1965, para. 41.

52 *Rent Rebates*, Circular no. 46/47.

53 Cmnd. 3073, op. cit., para. 12.

54 MoHLG, *Report for 1967 and 1968*, HMSO, 1968, p. 15.

55 *House of Commons Debates*, vol. 745, April 1967, col. 1301 and vol. 728, May 1966, written answers, col. 46.
56 S. Merrett, op. cit., 184.
57 *Fourth Report of the Estimates Committee*, op. cit., p. 55.
58 'Fair Rents', Joint Working Party Report, *Housing*, vol. III, no. 1, May 1967.
59 *Housing*, vol. II, no. 5, January 1967.
60 J. Macey, 'Housing policy and its implications, with particular reference to economic rents', *Housing*, vol. III, no. 1, May 1967.
61 J. Flemming, 'Basic housing problems and housing subsidies in this day and age', *Housing*, vol. II, no. I, May 1966.
62 *Fourth Report of the Estimates Committee*, op. cit., vols. II. and III.
63 ibid., vol. II, p. 105.
64 IMTA, *Housing Statistics, 1968–69*, June 1970, p. 11.

Chapter six

Reform and unreform in housing finance

The 1970s was a decade when housing finance came to the forefront of housing-policy debate, and it seemed for a while that there was a real prospect of fundamental cross-tenure reform. In practice, however, change was concentrated in the rented sectors, with owner occupation remaining immune to arguments for reform. As the previous chapter has shown, it was being argued in the late 1960s that local authority subsidy arrangements were anomalous and inequitable, and this position was strengthened by events in the private rented sector as fair rents spread through the stock. Controlled rents had always been well below local authority rent levels, but by 1970 it was clear that fair rents were being set at around twice the level of average council rents.[1] Moreover, the only source of subsidy for private tenants was through the supplementary benefit system, which excluded all those in employment.

An internal civil service review of housing subsidies was conducted in 1968–9, but the details never reached the public domain.[2] However, it seems that the recommendation must have been the introduction of fair rents in the public sector, an idea which Labour ministers were not prepared to implement.[3] As it turned out, fair rents became the dominant issue in housing finance in the first half of the 1970s, precipitating a major conflict between the Labour and Conservative parties, and between central and local government.

The Conservatives had eagerly espoused the idea of fair rents when in opposition,[4] and their victory in the 1970 general election set the stage for a radical reform of housing finance. Whereas in the past the problems of shortage and poor quality had been linked to the high cost of housing, the Conservatives now based their policy on the view that most tenants were not paying enough for housing. The new government set out the details of its proposed legislation in a White Paper, published in June 1971.[5]

'Fair deal for housing'

Entitled *Fair Deal for Housing*, the White Paper laid great stress on the promotion of fairness in housing finance. The government's housing policy objectives were stated to be:

a decent home for every family at a price within their means;

a fairer choice between owning a home and renting one;

fairness between one citizen and another in giving and receiving help towards housing costs.

The achievement of these objectives was, in the government's view, thwarted by several features of the public sector subsidy system in particular. First, the indiscriminate nature of local authority subsidies distributed assistance to tenants irrespective of their income. Second, subsidy was unfairly distributed amongst housing authorities, not being sufficiently related to local needs. Third, the burden of subsidies was unfairly distributed because ratepayers in many areas made no contribution towards council housing; 'But those who do [contribute] make a disproportionately heavy contribution towards the housing costs of some of their fellow ratepayers.'[6] Furthermore it was stated that 'many' taxpayers and ratepayers who made a contribution towards council housing were less well off than the recipients of assistance. Fourth, the subsidy system had created a pattern of rents which varied unfairly from place to place. Finally, the burden of subsidies was seen to rest heavily on the Exchequer, and the possible increase over the next ten years was described as 'a staggering addition to the nation's tax burden'.

The focus of the approach outlined in the White Paper was the extension of the fair rent principle to cover the remainder of the unfurnished private rented sector and the entire public sector. In relation to the private sector the government was able to draw on the report of the Francis Committee on the Rent Acts which was conveniently published in March 1971. The Committee concluded that the system of regulated tenancies was working well but that a number of changes should be made in particular to speed up the transition from rent control to regulation, with greater freedom for rents to be fixed by agreement between landlord and tenant without recourse to a decision by a rent officer.

The government's objective was to raise rent levels generally, so as to give a boost to the private market in rented housing and to reduce the subsidy burden arising from public housing. The intention was to bring rents in line with current money values and moderated market conditions, and to keep them there. The White Paper also outlined changes in the subsidy system and the introduction of a mandatory national rent-rebate scheme. In trying to unravel and understand what became a highly complex piece of legislation it is important to remember that these latter provisions stemmed from the commitment to fair rents. As the White Paper put it, 'In the Government's view, the right principle is first to determine a rent which is reasonable for the dwelling and then to consider whether the tenant needs help towards the rent. Any rent subsidy should be directed to the tenant rather than to the house.'[7] In future, general subsidy, if any, for local-authority housing in a given area would in essence be determined by the nature of the deficit arising after fair rents were charged. This required a new approach to subsidy, making Exchequer assistance flexible from year to year and from place to place. At the same time higher basic rents required a mechanism to channel assistance to those in need, in the form of a rebate scheme. In the private sector, similarly, the transition to fair rents all round required a means of assisting the less well off, and in this case it was termed a rent allowance scheme, just to distinguish it from the rebates for council tenants.

The White Paper was notably lacking in statistics. In particular there was no attempt to provide any indication of costing. The amount of increase needed, on average, to achieve a fair rent was not estimated; nor was the time-scale involved in reaching fair rents in the public setor; nor was there any indication of how many authorities were expected to move into surplus, nor when this was likely to begin to occur. On the level of subsidies overall the White Paper merely said, 'Under the new system total Exchequer subsidies for housing in England and Wales, instead of growing rapidly, will remain at about their present level (at current prices).'[8] Finally, there was no estimate of the cost of rebates and allowances, nor of how many people were likely to become claimants.

Fair rents for all

The Housing Finance Act 1972, broke from the tradition of separate acts for private and public rented housing, and as a result the Act was a long and very complicated measure, running to 108 sections, with 11 schedules.

The best way to approach this Act is to remember that the intention was to extend fair rents across rented housing as a whole, and that the various changes in rent setting practices and in subsidy and rebate provisions were all related to that purpose. The logical starting point for describing the new system is therefore the method of setting rents. As far as the public sector was concerned the Act introduced an entirely new rent and subsidy system, a completely fresh start after fifty years of accretion. The Act abandoned the notion of reasonable rent and made it the duty of local authorities to charge fair rents for all their housing accommodation, and established procedures for both the determination of fair rent levels and progression towards them. The determination of fair rents was to be based on the same criteria as applied in the private rented sector under the 1968 Rent Act. However, if the criteria for determining fair rents were the same, the procedures to be followed were rather different. Local authorities were to make provisional assessments of fair rents for all their housing stock within six months of the Act, and to publish the results for the information of tenants. After a period during which tenants could make representations, the authorities were required to submit the provisional rent assessments to Rent Scrutiny Boards for approval or modification. The Rent Scrutiny Boards which were especially created for the purpose of examining local authority fair rent assessments, were made up of members of the Rent Assessment Panel. This Panel already existed in the private sector to provide people to make up Rent Assessment Committees whose role was to hear appeals against rent officers' decisions. The Rent Scrutiny Boards had the power to make the final decision as to fixing of fair rents in the public sector, with no right of appeal by either councils or tenants.

It was freely accepted that fair rents would be much higher than existing council rents in many areas, and therefore the Act laid down detailed arrangements for the progression towards fair rent levels. Increases towards fair rents began in October 1972, and in the simplest terms the aim was to secure increases of £26 per dwelling per year (or 50p per week) until fair rents were achieved. The actual increase required in October 1972 depended on local rent decisions in the previous year or eighteen months, but the basic aim was still to obtain at least £26 per dwelling in the period up to 31 March 1973.[9]

In the private sector things were less complicated. The main mechanism for effecting the transition from controlled to regulated tenancies was by block transfer according to rateable value. Thus on 1 January 1973 all remaining controlled tenancies with rateable values of £95 or more in London and £60 elsewhere in England and Wales were transferred to regulation. There was then a timetable which envisaged the staged transference of all remaining controlled tenancies by 1 July 1975. Landlords were permitted to raise rents to fair rent levels in three annual instalments. Unlike local authorities, private landlords were not *required* to charge fair rents. Housing associations, too, were not required to charge fair rents, but were not permitted to charge more than the fair rent.

The national rent rebate scheme

The Act stipulated that from the beginning of October 1972 every housing authority had to operate a scheme of rent rebates for its own tenants in accordance with the model scheme set out in Schedules 3 and 4 to the Act, and regulations made from time to time by the Secretary of State. From January 1973 local housing authorities also had a duty to provide rent allowances for private and housing association tenants, again in line with the provisions of Schedules 3 and 4 to the Act, and subsequent regulations.

There was, however, freedom to increase expenditure on rebates and allowances by up to 10 per cent above the cost of the model scheme, thereby preserving a degree of local autonomy The model scheme outlined in Schedule 3 differed in a number of ways from the previous model offered to local authorities in 1967.[10] The new scheme was based on the calculation of a needs allowance, which was related to the size and composition of each household, and an assessed level of income. The income level was determined by taking into account gross household income. Where the needs allowance matched the assessed income, then the rent payable was fixed at 40 per cent of the standard rent, (i.e. fair rent or rent in progress towards that level) for the dwelling. In other words, the rebate (allowance) was set at 60 per cent.

In cases where the income was below the needs allowance, the rent was further reduced by 25 per cent of the difference between income and allowance. But where income exceeded the needs allowance, the rent payable was increased by 17 per cent of the difference.

This system meant that some tenants on very low incomes, or with several dependants, could be required to pay no rent at all. On the other hand, tenants with incomes well above the needs allowance continued to be entitled to some degree of assistance with their rent. The extreme case would be a large family of dependent children where even earnings of well above the industrial average would lead to entitlement to assistance. Once fixed, a rebate (allowance) remained payable for six months in the case of applicants under pensionable age, unless there was a change of circumstances in which case the tenant had a duty to inform the authority.

An issue which had been emerging for some years concerned the position of tenants who were were in receipt of supplementary benefit (SB). Many authorities had adopted the practice of refusing to pay rent rebates to SB recipients, on the grounds that the Supplementary Benefit Commission (SBC) had a duty to meet reasonable housing costs. It was argued that it was wrong for council tenants and local ratepayers to bear the cost of rent assistance for people who as SB claimants were the responsibility of the social security system and taxpayers as a whole. The SBC, not unnaturally, took the opposite view and received the support of both the Labour government in the late 1960s and the Conservative government which followed. However, it was not until the Housing Finance Act that local authorities were required to bear the cost of rebates for SB claimants.

The subsidy system

The changes in rent levels and methods for rent fixing and rent-rebate provisions required far-reaching revision of subsidy arrangements. The new subsidy system introduced in the Act was very complicated in its structure and operation, but to understand it it is important to keep in mind that the basic objective was to limit subsidy to the amount needed to balance the housing revenue account.

The new housing finance system abandoned the subsidies paid under previous acts and replaced them with eight new subsidies.

1 Residual (paid to the housing revenue account)

2 Transition

3 Rising costs } paid to the HRA and subject to limitation by reference to the state of the account.

4 Operational deficit

5 Rent Rebate } paid to the rate fund, and subject to limitation by reference to the state of the HRA

6 Rent Allowance

7 Town Development } paid to the rate fund

8 Slum Clearance

It is not necessary to enter into a long and detailed account of the roles of these various subsidies, but a brief explanation is required. The residual subsidy represented the consolidation of the various amounts paid in 1971–2 under earlier legislation. The Act set out a schedule for this subsidy to be phased out, leaving most authorities with zero entitlement within two or three years. Transition subsidy dovetailed in with the declining residual subsidy to provide support in situations where falling subsidy was not matched by rising rental income. Rising cost subsidy, on the other hand, provided for situations where costs rose faster than income. Given that rent increases were pegged to amounts determined in the Act it was necessary to have a variable element of subsidy to relate total income and expenditure. Rising cost subsidy was not a licence to spend, however; first because a rising proportion of deficit was to be covered by a rate fund contribution (planned to be 25 per cent by 1975–6), and second because only 'reckonable expenditure' was eligible for subsidy. In fact virtually all HRA expenditure was counted as reckonable and initially at least this was not a tight constraint.[11] Nevertheless, it is clear that rising cost subsidy was payable only where the HRA was in deficit, and that it was not expected to continue beyond the early 1980s.

Operational deficit was designed specifically to assist a small number of authorities which met the restrictive qualifying criteria. It too required a rate fund contribution.

Much more significant was the rent rebate subsidy. For the first time local authorities were given a subsidy specifically earmarked for rebate purposes. Previously they had been encouraged to use general subsidy for the payment of rebates but in the new system this was not permitted and a special subsidy was introduced. The rebate subsidy was set at 90 per cent of the cost of rent rebates (as determined by the terms of the mandatory scheme) in the first year, falling to 75 per cent by 1975–6. The balance had to be contributed from the local authorities' own resources, from the rates. Similar arrangements applied to the rent allowance subsidy for private tenants (although the Exchequer contributions were initially 100 per cent, falling to 80 per cent).

Having outlined the main subsidies introduced in the new system, we should reiterate that (apart from the residual subsidy) the three subsidies payable to HRA, and their associated RFCs, were due only in cases where they were necessary to balance the HRA. Where rental income was sufficient to cover expenditure, then none of these subsidies or RFCs was paid. More significant still was the provision (in schedule I to the Act) that once these subsidies and RFCs had been eliminated by rising rental income, then the next thing to be reduced was the 'model rent rebate contribution', i.e. the payment transferred from the rates fund in respect of the cost of rebates calculated according to the mandatory scheme. In other words, the cost of rent rebates was planned to be carried, in the longer term, once fair rents were reached, by council tenants themselves.

It was even envisaged that in some places there would be surpluses even after covering the full cost of rebates. Any surplus above £30 per dwelling was to be repaid to the Secretary of State, who was to use it to offset rent allowances to private tenants. And if there was still money left over, it was to be divided equally between the Exchequer and the local rates fund in the area generating the surplus.

The politics of the Housing Finance Act

The Housing Finance Act implied fundamental changes in the freedom of local authorities to set rents, and in the financial regime of public housing: general subsidy was intended to be reduced everywhere and eliminated in an increasing number of places, and in at least some places even means-tested assistance would be covered out of net rent income. Not surprisingly the government anticipated resistance at the local level, and the Act contained provisions for dealing with authorities which refused to co-operate. Councillors could be declared in default of their duties, fined, disqualified from public office, and replaced by a centrally appointed Housing Commissioner.

The struggle against the Act was widespread and bitterly contested, and in view of the scale and intensity of the campaign it is appropriate to refer to it, albeit briefly.[12] At the Parliamentary level Labour denounced the bill as 'the most reactionary and socially divisive measure that is likely to be introduced in the lifetime of this Parliament – and that is saying a good deal.'[13] From the outset of the Parliamentary process the Opposition was pledged to repeal the legislation on fair rents in the public sector. Labour members prolonged the Commons committee stage by presenting hundreds of amendments and taking the discussion into fifty-seven sessions over a three-month period, then a record in modern times. Their basic argument was that fair rents had no relevance in the public sector since the concept was designed to meet the requirements of landlords who needed to make a reasonable profit. Higher rents would inevitably result in greater reliance on means testing, but Labour argued that 'the only proper and sensible principle is to set rents at a level which most people can pay without a means test and without a rebate.'[14] On a more practical level, it was pointed out that fewer than 200,000 fair rents had been set in the private sector since 1966, yet provisional fair rents had to be set for 5.5 million council dwellings in under a year.

However, no matter how cogently the Opposition argued its case, the government was certain to win in the end. If the legislation was to be defeated it would have to be in the country and not in Parliament, but Sklair's detailed account of events shows that there were cleavages in the Labour movement which ultimately ruined any real chance of success. As with the poll tax in the late 1980s, the issue which divided the opposition was the rule of law: the national leadership of the Labour Party refused to support local councillors who defied the Act and broke the law.[15] It is not clear whether the leadership would have taken a different view if they had thought that local authorities would stand solidly together in defying the law. Equally, it is uncertain whether the authorities would have been more united and determined if they had been given a strong lead from the centre.

What is now clear is that local authority opposition began with widespread affirmation of resistance, which quickly melted away after the Act took effect in October 1972. Only a handful of authorities continued their resistance into 1973, and only two, Clay Cross, in Derbyshire, and Bedwas and Machen, in South Wales, maintained their stance through to 1974. In Bedwas and Machen the Welsh Secretary installed a Housing Commissioner very quickly and higher rents were soon being collected. But in Clay Cross the Secretary of State for the Environment took a different line, which led through the courts to the disqualification of the whole of the council, with the result that the name of Clay Cross became established as the symbol of defiance of central government attacks on local autonomy. The Clay Cross councillors skilfully exploited all opportunities to prolong their campaign and to generate maximum publicity for their cause. Their fight, however, taught central government some lessons in how to pursue policy objectives at local level, and subsequent legislation on rents and subsidies has avoided the mistakes of 1972.

The impact of the Housing Finance Act

In principle the approach based on fair rents, deficit subsidy, and rent rebates was simple enough, but in practice the Act was immensely complicated. Most of the complexity was associated with the *transition* to the new system, but it was also produced by an attempt to write into the Act itself provisions to deal with every contingency, an approach which was almost inevitably doomed to failure, given the ingenuity of local authorities and the tendency for conditions to change anyway.

Little previous work has been done on the impact of the Act, but there are a number of interesting points to be made. First, the Act began to have an impact even before it reached the statute book. This was because authorities knew it was coming and behaved accordingly. Some authorities took the return of a Conservative government as an indication that rents could be raised substantially (after the period of restraint in the late 1960s). Others took the view that, if the government proposed to raise rents then it should be seen to be wholly responsible for all increases that occurred. Thus in 1971–2 rents increased by around 25 per cent in one group of authorities and by very little in another group (some actually reduced rents).

Another response in advance of the legislation was to take account of the reintroduction of mandatory rate fund contributions. Some authorities in 1971–2 transferred large sums from housing into their rates funds, as a means of financing rate fund contributions in future years. A major source of funds for this manoeuvre was the repairs account; the Act made repairs accounts optional and so authorities were tempted to use accumulated balances to cushion the impact of the Act on local ratepayers. This is an example of a local response which was not anticipated and taken into account in the drafting of the legislation.

What the government did plan for was local authorities' holding down or reducing rents in advance of the Act itself. Overall rents increased by 25 per cent in 1972–3, and the government's objective was to secure additional rent of £26 per dwelling in that financial year. Authorities which had made reductions or very low increases in the first half of the year were required to make correspondingly larger increases in October 1972. Thus actual rent increases in October 1972 varied quite widely, depending on what decisions authorities had made in the previous year.

The available evidence (which is not perfectly reliable) suggests that rents rose most sharply in 1972–3 but in the following year the Act did not result in increases of the magnitude that many people had anticipated. The explanation for this would seem to be that the government failed to insist on a strict implementation of its legislation. By this stage (most authorities were due to make increases in October 1973) the government was pursuing a quite different economic policy from that in operation when the Act was conceived. Then interest rates had been falling and the Heath government tried to encourage industrial expansion by cutting taxes and easing credit restrictions. However, by 1973 inflation was rising above the levels which had been considered normal in the post-war period, and interest rates also rose, to very high levels. The Arab-Israeli war of October 1973 was followed by quadrupling of oil prices by the producer countries, and at the end of the year the miners' strike led to the imposition of a three-day working week. It is arguable, therefore, that the government's resolve in relation to council house rents was severely weakened by wider economic and political problems during 1973–4.

If the increase in rents was rather less than had been anticipated, the growth of subsidy was even less in accord with the intentions of the authors of the Act. One important factor in the growth of government financial support for council housing was the introduction of the mandatory rent-rebate scheme. Hitherto most local authorities had declined to pay rebates to supplementary benefits claimants, but subsequently they were required to do so in the case of claimants in receipt of benefit for more than eight weeks. As a consequence of the new arrangements for rebates the total expenditure rose rapidly. In the first quarter of 1972–3 local authorities spent £6.58m on rebates, but by the last quarter, i.e. after the introduction of the mandatory scheme and the absorption of SB claimants, the total was £23.54m, an increase of 258 per cent. Most (90 per cent) of this expenditure was covered by subsidy under the Act, and the balance was assisted by rate support grant.

The course of subsidy expenditure under the Act has been usefully summarised in the 1977 Green Paper and is worth quoting in full:

In the first year, 1972–3, the system began to work in the expected direction. Despite a sharp increase in expenditure on management and maintenance work, the imposed flat rate average increase in rents of 50p a week produced sufficient extra revenue to enable total general subsidies to be reduced in 1972–3 but nearly £20m in real terms. There was no net saving in public expenditure however, because rent rebates rose by over £40m in real terms. Even the saving in the general subsidy was short-lived. The combination of sharply rising land prices, construction costs, and interest rates produced a growing HRA deficit in virtually all authorities despite the increase in rents. And in 1974, as a counter-inflation measure, rents were frozen and the planned progression to fair rents came to an abrupt halt. The consequence was that total Exchequer subsidies began to rise again in 1973–4 at an accelerating pace, so that by 1974–5 they had almost doubled in real terms in two years. In the same two year period there was a four-fold increase, in real terms, in Rate Fund contributions. On top of these increases in general subsidy came a very sharp rise in total rent rebates – from £68m in 1972–3 to £193m in 1974–5 (in current prices).[16]

The point here is that, although the HFA was repealed before fair rents were reached in most places, it was already clear that the Act was not working as planned. Instead of subsidy levels falling, the Act was shown to contain, curiously enough, the capacity to respond flexibly to unforeseen conditions of rising costs by providing higher levels of assistance. An important feature of the transition to fair rents was that it broke the link between rents and costs. Previously, higher costs tended to be reflected in higher rents, but by imposing a system of regular increases towards fair rents the Act inadvertently shielded tenants from short-term increase in costs. With rents pegged to a non-indexed series of increases, when inflation pushed up costs so deficits rose and subsidies followed suit.

Assessing the Act

It is important to be clear about the status of the Housing Finance Act as a major turning point. On the one hand, it was a turning-point or watershed because it abandoned all the basic principles on which local authority housing finance had been based for many years. It greatly reduced local autonomy and opened up the prospect of a much more residualised public sector, as higher rents drove out the better off and rebates made council housing more affordable for the least well off. On the other hand, it can be seen as introducing a new set of policy instruments to facilitate objectives which had been in view for a long time. There was considerable continuity in policy objectives either side of the Housing Finance Act.

Basically it must be said that the Act was a bungled attempt to carry through the throughgoing reform of housing finance for which the Conservatives had been waiting since 1964. In fact the term 'reform of housing finance' was a euphemism for an attack on public housing, for as Parker pointed out at the time, fair rents and rent rebates were not the objectives for the Act but merely the means which served the wider purpose of shifting the balance of advantage and attraction in favour of owner occupation.[17] The Act was a bungled attempt because it failed both politically and administratively. Presented in the way that it was, laying down a timetable for compulsory substantial rent increases, removing local autonomy over rent setting, the Act provoked political hostility and failed at the point when the Labour Party committed itself to repealing the fair rent provisions.

The Act failed partly because of the way that it was drafted. The insistence on compliance with the Act, backed up by the threat of court action, invited defiance and enhanced the political opposition to the legislation. In practice the Government proved reluctant to use the courts against local authorities and, although many councillors were intimidated by the mere suggestion of fines and surcharges, the government could be made to look rather silly if it was challenged (as the Clay Cross councillors showed). Using the courts was a heavy handed way for one part of the state to carry on relations with another part. And it was highly visible to the public. The result of court action, even as a possibility written into the Act, was necessary only because of the absence of a *financial* means of ensuring that authorities complied with the Act. Financial mechanisms are much more effective and leave no scope for political campaigning and the creation of martyrs.

The Act also failed because, as previously explained, under conditions of growing political difficulties and worsening inflation it produced results which were contrary to the original intentions. The idea of fair rents, to be reached by fixed annual increases, appeared highly inflationary when it was unveiled in 1971, but by 1973 this mechanism was protecting tenants from inflationary pressure on rents. The Act failed because the government did not anticipate the rise in inflation, nor indeed should they have been expected to foresee the oil crisis of late 1973. However, the fact remains that the principles of the Act were conceived in the late 1960s and proved to be undone by the changed economic conditions of the late 1970s. It is ironic that an Act of such great complexity, containing provisions carefully designed to anticipate and thwart local authority resistance, should founder on the quite different problems posed by inflation. The attempt to anticipate every eventuality tied the government to such a complex system that there was no room for manoeuvre when an unexpected problem emerged. The problem addressed in the Act was that of ensuring that local authorities made increases beyond those dictated by costs. But when costs rose, the government was left with no way to raise the level of increases.

It seems reasonable to suggest, therefore, that the Act would have been abandoned or modified whatever the outcome of the 1974 general elation. Whereas the Conservatives in 1970–2 had not given priority to curbing inflation, by 1974 this was becoming a more urgent issue, and it has already been shown that the government did not press ahead with enforcing increases of the magnitude set out in the Act. As a measure designed to raise the real value of rents and to reduce subsidy the Act was a failure, but when defeating inflation assumed greater importance the Act was a liability.

The demise of fair rents in the public sector

The general election of February 1974 ushered in a period of Labour government, during most of which the government was dependent on the support of minority parties to secure its legislation. It was a time of considerable volatility and turbulence in political and economic affairs,[18] arguably not the best circumstance in which to try to introduce fundamental reform of housing finance. The Labour Party took office with a firm commitment to repeal the contentious parts the Housing Finance Act, but with no clear, coherent alternative model of housing finance. The new government showed none of the determination of purpose displayed by the previous administration. Whereas the Conservatives had moved boldly ahead with their version of the reform of housing finance, despite widespread opposition, Labour seemed intimidated by the prospect and uncertain of what to do anyway. However, whilst the period 1974–9 failed to generate fundamental reform in housing finance, there were significant changes.

As soon as the new government was formed it began the process of repealing the 1972 Act, initially by imposing a rent freeze for twelve months from March 1974, as part of counter-inflation policy. A second general election, in October 1974, gave Labour a small overall majority, and a Bill was then brought forward to repeal the 1972 Act, and to put it in its place a temporary subsidy system, pending the outcome of a thorough review of housing finance. The Housing Rents and Subsidies Act, 1975, swept away the concept of fair rents in the public sector, restored to local authorities their responsibility for setting reasonable rents, and reimposed the no-profit rule on housing revenue accounts. The national rent rebate scheme remained in place, however, indicating the non-controversial status of rebating by this stage.

The new subsidy system was in effect a reversion to the principles which had operated before 1972; the main element was a subsidy equivalent to 66 per cent of loan charges on all new investment. This was designed to facilitate the higher level of new building which the government wished to achieve, but it was recognised as a temporary measure since it had all the distributional deficiencies of the old system.[19]

The housing finance review

It was in November 1974, during the second-reading debate of the Bill to repeal fair rents in the council sector, that the Secretary of State, Anthony Crosland, announced the establishment of a fundamental review of housing finance. The terms of reference were initially:

> To review the arrangements for finance for the provision of housing and the assistance, direct or indirect, given from public funds; to consider what changes are desirable to facilitate adequate timely and economical provision to meet differing needs with reasonable freedom of choice, and to secure a more equitable and balanced distribution of assistance, and to make recommendations.[20]

The scope of the review was later widened to include fuller consideration of social aspects of policy, but as a vehicle for educating public opinion as to the need for far-reaching reform the review was enfeebled by the decision to have it carried out in private by civil servants.[21] It has also been argued that the political and economic situation in 1976 meant that the government had to let the review drag on,[22] and it was not until June 1977 that the report was published as a Green Paper. When it finally appeared the reaction in housing circles was generally one of disappointment, summed up in Lansley's statement that:

> For all the publicity gained during its 2½ year life and all the analysis presented in its 700 pages, the housing policy review is almost entirely a non-event in terms of its policy recommendations, and the housing situation in future years will suffer in consequence.[23]

The most remarkable feature of the Green Paper, given that it was a review established to make fundamental reform of housing finance a possibility, was that such reform was deemed to be unnecessary and undesirable. The Secretaries of State for the Environment and for Wales (there was a separate Scottish Green Paper, Cmnd 6852) set the tone by saying:

> we certainly do not believe that the household budgets of millions of families – which have been planned in good faith in the reasonable expectation that present arrangements would broadly continue – should be overturned, in pursuit of some theoretical or academic dogma.[24]

This immediately revealed how far attitudes and circumstances had changed since 1975. Then Crosland had spoken of the need for thoroughgoing reform of a system which was like a 'dog's breakfast' and 'whimsical in the extreme'. By 1977 the case for reform was airily dismissed as 'dogma'.

The text of the Green Paper itself is unremittingly positive about home ownership, repeatedly referring to its intrinsic merits, especially its capacity to impart freedom, independence, and mobility as well as financial advantage and psychological fulfilment to individual owners. This has been interpreted as evidence of convergence by the two main parties on housing policy. The Labour government's acceptance of the traditionally Tory philosophy of a property owning democracy has been more fully recognised than its similar movement towards public sector rent and subsidy policies which were in many ways acceptable to those of the Conservatives.

The Green Paper proposed to make no substantial changes to the highly inequitable system of tax relief for owner occupiers, but it did outline a new public sector subsidy system which was designed to deliver most assistance to those areas with greatest need, whilst reducing help for the rest.

The Government believe that there is a need for a new public sector subsidy system designed to achieve a more efficient and fairer use of subsidy. This could be done by reducing subsidy in areas where the need for it is declining in order to concentrate it more on authorities who need large investment programmes and whose costs are consequently rising.[25]

The Green Paper began the section on the new subsidy system by stating that the rights and duties restored to local authorities (the right to set 'reasonable' rents and the duty not to run a surplus on HRA) should be maintained. It went on to say that, 'payment of subsidy should be based on a regular appraisal of local housing costs, with the subsidy designed to help bridge the gap, *if any*, between those costs and a reasonable local contribution from rents and rebates.[26] [Present author's italics.] The government was proposing a deficit subsidy based on calculation of the relationship between current income and expenditure, as distinct from subsidies tied to loan charges irrespective of current rent income. In other words, the Labour government accepted one of the key principles underlying the 1972 Housing Finance Act – a major departure from the positions adopted both in the 1960s and in the early 1970s.

Explanation of the new system was rather tentative but contained four clear stages for the calculation of subsidy for each authority each year:

(i)   the starting point would be the authority's subsidy entitlement in the previous year;
(ii)   the increase in expenditure would be calculated according to a formula for determining expenditure that was admissible for subsidy;
(iii) the level of increase in 'local contribution' from rents and rates would be calculated;
(iv)   if the figure produced in (ii) was larger than the figure produced in (iii) then subsidy would be increased, and vice versa.

A key feature of deficit subsidy systems is that the government has a much closer interest in local income and expenditure than under systems that tie subsidies to loan charges. This was clearly recognised in the Green Paper:

Under this system, the rate of increase in the 'local contribution' – rents and General Rate Fund contribution – would be perhaps the most important decision to be taken annually. It would be the predominant factor in determining the total Exchequer subsidy bill and it would also be likely to influence the size of local authority rent increases, though the balance between rents and General Rate Fund contributions, and the fixing of individual rents, would remain a matter for local discretion.[27]

It is important to remember that one of Labour's main objections to the Housing Finance Act, 1972, was its removal of local autonomy in rent fixing. Thus in adopting a deficit system it was entering a difficult area. Under the 1972 Act rents were raised in specified amounts in a progression towards 'fair' rent levels, but the Labour government, not surprisingly, looked for an alternative yardstick to determine the rate of increase in 'local contribution', and settled for the principle that 'over a run of years rents should keep broadly in line with changes in money incomes'. It was also clear from the Green Paper that rent increases, rather than rate fund contributions, were expected to account for most, if not all, increases in local contributions.

The government recognised that one effect of a proposed deficit subsidy would be to ensure that areas of high levels of investment, and therefore rapidly increasing costs, would receive most assistance, whilst low-cost authorities (those with a relatively old housing stock and little new building) would receive less. In some cases entitlement to subsidy would gradually be eliminated by rising rents. This led the government to consider the idea of a minimum subsidy entitlement or 'subsidy floor', in order, it was said, to foster a sense of fairness between the owner occupied and public sectors. The idea would involve a reduction in subsidy entitlement in low-cost authorities only to a level which represented some agreed proportion of interest charges. Once this subsidy floor was reached Exchequer contributions would remain steady and, if costs relative to total income continued to fall then the real value of rents would also fall, 'as the tenants of the authority as a group enjoyed the full benefits of fixed historic costs in the same way in which home owners individually enjoy the full benefit of a gradually declining real level of costs under conventional mortgage arrangements.'[28] The Green Paper's proposals for rents and subsidies have been criticised in various ways. Merrett, for instance, refers to the increased control exercised over local authorities by central government in a deficit-subsidy system.[29] The same point is made by Lansley,[30] Harloe,[31] and Ginsburg.[32] Lansley also argues that the new system is unlikely to redistribute subsidies sufficiently to make a significant change in disparities in rents and RFCs. He points out that by taking the existing level of subsidy as the starting point, current disparities are built into the system. In this respect the Housing Finance Act was fairer because it eliminated the effect of existing RFCs in the calculation of deficits. Lansley is also critical of the idea of a 'subsidy floor', which he says would have a capricious effect on the distribution of subsidy. He can see no clear principle upon which the suggestion is based.

Housing finance and the management of the economic crisis

Meanwhile, as the housing policy review ground on, the British economy was going through a major crisis, unlike anything experienced since 1945.

129

Inflation, interest rates, public expenditure and unemployment all reached record levels during 1975–6, and Keynesian methods of economic management gave way to the ascendant prescriptions of monetarism, a perspective requiring cuts in public expenditure. As it happened, housing expenditure had been rising very rapidly and in 1974–5 it reached a peak which was 82 per cent higher in real terms than in 1972–3.[33] The cuts in subsequent years have to be understood in relation to the abnormally high level of 1974–5.[34] The main contributory factors on the capital side were increases in land prices, the higher than average increase in building costs, and the expansion of the house building programme. On the revenue side, there had been an increase in local authority repair and maintenance activity since 1972, interest rates were rising, thereby exacerbating the increased expenditure on new building, and council rents were frozen in 1974–5. In addition, it is appropriate to refer to the expansion of the housing association building programme and a substantial loan to building societies to hold down mortgage interest rates in 1974.

Having established that housing expenditure was at an all-time high in 1974–5, it is necessary to look at what happened subsequently. If we take the overall picture first, as represented in the 1979 public expenditure White Paper,[35] total public expenditure on housing declined by almost a fifth (19.0 per cent) between 1974–5 and 1978–9. Thus the programme which had increased fastest in the early 1970s, much faster than the general increase in public spending, declined at a faster rate in the rest of the decade. Total capital expenditure suffered the greatest reduction, being 35 per cent less in 1978–9 than in 1974–5. However, general Exchequer subsidy to local authority housing rose by 20 per cent, and total subsidy on rent rebates rose by 36.4 per cent. Within the overall reduction, therefore, there was a substantial shift from investment spending to consumption spending. An important development of the period was the declining proportion of local authority HRA expenditure covered by rents:

Table 6.1 Rebated rents and subsidies as percentages of housing revenue account expenditure (England and Wales)

	Rents	Exchequer subsidy	Exchequer subsidy and rate-fund contribution
1973–4	53.5	21.4	38.0
1974–5	43.8	30.6	50.1
1975–6	41.2	40.7	53.0
1976–7	39.9	43.7	53.5
1977–8	41.4	42.1	50.9
1978–9	38.6	41.4	51.3

Source: CIPFA *Housing Revenue Account Statistics*

Average net rents in local authority housing stood, by 1979, at a historically low level in relation to both costs and wages. During the 1960s rents had risen faster then pre-tax earnings and much faster than prices.[36] The Housing Finance Act of 1972 imposed further sharp increases in real terms, but the trend was halted by the rise in inflation and the imposition of a rents freeze in 1974. Thereafter rents fell in real terms, by an average of 4.3 per cent per year between 1974 and 1979;[37] and as a proportion of average earnings rents fell from 7.4 per cent to 6.7 per cent in the same period.[38]

It is quite clear that the changing balance between rents and subsidies, and the falling real value of rents, was not desired for its own sake; it was not part of housing policy, for, as has been pointed out above, the government's view was that rents should keep pace with wages. The surge in subsidy expenditure was necessary to protect tenants from the very rapid increase in interest charges during the period of high inflation. The argument had been made in the Green Paper,[39] and elsewhere,[40] that the growth of subsidies was, in effect, an accident of high inflation.

The Housing Bill, 1979

The previous section has shown that although the government failed to devise a coherent plan for the reform of housing finance during 1974–9, there was, nevertheless, a good deal of change. It was not until mid-March 1979, just before the government was defeated in Parliament and forced into a general election that a bill was published setting out a number of policy developments, including a new subsidy system in the council sector.

Little needs to be said about Labour's 1979 Housing Bill, but there are a couple of points worth making. First, the objectives of the Bill placed housing finance towards the bottom of the list:

> The main purposes of the Bill are to introduce a new code of rights for public sector tenants; to provide for further assistance towards the improvement and repair of homes, including grants for tenants and grants for repairs alone; to enable local authorities to give further encouragement to owner-occupation and to make amendments to the option mortgage scheme; to introduce a new scheme of subsidies for housing authorities; to provide for revised arrangements for housing association rents and other matters; and to make miscellaneous amendments to the law relating to leasehold houses.[41]

This was clearly not the bill to reform housing finance that might have been expected in 1975, and by continuing the convention of treating each tenure separately it perpetuated the confusion of which Crosland had complained.

New priorities had emerged, raising the idea of a tenants' charter to the high ground of housing politics. The tenants' charter, by the way, was an idea put forward by the Conservatives in 1976,[42] although it originated amongst tenants' organisations, and was only belatedly taken up by the Labour Party. Even in opposition the Conservatives were making the running in housing policy, with the Labour Government appearing to react rather than taking its own distinctive line.

Second, the new system of housing subsidies in the local authority sector reflected the scheme outlined in the Green Paper. That is, a single deficit subsidy was to be introduced, calculated on the difference between reckonable expenditure and rent income. Subsidy entitlement would begin with the existing level of assistance in the year before the new scheme came into operation. If the increase in reckonable expenditure was greater than the 'local contribution differential' (i.e. rent increase) then the subsidy would rise. Clause 45(7) stated that the calculation of the local contribution differential would be based on a general assessment of changes in the level of earnings and a determination would be made by the Secretary of State accordingly. However, in making such determinations he was required by Clause 45(8) to consult with the local authority associations. Beyond this, commentators at the time did make criticisms of the use of the existing level of subsidy as the starting point.[43] It was also predicted that there would be an overall reduction in subsidies and a redistribution towards inner London.[44]

Conclusion

The period which began with the great confrontation over the Housing Finance Act ended with Labour's proposing a subsidy system which was quite acceptable to the Conservatives. To the extent that there was true convergence, it was that Labour gave up opposition to deficit subsidy and the Conservatives abandoned fair rents. However, it seems that what was happening was that for the most part Labour (certainly the government as distinct from the party) was converging on the Conservatives, rather than there being a meeting on the middle ground. It is very important to recognise how the Green Paper of 1977, stripped to its conceptual bones, represents a replication of the views promulgated in the Tory White Paper of 1971. Both documents essentially take the position that owner occupation is highly desirable and that no major changes in financial arrangements are needed. On the other hand, both propose changes affecting council housing subsidy provisions, and despite the rhetoric of 1971–5 the proposals in the Green Paper have more in common than conflict with the principles of the Housing Finance Act. It is not just that the two sets of proposals for council housing are similar, but that each in combination with a policy of no change in the owner-occupation sector represents a residualist view of council housing.

The decision to set up the housing finance review has been criticised as a strategic and tactical error.[45] The basis for this claim is that 1975 was the right time to legislate for the reform of housing finance, in terms of the life of the Parliament. The political climate of 1974 had not yet faded and the risk was that a review followed by legislation would result in proposals being considered in a very different atmosphere, which, of course, is precisely what happened. The argument in favour of the review was apparently that it was necessary to carry public opinion and that this required some careful cultivation. Unfortunately the fact that the review was conducted in private (and not as a great public debate, such as that simultaneously undertaken in education) completely undermined that case.

An alternative view is that the housing-finance review, far from being a mistake, was the only option open to Labour, for two related reasons. First, the Party had strongly opposed the Housing Finance Act, committing the next Labour government to its repeal, without devising a proper alternative. Having repealed the Act, the Labour government had nothing to put in its place apart from a temporary measure. This reveals the intellectual bankruptcy of the Labour Party on housing policy, a position fostered by the Party's convergence on Conservative policy – in a political situation which called for a radical alternative vision of housing finance the Labour Party's commitment to home ownership left it totally adrift. The best that can be said for the housing finance review is that it was a genuine, albeit belated, attempt to find an alternative to Conservative policy on housing. It seems more likely, however, that a key function of the review was always to create a breathing space, a gap in time that might obscure the fact that the rents and subsidy policy actually implemented in succession to the temporary regime, was a redrafted version of the 1972 Act. It is possible that the Labour leadership was driven into a corner by the 1972 Act, by the crude legal draughtsmanship of the Act on the one hand and on the other the opposition to it from their own numbers, especially councillors and tenants at local level. Hence the commitment to repeal the Act, but the lack of an alternative vision.

The Labour government's thinking on council house rents and subsidies was hopelessly muddled, in sharp contrast to the Conservatives'. This was because the Tories had a clearer view of the role of the public sector, as a residual tenure for the least well off. For them there was no problem about housing revenue account surpluses, high rent levels, and a subsidy system that was obviously inequitable between tenures. Labour, however, was forced into a highly contradictory position, as described above, because of its commitment to the no-profit rule on the one hand and indexed rent rises on the other. And to make matters worse, the concern about maintaining a minimum level of public-sector subsidy to create some sort of equity with owner occupiers just added to the incoherence of Labour's position.

By their failure to come to terms with what had been happening in housing finance, the Labour governments of 1974–9 left the way clear for a radical reforming government of the Right. They almost succeeded in taking politics out of housing. But, more than that, they actually set up the network of controls on capital spending, and the outlines of a public sector subsidy system which provided the Thatcher governments with the tools they needed for their version of the reform of housing finance.

References

1 *Report of the Committee on the Rent Acts (The Francis Report)*, Cmnd. 4609, HMSO, London 1971. p. 27, Table 15, and IMTA, *Housing Statistics,* Part 1, 1970.
2 Evidence of MoHLG to Estimates Committee on 3 March 1969; *Fourth Report of the Estimates Committee, Session 1968–9*, vol. II, Evidence, p. 165.
3 A Crosland, speaking during the second-reading debate on the Housing Finance Bill, *House of Commons Debates*, vol. 826, November 1971, col. 49.
4 See the speech by Peter Walker at the Urban Research Bureau Housing Conference, *Second Thoughts on Urban Renewal*, Manchester, June 1969, p. 32.
5 *Fair Deal for Housing*, Cmnd 4728, HMSO, London, 1971.
6 ibid., para. 6(iii).
7 ibid., para. 20.
8 ibid., para. 66.
9 For more detail see J. Macey, *The Housing Finance Act, 1972*, Butterworth, London. 1972, pp. 279–81.
10 MoHLG, Circular 46/67.
11 *Housing Policy Technical Volume Part III*, HMSO, London, 1977, p. 50.
12 See also: D. Skinner and J. Langdon, *The Story of Clay Cross*, Spokesman Books, Nottingham, 1974; L. Sklair, 'The struggle against the Housing Finance Act', in R. Miliband and J. Saville (eds), *The Socialist Register 1975*, Merlin Press, London, 1975, pp. 250–92; P. Beirne, *Fair Rent and Legal Fiction*, Macmillan, London 1977; P. Malpass, 'The road from Clay Cross', *Roof*, January–February, 1989.
13 *House of Commons Debates*, vol. 826, November 1971, col. 48.
14 ibid., col. 54.
15 See *Report of Seventy-First Annual Conference of the Labour Party*, Blackpool, 1971, p, 152.
16 *Technical Volume Part III*, p. 41.
17 R. A. Parker, *The Housing Finance Act and Council Tenants*, CPAG, London, 1971, p. 12.
18 See M. Holmes, *The Labour Government 1974–9*, Macmillan, London, 1985, and N. Bosanquet and P. Townsend (eds), *Labour and Inequality*, Heinemann, London, 1980.
19 *Housing Policy*, Cmnd. 6851, op. cit,, pp. 82–3.
20 ibid., p. 133.
21 B. Kilroy, *Housing Finance – Organic Reform?*, Labour Economic Finance and Taxation Association, London, 1978, p. 9.
22 ibid., p. 9, and M. Harloe, 'The Green Paper on housing policy', in M. Brown and S. Baldwin (eds.), *The Year Book of Social Policy in Britain 1977*, Routledge & Kegan Paul, London, 1978, p. 6.

23 S. Lansley, *Housing and Public Policy*, Croom Helm, London, 1979, p. 218.
24 *Housing Policy*, op. cit., p. iv.
25 ibid., p. 36.
26 ibid., p. 83.
27 ibid., p. 83.
28 ibid., p. 87.
29 S. Merrett, *State Housing in Britain,* Routledge & Kegan Paul, London, 1979, p. 272.
30 S. Lansley, op. cit., p. 208.
31 M. Harloe, op. cit., p. 14.
32 N. Ginsburg, *Class Capital and Social Policy*, Macmillan, London, 1979, p. 155.
33 *The Government's Expenditure Plans Vol. II*, Cmnd. 6721–II, HMSO, London, February 1977, Table 2.7. But see also *Public Expenditure to 1978–9*, Cmnd. 5879, HMSO, London, 1975, Table 2.7.
34 E. Craven, 'Housing', in R. Klein (ed.) *Social Policy and Public Expenditure 1975: Inflation and Priorities*, Centre for Studies in Social Policy, London, 1975. See also E. Craven, 'The explosion in housing expenditure', *Housing Review*, July–August 1975.
35 *The Government's Expenditure Plans 1979–80 to 1982–83*, Cmnd. 7439, HMSO, London 1979, Table 2.7.
36 *Housing Policy Technical Volume Part I*, p. 187.
37 Calculations made by B. Kilroy and included in evidence to the House of Commons Select Committee on Environment, 1981. Unpublished.
38 Statement by Sir G. Howe to Treasury and Civil Service Committee, quoted in the *First Report of the Environment Committee*, op. cit., p. xi.
39 *Housing Policy Technical Volume*, I, p. 192–3.
40 D. Webster, 'Council house costs, why we should all calm down?', *Roof*, October. 1975, pp. 7–10.
41 *Housing Bill*, March 1979, Explanatory and Financial Memorandum.
42 *The Right Approach*, op. cit., p. 54.
43 H. Aughton, *Roof*, November 1978.
44 E. Howes, 'The new subsidy system', *CES Review*, 4, September 1978.
45 e.g. D. Webster in Bosanquet and Townsend, op. cit., p. 248.

Chapter seven

Residualism triumphant? Rents policies in the 1980s

The 1980s have been years of rapid change in British society, marked by government determination to turn away from the framework of public services established in the post-war settlement. The term 'Thatcherism' was coined to characterise the distinctive brand of right-wing politics which had been on the ascendancy in the Conservative Party since the mid-1970s. Thatcherism has been described as a combination of monetarist economics and authoritarian populism[1] which has 'changed the face of British politics'.[2]

Hall and Jacques argue that Thatcherism is not the same old Conservative Party in a suburban disguise, and warn against under-estimating its novelty as a political force:

> The historic mission of Thatcherism has not been to win this or that election....it is much more ambitious than that. Its project has been to reverse the whole postwar drift of British society, to roll back the historic gains of the labour movement and other progressive forces, and force-march the society, vigorously, into the past. It has made a number of damaging raids on the social democratic consensus. The main reference points of the postwar political settlement – already weakened and eroded in fact under successive Labour governments – have been contested *in principle*. One after another the old landmarks – full employment, welfare state support, equality of opportunity, the 'caring' society, neo Keynsian economic management, corporatist incomes policies – have all been reversed.[3]

Alternative critiques would argue that the retreat had begun under right-wing Labour governments in the 1970s,[4] and that despite the vigour of the Thatcherite assault on it, the welfare state has proved to be remarkable resilient. As Chapter 1 illustrated, housing has been a prime target for change.[5] In this chapter the focus is on local authority housing finance in the 1980s, and it is clear that a number of factors have combined to bring about changes which amount to a transformation. There has been a fundamental restructuring of the revenue side of local authority housing finance, and central government policy on rents and subsidies is just one of a bundle of influences which have affected the pattern of flows in and out of housing-revenue accounts (HRAs). In addition it is relevant to refer to:

the impact of high unemployment and general residualisation of council housing which have increased the numbers claiming means-tested assistance with housing costs;

cutbacks in new building and the impact this has had on the rate of growth of outstanding debt;

the sale of council houses and the revenue implications of interest on accrued capital receipts;

the introduction and subsequent modification of the housing benefit system;

the exercise of discretion by local authorities in the implementation of central government policy on rents and subsidies.

Some of these factors will be referred to in the course of examining the form and implementation of rents and subsidy policy since 1980.

Whilst the new Conservative government after May 1979 was clear and emphatic about certain aspects of its housing policy, such as the right to buy, it was highly evasive on other important issues such as estimates of housing need and likely rates of new building. On rents and subsidies, too, ministers were careful to give little away. The Chancellor spoke in 1980 about reversing the decline in the real value of rents, and the Secretary of State for the Environment hinted at a 10 per cent real increase in four years.[6] However, it was not until April 1981, when the new subsidy system came into operation, that the government was able to impose real pressure on rents.

The new subsidy system

In view of the amount of attention which focused on rents and subsidies during the passage of the Housing Finance Bill in 1972, it is remarkable how little discussion there was on these issues in the Housing Bill of 1980, especially bearing in mind the potency of the new system. This time the focus of public attention was the right to buy, and the one and a half pages of the bill which set out the new subsidy regime were deeply embedded in a location ensuring that little parliamentary time would be devoted to the topic. Thus Michael Heseltine's speech introducing the Bill's second-reading debate covers eighteen closely printed columns in Hansard, but just two paragraphs refer to subsidy reform, and there is no reference to rent levels at all.[7] However, the first Opposition speaker, Roy Hattersley, picked up this omission and expressed the fear that the bill heralded a period of continued and substantial council rent increase as part of the government's wider economic policy.[8] He recognised the similarities between the proposed subsidy system and the one contained in Labour's 1979 bill, but noted two differences: that the Secretary of State would not now be required to keep rent increases in line with earnings, and that housing revenue accounts would be permitted to generate surpluses. In this latter respect the bill resembled the 1972 Act, but whereas in 1972 the Act contained detailed provisions to explain what surpluses would be used for, in 1980 there was nothing in the bill on this issue. Hattersley unsuccessfully challenged the minister replying to the debate (John Stanley) to make clear the government's intentions on both rent increases and the fate of HRA surpluses.

Rather than spell out his own intentions Heseltine preferred to attack Labour's record, arguing that, 'The rent policies of the last Labour Government have been a major factor in the inability of local authorities adequately to meet housing costs, finance investment and maintain their existing stock.'[9] As long as they said nothing very precise about their rents policy, ministers were difficult to attack on the issue, for two main reasons.

First, as noted above, the system outlined in the Bill was very similar to the scheme put forward by Labour. And second, the Bill did no more than set up a *formula* for the annual calculation of local-authority subsidy entitlement – what actually happened to rents and subsidies would depend on the figures fed into the formula each year. Future trends in rents and subsidies would depend upon the way the formula was used, rather than the formula itself. The Bill was, in fact, an enabling measure, creating a framework within which the Secretary of State could manipulate council rents and subsidies without having to seek Parliamentary approval for his actions. In this respect it was a major departure from all previous legislation on rents and subsidies since 1919. In its lack of precision the 1980 system stood in marked contrast to the 1972 Housing Finance Act which, as Chapter 6 has shown, attempted to spell out provisions for all eventualities.

The key differences between the 1972 and 1980 systems were, first, the lack of any attempt in the 1980 Act to specify rent levels or even rent increases, and, second, the introduction of notional housing-revenue accounts as the basis for payment of actual subsidy under the 1980 Act. The abandonment of the fair rent principle and the use of notional HRAs gave central government considerable power and flexibility, but the success of the system, from the point of view of central government, depended upon the extent to which actual and notional HRAs remained closely aligned. Payment of actual subsidy was to be related to assumed movements in income and expenditure, an approach which combined powerful leverage on rents with avoidance of damaging public confrontations with defiant local authorities: the system avoided instructing local authorities to raise rents by a certain amount, thus leaving them with some semblance of discretion, whilst at the same time putting them in a position where a response more or less in line with the centre's aspirations was hard to resist.

The new system came into effect in April 1981, and under section 97 of the Act the formula for calculating the subsidy for each authority was that:

$$Subsidy = BA + HCD - LCD$$

where BA = base amount, HCD = housing costs differential and LCD = local contribution differential.

The base amount was the subsidy received in the previous year, starting from the amount received under previous legislation in 1980–1. The housing-costs differential was the amount by which each authority's 'reckonable' expenditure for the year exceeded that of the previous year. The main items of reckonable expenditure were loan charges incurred before April 1981, 75 per cent of loan charges on admissible projects incurred after April 1981, and expenditure on management and maintenance of dwellings in the HRA.[10] The starting point for calculating changes in management and maintenance expenditure in each authority was the average of the actual expenditure in the three years 1978–9 to 1980–1. The local contribution differential was the amount by which reckonable income for the year exceeded the authority's reckonable income for the previous year. The main item of reckonable income was aggregated rental income, starting from the actual rents charged in 1980–1.

Stripped of its rather cumbersome and indigestible terminology this simply meant that subsidy was related to the state of the HRA: if there was a deficit, then it was covered by subsidy, but, if income rose faster than expenditure and the deficit disappeared, then no subsidy was paid. It is important to note that the Act abolished the no-profit rule on HRAs, for it was clearly intended that many authorities would soon move into surplus. Under this system subsidy could be concentrated in areas of greatest need, i.e. where continued high levels of new investment led to costs rising faster than income. By the same token, subsidy could be withdrawn from areas with low levels of new building.

Although in principle the new system was much simpler than earlier subsidy regimes, especially the previous attempt to introduce a deficit-subsidy system in 1972, in practice it was complicated by the need to calculate reckonable and admissible amounts as distinct from actual amounts, and by the resultant fact that subsidy related to the notional rather than the actual deficit.[11] The use of notional HRAs arose from the need perceived by central government to limit its liability for subsidy; it could not give an open-ended commitment to fund any deficit, however high the expenditure and however low the rents. Subsidy entitlement was therefore based on central-government *assumptions* about changes in costs and incomes in each local authority.

The two key assumptions referred to changes in income from rents and expenditure on management and maintenance. Each year the Secretary of State decided the assumed rate of change in rents and management and maintenance costs for calculation of subsidy in the following year. In fixing a rent increase he was required by section 100 of the Act to 'have regard, among other things, to past and expected movements in incomes, costs and prices'. Before a final 'determination' could be made he was also required to consult with the local-authority associations.

In practice, proposals were announced in a consultation paper in November–December each year and then finally determined in a ministerial letter to local authorities in the new year, preceding the start of the financial year in April. The sets of determinations for the years 1981–2 to 1989–90 are shown in Table 7.1

Table 7.1 Ministerial determinations of increases in rent income and management and maintenance expenditure, 1981–2 to 1989–90 (England and Wales)

	Rent*	Management and maintenance**
	£	%
1981–2	2.95	9.0
1982–3	2.50	7.0
1983–4	0.85	7.0
1984–5	0.75	5.0
1985–6	0.60	5.0
1986–7	0.65	4.0
1987–8	0.65	3.75
1988–9	1.60	9.2
1989–90	1.95	10.25

* Average weekly increase per dwelling
** Average annual increase per dwelling

In 1981–2 it was assumed for subsidy purposes that rents would rise by £2.95 per week, but it was also announced that increases in unsubsidised costs would lead to a rise of a further 30p in rents. This dual forecast was not continued in subsequent years.

The impact of the very high determinations for rent increases in 1981–2 and 1982–3, and to a lesser extent in 1983–4, was that average rents rose very rapidly, and that total subsidy fell very rapidly.

Table 7.2 shows that the actual increase in rents in 1981–2 was greater than that assumed by the Secretary of State, and between April 1980 and April 1983 rents rose by 82 per cent in cash terms. Taking the government's first term as a whole, average unrebated council rents in England and Wales rose by 119 per cent, during a period when the retail-price index rose by only 55 per cent. Increases in the real level of rents were concentrated in 1981–2 and in 1982–3, but subsequently increases were broadly in line with the rate of inflation, and in relation to average earnings there was a slight

Table 7.2 Average local authority rents in England and Wales, April 1980 to April 1988

	Average rent	Average increase		Ministerial determination
	£	£	%	£
1980	7.71	1.31	20.5	
1981	11.39	3.68	47.7	2.95 (3.25)
1982	13.50	2.11	18.5	2.50
1983	14.01	0.51	3.8	0.85
1984	14.71	0.70	5.0	0.75
1985	15.60	0.89	6.0	0.60
1986	16.41	0.81	6.0	0.65
1987	17.24	0.84	5.0	0.65
1988	18.43	1.19	7.0	1.60

Source: CIPFA, *Housing Rents Statistics*

decrease in 1983–4 and in 1984–5. It is important to recognise that the government pursued a very different policy on rent increases after 1983, and to explain why this change occurred.

One factor to be taken into account must be the rapid withdrawal of subsidy, which fell by 84 per cent in real terms between 1980–1 and 1983–4.

Table 7.3 Exchequer subsidies to local authority housing revenue accounts (England and Wales)

	£m cash	£m at 1987–8 prices
1979–80 out-turn	1,274	2,237
1980–1 ..	1,423	2,106
1981–2 ..	906	1,224
1982–3 ..	536	674
1983–4 ..	280	336
1984–5 ..	342	394
1985–6 ..	409	444
1986–7 ..	534	561
1987–8 estimated out-turn	464	473
1988–9 plans	459	422
1989–90 ..	490	432
1990–1 ..	510	441

Sources: Column 1: 1979–80 to 1981–82, *The Government's Expenditure Plans 1985–86 to 1987–88*, Cmnd 9428, 1985, p. 107; 1982–3 to 1990–1, *The Government's Expenditure Plans 1988–9 to 1990–91*, Cm. 288, 1988, p. 149. Column 2: Ministerial written answer, *Hansard*, 31 October 1988, col. 541, quoted in *Inside Housing*, 4 November 1988

The impact of massive and very rapid withdrawal of subsidy varied from place to place, and this is explored in more detail later in this chapter. For the moment it is sufficient to note that the withdrawal of subsidy soon left a majority of authorities with no subsidy at all. The capacity to withdraw subsidy on the basis of assumed rent increase provided a very powerful mechanism to influence local authority decision-making. However, once subsidy was reduced to zero, such leverage was lost, but this was where the block grant mechanism was designed to come into action.

The block grant and housing

The Local Government, Planning and Land Act, 1980, introduced a new system for calculating the rate support grant (RSG). It is not necessary to explain the complexities of the block grant and associated target and penalty systems.[12] This discussion focuses on the interaction between the block grant and housing. 'Block grant' was the term introduced to refer to the main part of the RSG, previously known as the needs and resources element. Calculation of entitlement to block grant for each authority involved the production of a figure for grant related expenditure (GRE) which was an estimate of the level of expenditure required to provide a common standard of service. The aggregate GRE for each authority was composed of a large

Figure 7.1 Simplified diagrammatic representation of the progressive removal of housing subsidy and block grant, and its impact on rents

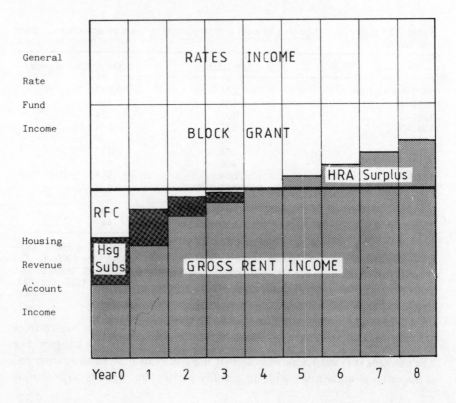

number of GREs for individual expenditure items. There were three housing GREs and one of them referred to the deficit rate fund contribution to the HRA, i.e. RFCs to the HRA were regarded as a subsidisable item of expenditure (and had been so since 1972). According to Bramley, 'It is little exaggeration to say that this item has generated more concern and heated debate than the whole of the rest of the 50 odd GRE formulae put together.'[13]

The reason that the GRE for HRA RFCs was so controversial was that it provided a mechanism through which central government could continue to put pressure on local authorities to raise rents, even after the removal of all subsidy. A positive GRE figure indicated that the HRA was in deficit, and that block grant would be payable to support any RFC as in year 0 in Figure 7.1. However, a negative GRE would arise in cases where rents rose to levels which put the HRA into surplus and where such surpluses were transferred into the rates, years 5–8 in Figure 7.1. In other words, the Department of the Environment (DoE) could calculate negative GREs for RFCs to the HRA and this would lead to a reduction in block grant, the scale of which would reflect the magnitude of the negative GRE (or the surplus on the HRA).

Figure 7.1 illustrates how the general rate fund and the housing revenue account were separate but interlinked; the heavy line across the middle represents the boundary between the two accounts, but it was a boundary which in the 1980s allowed money to flow across it in both directions. Year 0 represents the year before the start of the new system. In year 1 both subsidy and RFC are reduced, requiring rents to make up a higher proportion of income. By year 4 there is no subsidy or RFC, and the HRA is in balance. However, in years 5 to 8 the block grant is progressively reduced, putting pressure on the authority to raise rents beyond the level required to balance the HRA, the surplus being transferred into the general rate fund.

Although the simplest way to understand the role of the block grant mechanism in relation to council rents is to think of it as a device which took over *after* the elimination of subsidy under the Housing Act, the reality was more complicated, because in some places the block grant effect came into play before the elimination of subsidy. This arose out of the composition of an indicator called E7, which was used to calculate the GRE for deficit RFCs in 1981–2.[14] Included in E7 was the assumption that each authority was charging the average rent for its region of the country. E7 was the notional deficit (or surplus) on the HRA, derived from actual expenditure minus actual subsidy and minus the notional income derived from charging rents set at the regional average. This meant that for some authorities in 1981–2 the calculation of block grant assumed a bigger rent increase than was being assumed for purposes of calculating housing subsidy. In 1981–2 a total of 195 authorities were deemed to have a negative GRE–HRA deficit,[15] but only 21 authorities lost all subsidy in that year.[16]

The city of Worcester provided an illustration of how this could happen.[17] Worcester's rents averaged only £6.47 per week in 1980–1, and its subsidy was cut in line with the assumed rent increase of £2.95 per week, but leaving the authority still in receipt of £378,000 subsidy. However, the calculation of block grant assumed that Worcester's rents would rise by £5.77, generating a surplus on the HRA of over £700,000, and that this would be transferred into the general rate fund. Thus it was possible for an authority to be regarded quite differently by the same government department simultaneously: for Housing Act subsidy purposes Worcester's HRA was still in deficit, but for block grant purposes the HRA was assumed to be in substantial surplus.

In practice, the block grant mechanism was used only once, in 1981–2. In 1982 the government bowed to lobbying by the Association of District Councils whose mostly Conservative-controlled members were most vulnerable to centrally imposed rent increases beyond those necessary to balance the HRA. Since 1982–3, therefore, the minimum GRE for RFC to the HRA has been zero – there were no negative GREs and the government held back from using this powerful lever on council rents. The effect of the forbearance, however, was to release the majority of housing authorities from any central government pressure to raise rents, since only a small number of authorities still received subsidy.

Nevertheless, there were some authorities where the government could influence decisions about rents through the system of targets and penalties which operated until the end of 1985–6. It has been shown by Bailey[18] that authorities which made substantial RFCs to the HRA could thereby raise their total spending to such a level that they incurred severe penalties in the form of grant reductions, or 'hold-back'. These authorities, he argues, were under financial pressure to raise rents and reduce RFC, thus reducing total spending and reducing or avoiding grant penalties.

Despite the government's decision not to impose yet higher rents through the block grant it must be noted that most notional HRAs moved into surplus, and that this had a powerful disincentive effect on new building. Under the 1980 Housing Act, for the first time since the First World War, many local authorities arrived at the position that any new building was unsubsidised. This was because subsidy was only payable when there was a notional as well as an actual deficit on the HRA. Thus authorities which had substantial notional HRA surpluses would have to increase their expenditure considerably, and also their rents, before subsidy would be payable. This effect was reinforced by the provision that 75 per cent of new loan charges are eligible for subsidy.

Housing benefit

A longstanding objective of Conservative housing policy, chronicled in earlier chapters, has been to raise the basic level of council rents, to reduce general subsidy and to concentrate assistance on those in greatest need, by the use of means-tested benefits. So far this chapter has dealt with the first two parts of the policy on rents and subsidies since 1979 and it is appropriate to turn briefly to changes affecting means-tested housing benefits.

Since 1979 the rise in unemployment and the increase in rent levels have combined to produce a rapid growth in the numbers of council tenants claiming means-tested assistance with housing costs. Between 1979 and 1982 there was an increase of 35 per cent in the number of council tenants in England and Wales claiming rent rebates,[19] and an increase of 39 per cent in tenants in Great Britain claiming supplementary benefit.[20] By 1985 it was officially estimated that 66 per cent of all council tenants were dependent upon housing benefit,[21] compared with 44 per cent in 1976. Not only were a substantial majority claiming housing benefit, but only a small minority were in receipt of general housing subsidy. This represented a major reversal in the balance between general and means-tested assistance for council tenants.

Alongside its policies on rents and subsidies the Conservative government in the early 1980s brought about a major reorganisation affecting means-tested housing assistance. The background is described elsewhere,[22] and it is not necessary to go into detail here. To summarise, there had developed two separate ways in which low-income tenants could receive help with housing costs: (i) rent rebates (rent allowance for private tenants) and rate rebates administered by local housing authorities, and (ii) supplementary benefit, administered by the Department of Health and Social Security (DHSS). Many tenants were eligible for both, but from 1974 it was necessary for them to choose one or the other. This gave rise to the 'better-off' problem, i.e. it was not always clear which benefit to chose in order to obtain most help. The Supplementary Benefits Commission (SBC) campaigned with increasing vigour in the late 1970s for a unified housing benefit, to eliminate the better-off problem and to be administered by local authorities,[23] but in the event the government's consultative document[24] went only part of the way towards the proposals of the SBC.

Instead of introducing a truly unified housing benefit the government proposed to unify the administration at local authority level, and to unify the financial accounting within the social security budget of the DHSS. The old distinction between rebates and supplementary benefit was effectively continued in the new classification of standard and certificated housing benefit, each relying on its own means test. Enabling legislation (the Social Security and Housing Benefits Act, 1982) was passed which led to the introduction of the new scheme in a two-stage process, in November 1982 and April 1983. The speed with which the reorganisation was pushed through led to considerable criticism and a tendency to focus on the immediate administrative difficulties faced by the authorities as well as the problems of tenants in trying to secure the correct benefit.[25]

However, it is also important to locate housing benefit in the context of longer-term developments in housing policy. In this perspective the importance of the housing benefit reform is not that it was 'the biggest administrative fiasco in the history of the welfare state',[26] but that it marked a major turning point in the development of housing-subsidy policy. Historically, up to 1972, local authorities were given Exchequer housing subsidies which were related to construction costs and loan charges, but not to the financial means of individual tenants. However, they were permitted to distribute all or part of their subsidy income in the form of means-tested rent rebates. A conceptual distinction can be made between general subsidies and means-tested benefits. General subsidies refer to some notion about an appropriate price level applicable to all consumers, and in this sense they are clearly a part of housing policy, being a means by which the state influences the price of rented housing paid by consumers. A rent rebate, on the other hand, is related to the financial circumstances of individual tenants and can be seen as technically a form of income maintenance.

This distinction becomes more obvious and also more important in relation to the period after 1972. Since that date the Exchequer has separated general and rebate subsidies. As explained in Chapter 6, the objective behind the Housing Finance Act, 1972, was ultimately to raise rents to 'fair rent' level (i.e. moderated market rents), to eliminate general subsidy, and to rely on means-tested rebates for the least well off. In this situation rebates were clearly a form of income maintenance, albeit funded by what was regarded as a housing subsidy and administered by housing authorities.

The introduction of housing benefit marks the beginning of a third phase, in which the separation of means-tested assistance with housing costs was carried a stage further. It is relevant to note here that the Social Security and Housing Benefits Bill was brought to the House of Commons by the Secretary of State for Health and Social Services, Norman Fowler, and not the Secretary of State for the Environment. In this speech on the second reading Fowler said:

My right hon. Friends and I agreed that it is more appropriate for [the] responsibility [for housing benefit] to be placed with my Department. *Housing Benefit will be a form of income support* and it seems much better that future policies should be considered in that context of the social security benefit structure and developments as a whole. [Present author's italics] [27]

Thus the status of housing benefit as a form of social security was officially admitted. In keeping with this new orientation, expenditure on housing benefit was taken out of the housing programme and relocated within the social security budget in public expenditure White Papers. However, whilst the housing benefit reform was effectively removing the issue of means-tested assistance with rent from the area of housing policy altogether, at the same time the administration of housing benefit was being handed over to the housing authorities. This was a move which was clearly inconsistent with the recognition of housing benefit as a form of social security, but nevertheless the 1985 report of the review of housing benefit concentrated on the content and cost of the scheme.[28] The Social Security Act, 1986, left the administration of a simplified and much less generous housing-benefit scheme with the local authorities.[29]

The withdrawal of subsidy

When the Conservative government took office in 1979 all local housing authorities were in receipt of general housing subsidy, and the volume of subsidy was increasing. However, the Housing Act, 1980, provided the means to bring about major changes in both the level and distribution of subsidy. In its first year of operation, 1981–2, the new system removed all subsidy from 21 authorities, but in 1982–3 nearly 200 were without subsidy, and by 1985–6 the number was 258. The data are incomplete, but in 1985–6 only 95 authorities (fewer than 25 per cent) were still receiving subsidy, and the most reliable figures show 130 receiving subsidy in 1986–7.[30]

Subsidy disappeared first in small, predominantly rural and suburban authorities but in 1982–3 a much greater range of authorities was affected, including some major municipal landlords such as Leeds, Rotherham, Walsall, Wigan, Barnsley, Knowsley, and Doncaster (all of which were metropolitan authorities with more than 30,000 dwellings). Amongst the non-metropolitan authorities most of the biggest authorities lost all subsidy in 1982–3, including Bristol, Southampton, Hull, Stoke-on-Trent, Norwich, and Thamesdown (Swindon). In London only 3 outer boroughs (Barking and Dagenham, Bexley, and Richmond upon Thames) went out of subsidy in 1982–3.

By 1985–6, 6 London boroughs had no subsidy entitlement, but amongst the metropolitan districts only 12 were still receiving help. Amongst the English non-metropolitan authorities 58 received subsidy, plus 12 in Wales, but in 1986–7 the total number of non-metropolitan authorities in subsidy went up to 98.

On the question of the distribution of subsidy, it is clear that the effect of the system was to concentrate subsidy in London, as Table 7.4 shows.

Table 7.4 Distribution of subsidy by class of authority (percentages)

	London (inc. GLC)	Metropolitan districts	Non-metropolitan England	Wales
1980–1	35.6	22.9	37.0	4.5
1985–6	77.3	3.9	16.0	2.7
1988–9	76.3	7.4	13.7	2.6

Source: CIPFA, *Housing Revenue Account Statistics*, Actuals and Estimates.

In 1985–6, 78 per cent of the English non-metropolitan authorities receiving subsidy were south of a line between Gloucester and the Wash, an area containing 58 per cent of all non-metropolitan authorities. The same pattern was still evident in 1988–9, when 75 per cent of English non-metropolitan authorities receiving subsidy were in this southern region.

However, another interesting development was that the number of authorities claiming subsidy has increased, after rapid decline in the early 1980s, so that in 1988–9 as many as 172 authorities in England and Wales as a whole were due to receive subsidy. (The figure is unfortunately not a very reliable guide to entitlement to subsidy under the 1980 Housing Act because it includes authorities claiming under the Housing Defects Act, 1984.[31]) Nevertheless there is evidence that the number of authorities receiving subsidy increased in the late 1980s, an outcome which few would have predicted in 1981.

Changes in rents, 1980–8

The overall figures suggest that in the period 1980–8 rents increased broadly in line with the expectations of central government: the ministerial determinations amounted to £10.55 per week and rents rose by £11.03 between April 1980 and April 1988. It has been argued by Hills[32] that a system based on uniform flat-rate increases was likely to produce a narrowing of rent differentials, and that this effect was evident during the 1980s. There is some support for this view, in terms of regional rent averages, but a more detailed analysis suggests a different interpretation. Individual local authorities varied considerably in their responses to the ministerial deter-

Table 7.5 Authorities with the highest and lowest rents in 1988

	1988 rent	Increase since 1980		1988 rent	Increase since 1980
	£	£		£	£
Kensington and Chelsea	35.20	20.61	Sunderland	14.73	8.73
Wandsworth	32.27	20.82	St Edmundsbury	14.65	7.29
Westminster	28.41	18.04	Bromsgrove	14.64	6.63
Redbridge	27.18	15.66	Exeter	14.51	7.66
Hammersmith and Fulham	27.06	16.07	Oadby and Wigston	14.48	9.55
Bromley	26.74	14.57	Doncaster	14.37	8.18
Barnet	26.07	16.35	Stevenage	14.30	6.46
Harrow	25.46	13.13	York	13.83	9.12
Croydon	25.33	19.00	Wrexham Maelor	13.71	7.35
Enfield	25.16	15.70	Hereford	13.63	7.65

Note: Data based on CIPFA, *Housing Rent Statistics*, showing the top and bottom of the range of authorities for which 1980 and 1988 data are available

minations, sometimes because removal of all subsidy left them free from centrally imposed leverage on rents, and sometimes because they chose to increase rents faster than subsidy withdrawal required.

A look at the authorities with the highest and lowest rents in 1988 makes it is clear that there is very wide variation, as Table 7.5 reveals. These figures show not only the very wide variation between the highest and lowest rent areas, but, more significantly, that the top ten all increased their rents by substantially *more* than the aggregate determination, whereas the bottom ten all increased rents by *less* than that amount. Moreover, all but one of the top ten started from a position of rents above the London average in 1980, so their subsequent rates of increase cannot be seen in terms of catching up. On the other hand, of the low rent group eight out of ten started from rent levels in 1980 which were below the average for their class of authority.

Another way of putting it is to say that the average rent in the ten lowest rent authorities in 1980 was £5.21, which was £6.74 below the average of the top ten, but by 1988 the gap had widened to £13.71. It is clear, then, that at both ends of the range, authorities diverged from government's expectations in ways which amplified rather than narrowed rent differences.

In considering the apparent link between rent level in 1980 and subsequent increases, it is relevant to look at whether authorities were in receipt of subsidy. Thus the group of ten with the highest rents in 1988 contained six authorities which received subsidy in 1986–7 (the latest year for which reliable data are available), whereas only two of the lowest ten authorities received subsidy.

In the case of the group of non-metropolitan authorities which lost all subsidy entitlement in 1981–2, the very first year of the new system, a pattern of relatively low rents already existed and continued in subsequent years: 15 out of 16 providing information about rents in 1988 had average rents below the average for non-metropolitan authorities. On the other hand, there were 98 non-metropolitan authorities in receipt of subsidy in 1986–7; 60 per cent had started with rents above the average in 1980 and by 1988 the proportion had risen to 77 per cent. Almost three-quarters (73 per cent) had raised rents by more than the ministerial determinations.

The data suggests that in practice the 1980 system was effective in removing subsidy from low cost areas, but not very effective in raising rents in those areas. On the other hand, while the system concentrated remaining subsidy in the high cost areas, it failed to keep rent increases in line with ministerial determinations. In other words, a system which initially appeared to have major implications for local autonomy was soon characterised by wide variation in local impact and outcomes as councils found ways of exercising discretion in implementation.

The changing structure of housing revenue accounts

Table 7.6 shows how the structure of the income side of the national housing revenue account changed in the 1980s. These figures indicate how

Table 7.6 The national housing revenue account, 1980–1 to 1988–9 (percentages)

	Exchequer subsidy		Net rent	RFC	Other	Interest
	General	Rebate				
1980–1	31.2	8.1	37.0	13.0	11.0	—
1981–2	17.7	8.1	51.8	9.7	7.4	6.2
1982–3	8.5	12.5	52.2	8.6	9.3	8.8
	Exchequer subsidy	Housing benefit				
1983–4	7.0	31.0	35.0	9.0	9.0	9.0
1984–5	7.0	33.0	33.0	9.0	9.0	9.0
1985–6	6.0	35.0	32.0	5.0	11.0	11.0
1986–7	7.0	36.0	32.0	8.0	6.0	11.0
1987–8	8.2	35.9	31.0	8.7	5.9	10.3
1988–9	7.4	35.7	33.5	7.7	5.8	10.0

Source: CIPFA, *Housing Revenue Account Statistics*

in 1980–3 there was a major reduction in subsidy and an increase in income derived from rents. The introduction of housing benefit made comparisons difficult, but it is clear that, in the period as a whole, central government support has been shifted from general subsidy into income related assistance. It is also important to note that in the late 1960s rebated rents provided as much as three-quarters of HRA income, more than twice the proportion in the late 1980s. This turn-around is a direct outcome of the residualisation of council housing, in terms of both the composition of the tenants and the structure of policy.

Another point to draw out of this table is that historically Exchequer subsidy always far exceeded rate fund contributions, at the aggregate level if not always at the local level. During the 1980s, however, rate fund contributions became the main form of general subsidy for council housing.

It is also important to recognise differences amongst different types of authorities. Table 7.7 provides an indication of how the different classes of authority varied from each other. The main points to note in this table are, first, the continuing relatively high levels of Exchequer subsidy and RFC in London compared with both the other classes of authority, and the correspondingly lower proportion of income provided by rents. This reflects the

Table 7.7 Housing revenue accounts by class of authority in England and Wales (percentages)

	Exchequer subsidies		Net	RFC rent	Other	Interest
	General	Rebate				
London						
1980–1	35.4	4.4	23.4	21.3	12.5	3.0
1981–2	28.1	4.3	32.0	18.1	12.9	4.6
1985–6	14.1	20.7	21.2	10.8	24.8	8.4
1988–9	19.9	24.3	24.5	16.3	6.1	8.9
Metropolitan districts						
1980–1	29.6	10.6	40.2	8.1	8.3	3.2
1981–2	13.9	9.9	58.3	8.9	4.9	4.1
1985–6	1.0	48.5	33.0	5.1	4.5	7.9
1988–9	2.3	45.2	34.0	9.8	4.5	4.2
Non-metropolitan districts						
1980–1	29.1	9.2	43.9	5.7	6.0	6.1
1981–2	12.7	9.8	61.3	2.3	5.5	8.4
1985–6	2.3	37.6	38.1	1.9	5.9	14.2
1988–9	2.5	37.6	38.6	1.6	6.2	13.5

Source: CIPFA, *Housing Revenue Account Statistics*

much higher costs in London, for as the previous section showed, rents are generally higher in London than elsewhere. The average expenditure per dwelling in London is virtually twice as high as in the metropolitan districts. Expenditure was higher on all main items, debt charges, repairs, and management.

Second, RFCs are lower in the non-metropolitan authorities than in the metropolitan authorities, continuing the long-running tendency for the smaller, more rural councils to pay less to housing from the rates. Indeed, as will be shown below, these authorities are more likely than others to make payments *from* housing to the rates fund.

Third, interest from the sale of council houses is much more significant in the non-metropolitan areas, reflecting the larger number of sales in these areas.

An important feature of the new housing finance policy introduced in the 1980 Housing Act was the abolition of the 'no-profit' rule on HRAs. This released authorities to make surpluses on their HRAs and to make unconstrained transfers to the general rate fund. A growing number of authorities have taken advantage of this freedom. Table 7.8 shows the numbers and sums involved.

Table 7.8 Transfers to the general rate fund, 1981–2 to 1988–9

	London boroughs		Metropolitan districts		Non-metropolitan districts England		Wales	
	£m	No.	£m	No.	£m	No.	£m	No.
1981–2	1.4		—		16.4		—	
1982–3	6.3		1.1		16.4		—	
1983–4	9.0	10	1.2	2	18.5	79	1.1	2
1984–5	10.4	8	5.4	5	26.8	93	0.9	3
1985–6	14.5	7	8.8	5	30.9	98	1.0	5
1986–7	23.9	10	36.2	7	48.3	108	0.6	3
1987–8	22.5	9	5.0	3	37.4	111	0.3	3
1988–9	52.4	11	7.3	4	47.0	114	0.1	1

Source: CIPFA, *Housing Revenue Account Statistics*

Most authorities transferred relatively small sums into their rates funds, but there were some notable exceptions. For instance, in 1986–7 Sheffield transferred £22.7m.; however, this should be seen as an unwilling move by a rate-capped authority which had no previous record of drawing from the HRA. In general, authorities making HRA surpluses and using housing to subsidise the rates did so voluntarily, as a matter of locally determined policy, and in many cases transfers occurred year after year. Table 7.9 shows that in 1988–9 there were 21 payments of £1 million or more.

Table 7.9 Authorities transferring £1 million or more from the housing revenue account into the general rate fund in 1988–9

	£million		£million
Wandsworth	7.487	Windsor and Maidenhead	1.814
Barking and Dagenham	6.257	Castle Point	1.658
Redbridge	6.120	Epsom and Ewell	1.499
Merton	5.475	Bracknell	1.472
North Tyneside	5.000	Colchester	1.300
Hillingdon	3.629	South Tyneside	1.225
Bromley	3.313	Wansdyke	1.184
Runnymede	2.500	Reigate and Banstead	1.165
Torbay	2.476	Woodspring	1.152
Havering	2.363	West Oxfordshire	1.000
Epping Forest	2.200		

Source: CIPFA, *Housing Revenue Account Statistics, 1988–89 Estimates*, 1988

The total number of authorities making transfers to the rates increased year by year, from 84 in 1982–3 to 130 in 1988–9. English non-metropolitan and outer London authorities were more likely to make transfers than metropolitan, inner London or Welsh authorities. And amongst the English non-metropolitan districts, southern ones were more likely to make transfers than northern authorities. This southern bias is reflected in Table 7.9 which shows that 19 of the 21 authorities making the biggest transfers were clearly in the south of England. Transferring authorities tended to be concentrated in counties such as Surrey, Sussex, Berkshire, and Essex, but also further west in Dorset, Somerset, and Devon.

A remarkable feature of the 1980 system was that authorities could receive subsidy on a *notional deficit*, whilst the *actual* HRA was in surplus.

Table 7.10 Local authorities in subsidy and making transfers to their general-rate funds

	London boroughs	Metropolitan districts	Non-metropolitan districts England	Wales
1983–4	7	0	18	2
1984–5	7	1	25	1
1985–6	6	1	21	1
1986–7	5	2	33	2
1987–8	5	0	28	2
1988–9	8	2	46	0

Note: The 1988–9 figures may include authorities receiving subsidy under the Housing Defects Act, 1984, but not under the Housing Act, 1980
Source: CIPFA, *Housing Revenue Account Statistics*

The English non-metropolitan authorities receiving subsidy and making transfers were overwhelmingly concentrated in the south, including places like Bournemouth, Brighton and Eastbourne. Some authorities transferred sums equivalent to only part of their subsidy entitlement, but others regularly passed the whole of their subsidy income straight through the HRA into the general rate fund. The London Borough of Merton, for example, did this every year between 1983–4 and 1988–9, receiving the total of £3.6m. in subsidy but making aggregate transfers of over £15m.

It is also relevant to note that working balances (i.e. income carried forward in the HRA from one year to the next) increased significantly as a proportion of HRA income during the 1980s. In the early 1980s balances amounted to less than 2 per cent of income, but by 1986–7 they accounted for 7.5 per cent, and in 1988–9 balances brought forward from the previous year added up to £394 million. Together with the sums actually transferred into the rates, these working balances show that large amounts of money entered HRAs, from various sources, but were not spent on providing housing services for council tenants, as a direct result of decisions taken at the local level.

The criticism is often made that local councillors choose to keep rents low and to skimp on repairs, but the evidence presented here shows that in the 1980s a growing number of authorities deliberately chose to raise rents by more than was necessary to balance their accounts and to divert surplus income into non-housing purposes.

Discussion

The 1980 system represented an amalgam of ideas from the old, pre-1972 arrangements and the Housing Finance Act, 1972. The mandatory national rent rebate scheme, along with the use of deficit subsidy, survived from the Conservatives' previous attempt at reform, but fair rents were abandoned and local authorities retained their old freedom to set reasonable rents. The real potency of the new system lay in the deficit subsidy, which can be seen as a kind of reinvigorated rent pooling device for exercising leverage on rents. The similarity lay in the way that both methods of calculating subsidy relied on financial measures rather than administrative and judicial instructions to local authorities in respect of rent levels. Both rent pooling and the 1980 system put pressure on rents by calculating *actual* subsidy by reference to *assumed* increases in income and expenditure. In this sense the 1972 Act appears to be not just a failed system but also a digression from the main path of rents and subsidy policy. However, the 1972 Act did establish a crucial break with past conventions, in particular the inviolability of existing subsidies and the no-profit rule. Thus, although the 1980 system was similar to the old rent pooling device, it differed in two key ways: (i) whereas under rent pooling governments could only put pressure on rents by *reducing the rate of increase* in subsidy, under the 1980 system they could remove existing subsidies; (ii) so powerful was the system that subsidy could become negative, forcing HRAs into surplus.

The key feature of the 1972 system was that it was led by rents policy, with subsidy reflecting the progression towards fair rents. The 1980 system, on the other hand, was subsidy led; it was very effective in removing subsidy and thereby *raising* rents, but it contained no principled approach to rent *levels*. It was essentially characterised by pragmatic short-term considerations, more related to cutting public expenditure and providing tenants with an incentive to buy their homes than to establishing a credible, coherent and durable policy on rents. The pragmatic short-term approach was typified in the way the system took as its starting point the existing highly varied pattern of rents, subsidies, and rate fund contributions on the income side, and the equally varied pattern of management and maintenance expenditure on the other side.[33] On to this situation was imposed a series of standard assumptions designed to bring about an orderly advance, but doing nothing to remove the inequalities in the positions from which different authorities started to move forward.

For all its deficiencies, the 1972 Act at least set out the criteria for rent setting and a method for moving towards fair rents. By completely avoiding the issue of rent levels, as distinct from rent increases, the

1980 system failed to address one of the main points raised by advocates of reform over many years. Nevertheless, the system was very powerful and difficult for local authorities to resist. It contained none of the opportunities for public campaigning and acts of open defiance which were created in 1972. In this respect, therefore, the 1980 system did represent a distinct advance, from the point of view of central government. But from the local authority point of view, the system combined minimum freedom and maximum uncertainty about where they were being taken.

If the short-term objectives underlying the 1980 system implied that further legislation would be necessary fairly soon, the way the system was operated made this even more probable, and it is remarkable that the system lasted as long as it did. Predictions of further reform were being made as early as 1984,[34] as a result of the way the system was working in practice. The successful implementation of the system depended upon both parts, the housing subsidy and block grant mechanisms, working together. The 1981 decision not to deploy block grant leverage on rents, via the imposition of negative E7s, ultimately undermined the coherence of the whole system, because it greatly weakened central government's power to influence local rents policies, and led to a pattern of outcomes at variance with government aspirations.

By not using the power of the block grant the government released some of the upward pressure on rents in areas that were out of subsidy, and this returned to a large number of local authorities a significant degree of discretion in rents policy. The result was that in a growing number of authorities the actual and notional HRAs moved further apart. It also meant that any HRA surplus remained with the local authority, to use as it wished. Thus the system which had initially appeared so powerful and irresistible very soon gave way to local demands, thereby opening up the possibility that variation would increase from place to place. Meanwhile, authorities still in receipt of subsidy continued to be vulnerable to pressure to raise their rents.

The outcome was that authorities that went out of subsidy first tended to have low expenditure and low rents, and they continued to have relatively low rent increases. At the same time, authorities remaining in subsidy tended to have higher rents and higher expenditure, and their rents increased most. In addition, it has been shown above that an increasing proportion of authorities chose to raise rents by more than the amounts required to balance the HRA. It is very important to avoid the assumption that rent increases were everywhere imposed on unwilling local authorities. The evidence clearly shows that a considerable number of authorities during the 1980s were willing to raise rents beyond the centrally required levels. The crucial issue was not the amount of increase but the destination of any surplus. Local opposition to the block grant mechanism was essentially about the retention of HRA surpluses at the local level, for the benefit of ratepayers as a whole.

It can be concluded that in practice four categories of local authority were produced (not necessarily intentionally) by the operation of the 1980 Act:

1. Authorities continuing in subsidy and subject to centrally imposed rent increases, irrespective of local political preferences. Rents here tended to be above average, having been relatively high in 1980.
2. Authorities with no subsidy who raised rents only enough to balance the HRA. Rents were generally below average amongst this group.
3. Authorities with no subsidy who raised rents by more than enough to balance the HRA, generating surpluses for transfer to the general rate fund. Rents here were often above average.
4. Authorities receiving subsidy who raised rents by more than enough to balance the HRA, generating surpluses for transfer to the general rate fund. Rents here were also likely to be well above average.

In addition to the amplification of local variation as a result of the way the system was operated, it is necessary to refer to the extent to which central government itself actually, but unintentionally, funded HRA surpluses through the housing benefit system. By not recycling surpluses back to the Exchequer via reductions in block grant, the government in effect permitted the use of DHSS (DSS) contributions in respect of housing benefit to be used to subsidise ratepayers. It seems likely that the much lower rent determinations after 1982–3 were due to Treasury and DHSS objections to increasing central government assist- ance towards higher rents where the beneficiaries were ratepayers as a whole. During a period when the DoE was attempting to contain local expenditure and to cut back on rate support grant, it was rather anomalous for DHSS resources, which were supposed to be targeted on the least well-off tenants, to be channelled into the rates for the indiscriminate benefit of ratepayers as a whole. On the other hand, there was a conflict of interest between the DoE preference for higher basic rents (to stimulate sales) and the DHSS desire to contain expenditure on housing benefit.

The 1980 system was, in fact, open to the charge that it was very inefficient in terms of targeting. First, although the system was effective in channelling a high proportion of total subsidy into the high cost London authorities, it failed to recognise and take account of the whole of the deficit in such areas. This was because of the adoption of the actual position in 1980–1 as the starting-point; the subsidy system was blind to the high levels of rate fund contribution which were then found in a majority of London authorities.

Second, outside London a pattern soon emerged in which a majority of authorities still receiving subsidy were low-need, high rent authorities in the south. The evidence on location and rent levels has been referred to above, and in addition it can be said that more than three-quarters (76.4 per cent) of English non-metropolitan authorities receiving subsidy in 1987–8, had negative housing Z scores, which meant that the official index of housing deprivation defined their condition as better than average.[35] This situation arose because the subsidy system channelled resources to authorities according to their current financial position rather than their housing investment needs. Thus areas of above-average deprivation, where new building or renovation was very necessary, sometimes found themselves unentitled to subsidy, with the result that there was a powerful disincentive to further investment in precisely the areas where it was most needed.

Third, the subsidy system was poorly targeted in the sense that it was capable of giving assistance to authorities where there was already a surplus on the HRA, and in other cases it gave subsidy in larger amounts than were justified by the actual (rather than the notional) HRA deficits. A third of all authorities assumed to be in deficit actually had a surplus in 1988–9, and amongst English non-metropolitan authorities the proportion was even higher, at 38.6 per cent.

Fourth, in principle the 1980 system permitted central government to be highly sensitive to variations in local needs and resources, but in practice it was operated as a very blunt instrument, using a single set of national determinations for changes in income and expenditure each year.

The final point to be made in this discussion is that the subsidy system was operated in a way which tended to convert the income from higher rents into a benefit for taxpayers rather than better services for council tenants. In this sense the government was itself the agent of growing disrepair in the public sector. This was most obviously the case in 1981–3 when rents were assumed to rise far faster than expenditure, with the result that subsidy fell rapidly.

In the period 1981–2 to 1988–9 the compounded percentage increase in allowable expenditure on management and maintenance was 60.5 per cent,[36] whereas the determined increase in rents was 137 per cent. If the government had wanted councils to attend to repair and maintenance problems it could have made different assumptions about expenditure, allowing more of the extra income to be spent locally. However, from the government's point of view the main objectives were to raise rents and reduce subsidy, which meant that it had to squeeze repair and maintenance expenditure. Leverage on rents could only be achieved by withdrawing subsidy; if the government had made matching assumptions on income and expenditure, then this would have left local authorities with much more discretion, and perhaps lower rent increases. This leads to two general propositions about deficit-subsidy systems as a method of influencing local policy; first, the closer the income and expenditure determinations are to each other, the less the leverage on rents, and second, it is possible for central government to make authorities spend less on repairs and maintenance but not to make them spend more.

Conclusion

Finally, to return to the themes of continuity, residualisation, and local autonomy, there are just a few brief points to make. In terms of continuity with past trends in rents and subsidy policy, it is important to recognise similarities with the past in respect of both methods and objectives. On methods, it has been shown here how the 1980 system was similar to the pre-1972 rent pooling mechanism for exercising leverage on rents. And on objectives the 1980 system represented an important step towards the long-standing aim of reliance on income-related rather than general subsidy. It even appeared for a while, in the early 1980s, that general subsidy would soon disappear virtually everywhere outside London. However, the element of continuity was overlain by short-term goals and pragmatic design, which left the system vulnerable to criticism from various directions. Local resistance soon manifested itself, albeit in ways that were very different from the public campaigns of the early 1970s, but nevertheless it was local opposition to the implications of the system which led to its disintegration. It is arguable that the 1972 system foundered on the rocks of local resistance and the complexities inherent in the transition to the new regime, but that the 1980 system proved much more effective in dealing with problems of transition and was powerful in the short term, only to crumble in the face of renewed local opposition.

On the question of residualisation, the 1980 system hastened the transition to a situation in which assistance with housing costs in the public sector was dependent upon proof of low income, while assistance to mortgaged home owners continued to be indiscriminate. The hike in rents in the early 1980s was clearly linked to the policy of encouraging home ownership through the right to buy. Discounts and the right to a mortgage were linked to higher rents in the form of a carrot-and-stick policy designed to maximise sales. Better-off tenants were put in a position where the shift to housing benefit denied them assistance with housing costs, but by exercising the right to buy they immediately became eligible for tax relief on mortgage interest.

The fact remains, however, that within two or three years of its introduction the 1980 system was producing outcomes which were in certain important ways at variance with government's intentions and aspirations. The system was allowed to drift during the Conservatives' second term in office, as housing policy planning returned to the long-standing Tory preoccupation with deregulation of the private rented sector. During the 1987 general election campaign it emerged that the government intended to act on local authority housing finance, and the next chapter takes up the narrative from that point.

References

1 I. Gough, 'Thatcherism and the Welfare State', in S. Hall and M. Jacques (eds), *The Politics of Thatcherism*, Lawrence & Wishart, London, 1983, p. 154.
2 M. Jacques, 'Thatcherism – breaking out of the impasse', in Hall and Jacques, op. cit., p. 41.
3 S. Hall and M. Jacques, op. cit., p. 11.
4 M. Harloe and C. Paris, 'The decollectivisation of consumption', in I. Szelenyi (ed.) *Cities in Crisis: Public Policies*, Sage, London, 1984, pp. 70–98.
5 See also P. Malpass and A. Murie, *Housing Policy and Practice*, Macmillan, London, 2nd edition 1987, Chapter 5.
6 Quoted in *First Report of the Environment Committee, Session 1979–80*, HMSO, London, 1980, HC 714, p. xi.
7 *House of Commons Debates*, vol. 976, 15 January 1980, cols 1443–60.
8 ibid., col. 1464.
9 *House of Commons Debates*, vol. 979, 21 February 1980, col. 667.
10 *Local Authority Housing Subsidy System Consultation Paper*, DoE, mimeo, 1979.
11 For a fuller discussion see: G. Bramley, P. Leather, and M. Hill, *Developments in Housing Finance*, WP24, SAUS, University of Bristol, 1981, Chapter 2; and D. McCulloch, 'The new housing finance system', *Local Government Studies*, May–June, 1982.
12 J. Gibson, 'The block (and target) grant system and local authority expenditure – theory and evidence', *Local Government Studies*, May–June, 1982.
13 G. Bramley, P. Leather and M. Hill, op. cit., p. 31.
14 For a fuller discussion of E7 see ibid., pp. 31–4, and J. Gibson, *The New Housing Subsidy System and its Interaction with the Block Grant*, revised edition, INLOGOV, University of Birmingham, 1981, Chapter 5.
15 S. Bailey, 'The relationship between cities' housing rents and block grant', *Urban Studies*, vol. 22, 1985, pp. 237–48.
16 CIPFA, *Housing Revenue Account Statistics, Estimates, 1981–2*.
17 J. Kemeny and J. Rudd, 'Fair rents revisited', *Roof*, May–June 1981.
18 S. Bailey, op. cit.
19 CIPFA, *Housing Rents Statistics*, HMSO.
20 *tatistics 1983*, HMSO.
21 *Local Authority Housing Subsidy System, Determination of Reckonable Income for 1986/87*, DoE Consultation Paper, November 1985, p. 3.
22 P. Malpass, 'Housing benefits in perspective', in C. Jones and J. Stevenson, *The Year Book of Social Policy in Britain 1983*, Routledge & Kegan Paul, London, 1984; P. Kemp, 'The Housing Benefit Scheme', in M. Brenton and C. Jones (eds), *The Year Book of Social Policy in Britain 1984–5*, Routledge & Kegan Paul, London, 1985.

23 D. Donnison, *The Politics of Poverty*, Martin Robertson, Oxford, 1982, Chapter 7.

24 *Assistance with Housing Costs*, DoE 1981.

25 For example: P. Kemp, *The Cost of Chaos*, SHAC, London, 1984; P. Kemp and N. Raynsford (eds), *Housing Benefit: the Evidence*, Housing Centre Trust, 1984; M. Hill, 'The implementation of housing benefit', *Journal of Social Policy*, vol. 13, no. 3, July 1984, pp. 297–320.

26 *The Times*, 20 January 1984.

27 *House of Commons Debates*, 23 November 1981, vol. 29, col. 651.

28 *Housing Benefit Review*, HMSO, Cmnd. 9520, 1985.

29 P. Kemp (ed.), *The Future of Housing Benefits*, Centre for Housing Research, University of Glasgow, 1986.

30 CIPFA, *Housing Revenue Account Statistics 1985–6 Actuals*, and *Housing Revenue Account Statistics 1986–7 Actuals*, 1988.

31 CIPFA, *Housing Revenue Account Statistics 1988–9, Estimates,* 1988.

32 J. Hills, *Twenty-First Century Housing Subsidies: Durable Rent Fixing and Subsidy Arrangements for Social Housing*, Welfare State programme, paper 33, London School of Economics, 1988, pp. 22–3.

33 ibid., p. 87.

34 P. Malpass, *Beyond Deterrent Rents: An Alternative Approach to Housing Finance*, paper presented to the ESRC-Rowntree Conference, 'Housing Research: Building a New Agenda', SAUS, University of Bristol, 1984.

35 Inner Cities Directorate, DoE, 1981 Census, Urban Deprivation Information Note No. 2. n.d.

36 J. Hills, op. cit., p. 86.

Chapter eight

The 'new regime' for local authority housing finance

It was shown in the previous chapter that the 1980 legislation was very effective at raising council rents in the short term, but that it soon began to lose its potency and eventually led to a pattern of outcomes which was largely unintended. This raises the questions 'Where do we go from here?' and 'What are the issues to be confronted in devising a system that is efficient, equitable, and durable?' The first part of this chapter looks at some of the proposals which have been put forward as blueprints for reform, and then considers the implications of the historical analysis of policy development recounted in earlier chapters. This leads into a description and critical evaluation of the government's proposals for local-authority housing in the 1990s, the so-called 'new regime'.

Subsidies, rents and local autonomy

A considerable amount of academic and professional effort has been devoted to the production of a series of blueprints for the reform of housing finance. Responding to the incoherence, inefficiency, and inequity in existing arrangements, a line of argument which is strongly represented in the literature is that it is necessary to adopt a comprehensive approach, embracing analysis and action in all tenures, and to adopt a consistent set of principles for pricing, taxation, and subsidy across all tenures. These are seen as basic conditions for a system which is efficient, equitable, and durable.

Underlying most of the proposals based on these conditions is the notion of tenure neutrality. This describes a situation in which investment and consumption decisions are not distorted by pricing, taxation, or subsidy arrangements which make one tenure more or less attractive than another.[1] It is related to the wider notion of fiscal neutrality, which refers to neutrality in the tax treatment of all investments (removing, for instance, the privileged tax position of a person who invests in owner-occupied housing as compared to a person who invests in the stock market or antiques). Pursuit of tenure neutrality requires a decision as to the correct definitions and measures of subsidy in the various tenures. Market economists tend to take the view that the correct definition of subsidy in the owner-occupied sector is absence of tax on imputed rental income, rather than tax relief on mortgage interest. This stems from the prior decision to treat owner-occupied housing as investment rather than consumption; the subsidy is thus related to the tax-free status of the investment.

In the case of rented housing, the market economics definition of subsidy is the difference between the actual rent and the rent that would arise in a free market.[2]

Advocates of tenure neutrality normally argue that the goals of efficiency and equity are best pursued by removing all exiting subsidies. Thus Berthoud and Ermisch[3] suggest that:

Treating all tenures alike would involve the following changes:
– for council properties, the substitution of market for political control of rents;
– for private rentals, the freezing of rents from regulation and control;
– for owner-occupation, taxation of the 'occupier' on the rental value of his [sic] home; tax relief for the 'owner' on his costs, namely mortgage interest payments, depreciation and repair and maintenance.

Tenure neutrality is essentially a market-based idea, grounded in the belief that efficiency stems from the free play of market forces. However advocates of this approach acknowledge that the general effect of their proposals would be an increase in consumer costs: for tenants in all tenures rent would tend to rise, and for owners there would be additional tax liabilities. Therefore, alongside the removal of subsidies, tenure neutrality implies some sort of allowance scheme to assist low income consumers in all tenures. In this respect tenure neutrality relates to the old rallying cry of the right that it is better to subsidise people rather than houses.

Thus, the issues identified in relation to the development of a system of housing finance that is efficient, equitable, and durable are to do with the taxation of owner occupation, the deregulation of private renting, and the removal of general subsidy in the public sector. In addition, it is necessary to devise a housing-benefit system which can be applied equitably across all tenures. There are different interpretations of this basic package, with advocates of a robust approach, such as Ermisch,[4] arguing for market rents in the public sector, while others, such as Atkinson and King,[5] the Report of the Inquiry into British Housing,[6] and Hills,[7] make the cases for moderated market rents. The issue here is essentially about the desirability and feasibility of charging full market rents in the public sector, and the basis on which income related housing benefit should be provided and regulated.

Standing somewhat apart from market-based approaches are proposals for setting public sector rents in relation to aggregate costs (expenditure), rather than current value. One version, originally set out out by the Housing

Centre Trust in 1975,[8] and revived by Kelly,[9] is national rent pooling. This seeks to extend the system of local pooling to the national level, thereby requiring transfers amongst different local authorities.[10] In addition it is appropriate to refer to the idea of a universal housing allowance as an alternative to means-tested benefits. This has been discussed over a number of years,[11] most recently in a report from the Association of Metropolitan Authorities.[12]

It is not necessary here to engage in the debate amongst the advocates of these various proposals. Rather than examining differences between them, the intention is to draw out the similarity of approach, in the sense that in general the writers in this field tend to discuss the overall cost, investment implications, and distributional effects of their proposals, but not the important question of implementation. Their efforts are concentrated on questions of principle and theoretical rectitude, somehow implying that if these issues were resolved, then a political consensus would be achieved and implementation of a durable system could be taken for granted. It is interesting that the major obstacles to coherent reform are usually seen to be cost and the resistance by home owners to the imposition of taxes on their investment gains. The latter in particular has been seen by politicians of all parties as an insurmountable problem. For instance, in 1977 Labour ministers defended their refusal to reform housing finance on the grounds that 'we certainly do no believe that the household budgets of millions of families – which have been planned in good faith in the reasonable expectation that present arrangements would broadly continue – should be overturned, in pursuit of some theoretical or academic dogma.'[13] Later, when in 1985 the Inquiry into British Housing advocated the phasing out of tax relief (on the grounds that the public would resent and not understand taxation of imputed rental income), it was Conservative ministers who dismissed the idea within hours of publication.[14]

In practice, over the last fifteen or twenty years, governments have shown themselves to be much more interested in short-term feasibility than long-term ideals, and they have been increasingly motivated by a desire to promote the growth of home ownership and to hasten the decline of council housing. The conclusion has to be that tenure neutrality is not the issue and home owners are not the stumbling block. The issue is tenure restructuring and the stumbling block is local autonomy.

The analysis in previous chapters has shown that Conservative governments since the mid-1950s have adopted a consistent policy of seeking to raise the real level of council rents. During most of that time they have been more concerned to apply pressure to keep rents rising, rather than to establish clear principles about the appropriate level of council rents. For some years after 1955 rent pooling proved to be an effective and successful device. The success of rent pooling lay in the way in which it combined leverage on rents with both local autonomy in rent setting and fixed

Exchequer liability. However, attempts to move towards current value pricing and deficit subsidy since 1972 have been attended by severe implementation problems, which, in various ways, are related to the autonomy of local government. Any method which seeks to relate rents to current values and to base subsidy on the overall deficit inevitably gives central government a closer interest in local decisions on rents and expenditure on repairs, maintenance, and management.

The key implementation problem is how to ensure that local authorities comply with the national policy criteria. This problem arises in relation both to the arguments in favour of consistent approaches to pricing policy in all tenures (whether market-based or not), and for governments seeking to control public expenditure and local housing policy. The evidence presented in earlier chapters clearly shows that it is very difficult to devise a policy which can be implemented through democratically elected local authorities and yet produce consistent outcomes that are in accordance with overall policy. This important issue is one on which the advocates of various proposals for reform are either silent or naïve. Ermisch, for instance, refers to local authority housing administrators' being instructed to set economic rents.[15] But what if the local authority resolves *not* to instruct them to set economic rents? Local councils inevitably vary in their political composition and their attitudes to housing and rents. Attempts by central government to impose market-related rents cut across this variation, seeking to remove rent setting from the arena of local politics and to substitute the disciplines of the market. Market-related rents policies imposed from the centre deny expression of variation in political outlook, removing an important area of local autonomy and inevitably provoking resistance amongst some local authorities on either, or both, of two grounds: first, that market-related rents are inappropriate in council housing and, second, that decisions about rents are properly made by the local authorities as landlords which, just like private landlords, should have the freedom to set rents at below market levels.

Policies which seek to impose higher rents and a constant set of criteria for rent fixing violate the notion of local responsibility for rents and therefore require some sort of sanctions or mechanism to ensure that local authorities comply with central government's requirements. The Housing Finance Act, 1972, represented one approach to this problem, relying on administrative and judicial methods of control. As explained in Chapter 6, this Act failed because it was so provocative, generating widespread opposition. It was also very cumbersome, requiring each rebel authority to be dealt with individually via the installation of housing commissioners and, if necessary, court action.

The 1980 system represented an alternative approach, attempting to defuse central–local conflict by removing the emphasis from instructions about rent increase, using instead financial means of control. In this case the emphasis was on the calculation of subsidy entitlement, leaving the final decision about rents to the local authority itself. Councils could choose to increase rents by less than the amount assumed by central government, but only if they were prepared to spend less on housing repairs and maintenance, or to draw more from the general rate fund. This system also ran into difficulties arising from local authorities which were resistant to the idea that the benefit of housing revenue account surpluses should accrue to the Exchequer rather than local ratepayers. Thus both the 1972 and 1980 policies were undermined by local resistance and the assertion that local authorities should control income and expenditure.

Implementation of the 1980 system exposed other weaknesses of attempting to control local authorities by financial means. Since the system operated on the basis of leverage it could raise rents only by removing subsidy; when all subsidy had been removed, it depended upon what was described in the previous chapter as the block grant mechanism. Leverage on rents required that the determinations for changes in income and expenditure were widely different; the degree of leverage varied with the difference between determinations. Thus, if the determinations were the same, there was no leverage and local authorities could decide how to increase expenditure. The implication of this was that central government could raise rents only by assuming that additional rent income would accrue to the Exchequer in lower subsidy, rather than to the tenants in repair and maintenance expenditure. The system was good at taking away resources that could have been invested in the housing stock, but it was incapable of making authorities spend more on repairs and maintenance. In this sense it can be seen as a negative approach, depending upon the use of asymmetrical determinations.

The 1980 system also exposed the difficulty of securing consistency of outcomes from a uniform policy applied to a very uneven surface. As a result of the past exercise of local autonomy in relation to new building, repairs, modernisation, and rents, local authorities vary considerably in their expenditure on debt charges, management, and maintenance.[16] This variation in circumstances meant that the uniform determinations for rent increase and for management and maintenance expenditure had different impact in different places. The system made no attempt to relate rent increases to variations to pre-existing rents, nor to relate approved expenditure increases to the need existing in different localities. Over time this had a cumulative effect, applying different amounts of pressure to different authorities, permitting actual and notional housing revenue accounts to diverge. The key point here is that to secure consistency of outcomes it is necessary to have highly differentiated policy inputs. But to make the policy inputs more sensitive to the pattern of variation in local circumstances would require considerable additional administrative resources in central government, and a much more detailed knowledge of, and intervention in, each local authority. This, of course, would run the risk of further local resistance to yet more central control of local affairs.

To conclude this section, there are two main points which have been made: first, that the various proposals for reform of housing finance generally ignore or take for granted the question of implementation; and second, that governments are motivated primarily by short-term goals and are heavily influenced by· implementation issues. Historical analysis suggests that it is local autonomy and variation in circumstances which have thwarted successive rents and subsidies policies. From the point of view of central government, therefore, the key problem remains that of gaining control of local-authority housing finance.

'Ring fencing' the housing revenue account

It was in December in 1986 that the then Minister of Housing, John Patten, announced a review of the system of local authority housing revenue accounts to be carried out by Department of the Environment (DoE) officials, and representatives of the local authority associations. The working party was assisted by a report commissioned by the DoE and produced by accountants Coopers and Lybrand.[17] This report looked at advantages and disadvantages of the various accounting conventions used in council housing, housing associations, and private property companies. It concluded that:

> Housing revenue accounts were originally developed over 50 years ago and it is now widely recognised by local authorities and other interested parties that their present form and presentation are inappropriate and changes are required to improve accountability and the clarity of content and presentation. The improvements envisaged could have far reaching effects.[18]

The concept of 'ring fencing' was first applied to housing in a press briefing by Nicholas Ridley during the 1987 general election campaign.[19] The Secretary of State referred to the intention to introduce new-style housing accounts, but gave no details, apart from a clear commitment to banning local authority rate fund contributions to housing revenue accounts. Soon after the election the newly appointed Minister of Housing and Planning, William Waldegrave, addressed the annual conference of the Institute of Housing, an occasion that invited a major policy statement from the government. The minister spoke of the need 'to get people off the most deadly of all social drugs, the drug of dependence – on the state, or bureaucracy, or whoever. ... It is essential to introduce a much greater element of choice into the rented sector.' [20] This meant reviving private renting by removing rent regulation and encouraging council tenants to opt for new landlords. However, on rents, although it was obvious that the Tory strategy for the private sector implied higher rents for all, the minister was not very forthcoming in his discussion of plans for local authority housing finance. He merely referred to the need to run local authority housing in a businesslike way, and said that 'The Government propose to revise the financial and accounting framework within which councils discharge their landlord operations so that they can operate much more like a trading body.' He went on to say that the new trading-style structure would embrace capital as well as current expenditure.

The subsequent White Paper on housing added little to these rather cryptic ministerial comments. It did not use the term 'ring fencing', but it did refer to the need to keep rents at an affordable level, 'without excessive and indiscriminate subsidies.'[21] It also said that 'the aim is to move away from the present indiscriminate subsidies to tenants through rate fund contributions, Exchequer subsidies and unjustifiably low rents, and to rely instead on the assistance with housing costs available through housing benefit to those tenants who really need help.'[22] The lack of detail on the future of local authority housing finance constituted a major gap in the White Paper, but a consultation paper was promised ('around the turn of the year'), setting out 'proposals for a new financial regime which will reinforce the present statutory distinction between the provision of housing and other local authority functions and replace the existing housing revenue accounts by arrangements which are more in accord with modern accounting practice.'[23]

Ridley's commitment to banning rate fund contributions now looks like a statement that was made specifically for election purposes, for the government had much wider reforms in mind. In the context of the general election it was tempting for Ridley to focus on rate fund contributions, given that the majority of authorities making substantial RFCs were Labour-controlled London boroughs, such as Camden, Hackney, Lambeth, Lewisham, Brent, and Haringey. Altogether, in 1987–8, 14 London authorities made RFCs equivalent to more than 10 per cent of HRA income.[24] In the whole of the rest of England and Wales only 17 authorities made RFCs exceeding 10 per cent. As Figure 8.1 shows, more than 250 authorities made RFCs that were nil or less than 1 per cent of HRA income. Nevertheless, in aggregate terms in the 1980s, RFCs became a more significant proportion of general (or 'indiscriminate') assistance. Table 8.1 indicates how RFC became the major component of general subsidy, for the first time since the introduction of Exchequer subsidies in 1919.

It is important to say that in every year in the 1980s well over half the total RFC was due to London authorities, and to establish that the main reason for this was differences in loan charges; in 1987–8 average weekly loan charges per dwelling in London were £24.03, compared with £11.00 in metropolitan districts and £11.75 in English non-metropolitan districts.

Figure 8.1 Number of authorities making rate fund contributions (RFCs) of differing magnitudes in England and Wales, 1987–8

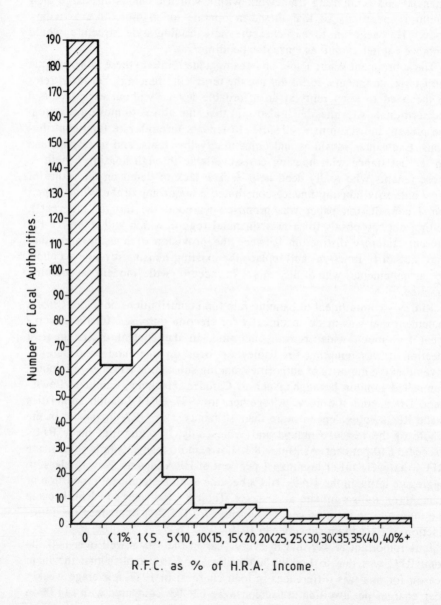

Source: CIPFA, *Housing Revenue Account Statistics, 1987–8, Estimates*

Table 8.1 Rate fund contributions and general Exchequer subsidy in England and Wales, 1980–1 to 1988–9 (£ million)

	Rate fund contribution	Exchequer subsidy
1980–1	446.1	1458.6
1981–2	432.0	900.6
1982–3	445.4	454.5
1983–4	503.9	343.1
1984–5	454.1	368.7
1985–6	347.2	475.3
1986–7	460.1	379.5
1987–8	542.5	509.8
1988–9	490.6	468.1

Source: CIPFA, *Housing Revenue Account Statistics 1980–1 to 1986–7*, Actuals, 1987–8 and 1988–9 Estimates

Despite the tendency for RFC to be higher in London, rents were also generally higher in the capital, and a straightforward ban on RFCs would have led to some massive rent increases in areas where rents were already high (albeit balanced to some extent by cuts in rates). On 1987–8 figures, a ban on RFC would have led to rent increases of more than 50 per cent in eight London authorities, with the highest increase being 183 per cent, in Camden. It is also important to remember that ministers referred to a ban on RFC, but not on the transfer of surpluses from housing into rates funds.[25]

The new regime

It was not until July 1988 that the government issued a consultation paper outlining its proposals for the 'new regime' in local authority housing finance,[26] together with a separate paper dealing with local authority capital expenditure as a whole.[27] The fact that two consultation papers were produced was evidence of a retreat from the sorts of fundamental reform that ministers had been hinting at in references to a more businesslike, trading-style structure and modern accounting practice. What eventually emerged was something very different from the fundamental reform of the whole basis of local authority housing finance. Once again priority was given to feasibility rather than principle.

Before we look at proposals for rents and subsidies, it is necessary to refer to the capital expenditure side, because there are important revenue implications in the changes planned for capital. The consultation paper explained that the need for change arose from the problems in the system for controlling capital spending which was introduced in 1980. The difficulties were mainly related to capital receipts from council house sales. First, it proved to be difficult to forecast capital receipts with any accuracy, so that there were problems in keeping total capital spending in line with overall public expenditure targets. Second, the drafting of the Local

Government, Planning and Land Act, 1980, was defective, from the government's point of view, in that whereas the original intention had been that authorities would be able to use only a proportion of receipts to justify new expenditure, with the remainder being used to redeem existing debts, in practice it emerged that authorities could carry forward an entitlement to spend a proportion of unused receipts accrued in previous years. This became known as the 'cascade effect', and it came to have a seriously distorting impact on local authority capital expenditure.

A third aspect of the growth of capital receipts was that the 1980 system did not permit the government to take into account an authority's accumulated receipts when deciding the annual housing investment programme borrowing allocations. The problem here was that capital receipts tended to be highest in areas with the least need for new investment, and so the targeting of resources was greatly impaired.

The final point to be made is that, although authorities were permitted to use only a limited proportion (20 per cent since 1985–6) of receipts for new investment, they could utilise the remainder for capitalised repairs to their housing stock, and carry forward a permission to spend, even though the cash had been spent in previous years. This meant that an increasing proportion of accumulated capital receipts was notional, no longer backed by cash.

It was clear that, from a range of points of view, the arrangements for capital expenditure were highly unsatisfactory. The new system, to operate from 1990–1, introduces a number of important changes.[28] First, authorities will receive 'basic credit approvals' (together with 'special credit approvals') which will set the maximum that can be raised through conventional borrowing and other credit arrangements. An important development is that the government will be able to take account of capital receipts at the local level when setting the credit approvals, and this should facilitate much better targeting of resources.

Second, authorities will be required to use 75 per cent of accumulated capital receipts, plus the same proportion of receipts in the current year, to redeem outstanding debt, or to finance future commitments.

Third, the consultation paper outlined a proposal to require authorities to repay outstanding loans by 'equal instalments of principle'. This represented an important departure from conventional methods of debt repayments, implying higher expenditure in the early years of a loan. In aggregate terms the Association of Metropolitan Authorities estimated that the cost would be an additional £800m. in 1990–1, and naturally this was condemned by the local authority associations. The government responded to the objections by issuing proposals for an alternative approach, known as the 'reducing-balance method' requiring authorities to make charges to their revenue accounts of not less than a fixed percentage of capital indebtedness at the start of each year.[29] This was designed to permit a less burdensome repayment regime, with less disruptive implications for local housing revenue accounts.

In general, the impact of the new capital controls will vary from place to place, but it is clear that the intention is to give central government much tighter control over local authority expenditure. The application of capital receipts to the redemption of debt will severely constrain capital programmes in many areas, but it will also have the effect of reducing debt charges falling on the housing revenue account. On the other hand, the elimination of the cascade effect will place considerable pressure on rents to support continued expenditure on maintaining and refurbishing existing council stock.

On the revenue side, it is important to state that what is proposed for the 1990s is essentially a revised and tighter version of the 1980 system, rather than a fundamental reform. Nevertheless, the new system departs from the old in at least two significant ways, breaching well-established principles. These main changes refer to the banning of rate fund contributions and the bringing together of housing subsidy and rent rebate subsidy. The rationale for the new regime is based on a critique of the 1980 system, as explained in the consultation paper of July 1988.

First, the paper refers to the multiple sources of support for council housing: housing subsidy, rent rebate subsidy, and rate support grant. Assistance through rate support grant is in respect of centrally approved rate-fund contributions, but in addition local authorities can make discretionary contributions from the rates, unsupported by RSG. The consultation paper refers to the diverse pattern of assistance, arising from the exercise of local autonomy: in 1987–8 a group of 133 authorities made rate fund contributions totalling £106m. more than the level assessed as appropriate for RSG purposes; meanwhile, 62 authorities were able to balance their HRAs with rate fund contributions totalling £115m. less than the assessments on which they received RSG.[30] The government's point here is essentially that actual and notional HRAs have moved out of alignment, resulting in a recurrence of the old pattern of inequitable distribution of subsidy.

Second, the consultation paper refers to the way in which the 1980 system tended to produce distortions in the incentives to efficiency and good management. This is an acknowledgement of the extent to which the system produced disincentives to new investment in areas with no subsidy entitlement. In addition, however, it is argued that the freedom to make unconstrained rate fund contributions can provide a cover for inefficiency in housing management. The same sort of argument is used in reverse, in relation to authorities generating surpluses on the HRA, when it is stated that 'It is essential that those surpluses should not be available to be used as a cushion for bad practices and inefficiency.'[31]

With these criticisms of the 1980 system in mind, the consultation paper sets out three objectives for the new regime: that it should be simpler, fairer, and more effective. A simpler system, it is said, should produce subsidy arrangements which work in a more intelligible way and give consistent incentives. Fairness is referred to in relation to the balance between tenants and poll tax payers, and between tenants in different areas. And an effective system would direct available resources to areas of need, and provide an incentive for good management rather than a cover for bad practice and inefficiency.[32]

To achieve these objectives it is proposed to establish a more tightly defined (ring-fenced) housing revenue account, into which will be paid just one subsidy, the housing revenue account subsidy. The new subsidy will combine and replace existing forms of subsidy:

HRA Subsidy
{
Entitlement under Housing Act, 1980
Rate fund contribution (including
    any rate-support-grant element)
Rent-rebate subsidy
}

From 1990–1 the main components of the HRA will be:

Income	*Expenditure*
Rebated rents	Loan charges
HRA subsidy	Management and
	maintenance spending
	Contributions to
	capital expenditure

Thus the new regime is characterised by two key features: a ban on payments to or from the general account, and a major redefinition of subsidy. The most important point here is that together these two elements give central government much greater control over HRA income and, therefore, rents. Under the 1980 system, at least as it was operated after 1982–3, central government had little real control over rate fund contributions or rent rebate subsidy, the former being a matter for local decision, the latter being determined by tenants' incomes and unrelated to the state of the HRA. Under the new system, however, HRA subsidy will be limited by the state of the account, and will be paid only in accordance with the notional deficit on the account.

It will be illegal for authorities to budget for a deficit before the start of a financial year, but where a deficit turns out to be unavoidable, then it must be carried forward, to be eliminated in the following year. All HRA expenditure must be covered from permissible income (not including transfers from other accounts) and all HRA income must be spent on housing services, or carried forward within the account.

The prohibition of rate fund contributions ends a freedom which local authorities have enjoyed since the very beginning of council housing, while the corresponding ban on the discretionary transfer of HRA surpluses ends a freedom which has existed since 1981–2.

Despite these important reductions in local autonomy, it is said to be essential that the introduction of the new system should not of itself produce sharp changes in rents or expenditure. It is necessary here to distinguish between the impact of the new system itself and the impact of the way it is operated year by year. In order to minimise disruption at the local level it is proposed that in the first year, 1990–1, entitlement to HRA subsidy will be based on:

(i)   entitlement to main housing subsidy under the Housing Act, 1980, for 1989–90, updated to 1990–1;

(ii)   estimated entitlement to rent-rebate subsidy for 1990–1;

(iii)   actual rate fund contributions to the HRA averaged over three recent years and updated to 1990–1.

In the case of rate fund contributions, the Exchequer is to take over responsibility for a sum reflecting actual contributions in the two years 1986–7 and 1987–8, plus the budgeted contribution for 1988–9. This means that local authorities cannot influence the size of the liability handed over to the Exchequer. With respect to prohibition of transfer of surpluses from housing into the general rate fund, the effect will be cushioned by transitional arrangements through central government support for poll tax revenues. Over a four year period Exchequer support to cover lost income from the HRA will be gradually phased out, implying a corresponding increase in poll tax. A third feature designed to effect a smooth transition to the new system is the proposal that the calculation of subsidy entitlement in 1990–1 will assume a minimum entitlement of zero under the Housing Act, 1980. This will avoid substantial rent increases in areas with notional HRA surpluses (or notional negative subsidy), but it will do nothing to address the issue of widening variations in rents during the 1980s.

In various ways, then, it is intended to avoid the sudden very large increases in rents or poll tax that would arise in some areas if the HRA were to be ring fenced without any transitional arrangements.

However, this does not mean that there will be no short-term impact on rents and housing expenditure. The introduction of the new system will not of itself impose big changes, but the actual increases in rents and housing expenditure will depend upon the values fed into the revised formula. As in the 1980 system, the subsidy paid to a local authority will reflect assumptions about changes in rents and management and maintenance expenditure. The consultation paper explains that:

HRA Subsidy will be designed to meet the notional deficit on the account, irrespective of an authority's actual decisions on rents and maintenance, or its managerial efficiency. This will ensure direct *financial incentives to efficient management* because any inefficiency (as for example, a high level of rent arrears) will put pressure on rents or on maintenance expenditure and other aspects of service to the tenants, while any increase in spending on management or maintenance will not in itself bring about reductions in subsidy.[33]

It is important to recognise that in some ways the new regime represents only a minor departure from the 1980 system, and yet in other ways it amounts to a major departure from past principles. The links with the old system lie in the fact that, first, the basis for calculating notional management and maintenance expenditure will continue to be the uprated expenditure levels derived from actual local expenditure in the period 1978–81; and second, increases in rents will be based on the pattern of variation which has emerged over the years. The starting point for the new regime will be the position arrived at under the old system, and the new regime is essentially the old system rolled forward, but with two crucial differences: the prohibition of transfers to or from other accounts, and the definition of what counts as subsidy. Both represent an erosion of local autonomy.

The redefinition of subsidy is a key feature of the new regime, yet it conflicts with the distinction between housing subsidy and income maintenance that was introduced by a previous Conservative government in 1972, and reinforced by the present government in the early 1980s. There is a real difference between a subsidy given to a landlord to bridge the gap between overall income and expenditure, and a rebate awarded to particular tenants to enable them to pay the full rent. Since 1972 rent rebates have been separate from general housing subsidies, and since the introduction of housing benefit the cost of rebates has been shown in the public expenditure White Papers under the social security budget rather than housing (see Chapter 7 above). By combining general subsidy (including rate fund contributions) with rent rebates in the new HRA subsidy, the government is ignoring the important principle that distinguishes subsidy from income support.

Why, then, should ministers wish to make this retrograde step? The answer lies in the priority given to the control of local authorities and public expenditure, rather than the construction of a principled housing finance system. From the point of view of the government, the proposed system deals with two growing problems in the 1980 system. Ministers were aware that the decline in general subsidy gave them diminishing leverage over council rents, and that as subsidy fell so rent rebate costs tended to rise, even in authorities which were in surplus on the HRA. Authorities continued to receive substantial sums in the form of rebate subsidy because the aggregate amount tended to rise as rents rose, and because entitlement was tenant-based rather than being limited by reference to the state of the HRA.

The new regime overcomes these problems by shifting to a definition of deficit and subsidy which is based on *net* rebated rents, rather than *gross* unrebated rents. By widening the definition of HRA deficit and expanding the volume of subsidy, yet without increasing public expenditure, the government is able to bring virtually all local authorities back into subsidy. This ingenious move restores central-government leverage on council rents, a measure of which can be obtained by comparing the leverage available in 1988–9 with what it would have been if the new regime were in operation. Aggregate subsidy under the Housing Acts in 1988–9 amounted to £468m., or just 7.4 per cent of total income. Under the new regime the measurement of subsidy would bring in a further £490m in rate-fund contributions and £2,268m in rebate subsidy, amounting to almost £3,250m. This represents just over 50 per cent of total HRA income, giving the centre nearly seven times as much leverage on rents.

The new regime provides for HRA subsidy to make good any deficit arising from the relationship between notional expenditure and notional net rents. Thus, if net rent income is assumed to increase faster than expenditure, subsidy will fall, and over time it is envisaged that a growing number of authorities will have a nil entitlement. In this situation the whole of the cost of rent rebates will fall on the HRA, and the whole of the benefit from the excess of gross rents over expenditure will accrue to the Exchequer. The consultation paper refers to the possibility that net rent income could exceed expenditure, and in these circumstances the Secretary of State would specify an amount to be transferred to the local authority's general fund. It should be noted that this breach in the ring fence does not involve any local discretion.

Implications of the new regime

In trying to understand and evaluate the new regime it is important to say that its impact will depend to a large extent on the way it is operated in practice. Like the 1980 system it permits a wide range of possible outcomes, the precise pattern of which will reflect the determinations fed into the annual round of subsidy calculations. A further factor to be recognised is that the consultation paper of July 1988 represented a partially formed policy in which there were numerous unresolved issues. This was reflected in the need to issue a further note in October 1988,[34] and six weeks later a letter to local authority associations outlining a revised method of debt repayment. Difficulties in finalising the details of important operational aspects of the system resulted in a delay of several weeks in the publication of the Bill, thereby squeezing Parliamentary debate and scrutiny into a much shorter time period.

Nevertheless, the broad outlines of the policy are clear, making it possible to discuss the implications in general terms. For convenience of presentation it is appropriate to look at the implications for tenants, local authorities, and the government itself.

Tenants seem certain to face higher rents, although perhaps not much higher in real terms until after the next general election, which is due in 1992 at the latest. The consultation paper was notably reticent about rents policy, saying only that:

> Rents generally should not exceed levels within the reach of people in low paid employment, and in practice they will frequently be below market levels. They should, however, be set by reference to these two parameters: what people can pay, and what the property is worth, rather than by reference to historic cost accounting figures.[35]

This raises questions about affordability and how existing variations in rents can be transformed into a more equitable pattern, related to current values rather than past investment decisions at local level or the impact of past subsidy policies. In one sense the consultation paper's brief statement on rents can be interpreted as the reintroduction of fair rents in the council sector, at the very time that fair rents are being phased out elsewhere. This time, however, there is to be no return to the rigid structure for setting and moving towards fair rents that proved so problematic in the early 1970s. Instead, ministers will rely on financial leverage to move towards affordability and value-based rents. Questions remain as to the method of determining affordability and value, and whether these should be related to incomes generally or more specifically tied to conditions in each region or locality. How should council houses be valued for purposes of rent setting? And how should the system respond to the very wide variations in values in different regions? In London, the south-east, and perhaps some other areas, the gap between affordability and value may prove unbridgeable.

The inference must be that, given historical trends and the contemporary shift towards market rents in the 'independent' rented sectors, council tenants in general face higher rents, but it is not clear that the pattern of increases will be fair and equitable.

For those tenants who are not in receipt of rebate assistance, or who receive very little such assistance, the situation will appear distinctly unfair because of the capacity of the system to transfer the cost of rent rebates from the Exchequer to the HRA. As rents rise relative to expenditure, so HRA subsidy will fall, and the better-off tenants will inevitably see themselves as paying for the rebates of their less well-off neighbours. This will reinforce the incentive to opt out of council housing, either through exercising the right to buy or opting for an alternative landlord. Tenants who buy will relieve themselves of the burden of subsidising their poorer neighbours, and will themselves become eligible for assistance through mortgage interest tax relief. The implication for remaining tenants must be an intensification of the residualisation process.

From the point of view of local authorities, it is clear that the impact of the new regime will vary considerably from place to place. Most authorities make no rate-fund contribution at all, or just a very small amount, and so for them the ring fence will make very little difference. Equally, most authorities do not transfer HRA surpluses into their general rate funds. However, the ring fence removes the capacity to respond flexibly to changing circumstances. The authorities most affected by ring fencing will be the fifty or so which make large rate fund contributions and the rather smaller number making substantial transfers of HRA surpluses. Given the regressive nature of the poll tax, the introduction of the ring fence will bring real benefits to the least well off in some areas, notably inner London, but probably only in the short term. For the majority of authorities the most important feature of the new regime will be the capping of rent-rebate subsidy, because of the way that rolling this in with housing subsidy and rate fund contributions returns virtually all authorities to a position where they are vulnerable to pressure to raise rents. Authorities will be in a weaker position than they were under the 1980 system because they will have no flexibility to counter subsidy withdrawal by means of a rate fund contribution instead of a rent increase. The consultation paper referred to authorities being made more accountable to tenants, but the reality is that they will be even more accountable to central government, and less accountable to tenants to the extent that they will have fewer policy options.

Local authorities will also face more detailed intervention from the centre. This arises from the government's recognition of the need to devise a more sophisticated and sensitive system of determinations for changes in rents and management and maintenance expenditure. As described in the previous chapter, the system of uniform determinations since 1981–2 was crude and unsatisfactory, but it did have the advantage of simplicity. In a ring fenced regime the need for a more sensitive system is even greater, because authorities will not have the capacity to compensate for the inevitable inaccuracies in central government's assumptions about local needs and resources. In order to tailor subsidy accurately to local circumstances, central government will require far better and more detailed knowledge of a complex set of variables in each local authority area. This could involve local authorities having to collect detailed information on the housing stock and the social composition of its tenants, including income levels, in order to establish the basis of subsidy entitlement. However, devising the details of possible schemes for differential determinations, whether by region or type of dwelling stock, proved to be a very difficult task for DoE officials to resolve. Whatever the scheme actually adopted, the implication is that local authorities will become more accountable to central government.

Nevertheless, it is also clearly stated in the consultation papers that local authorities will not be compelled to set rents and expenditure in line with the ministerial determinations. They will be free to raise rents by more or less than the determination but, whatever they do, the consequences will be contained within the HRA. Over time it seems certain that there will emerge a growing divergence between actual and notional HRAs, but on a much smaller scale than under the 1980 system.

The implications for central government are that there will be much greater control over the rate of increase in council rents, and that the benefits of rent income in excess of expenditure will accrue to the Exchequer rather than to ratepayers. On the other hand, both of these features of the new regime aroused opposition from amongst local authorities as soon as the proposals were revealed. It is to be expected that authorities will devise a variety of ways of opposing or circumventing the system. For instance, despite the existence of the ring fence, there are numerous opportunities for funds to flow between the HRA and the general fund, in the form of charges for services rendered. Formal, declared transfers cannot be banned without raising the complex issue of what should properly be charged to the HRA and what should be carried by the general fund. This was investigated at great length in the late 1960s,[36] but the problem was not resolved, and re-emerged in the 1986 report of the Audit Commission.[37] In the DoE note of October 1988, in which an attempt was made to clarify the earlier consultation paper, it was recognised that authorities varied in the way they allocated credits and debits to the HRA or general fund. Given this variation it was not intended to attempt a detailed prescription of future practice, a stance which left the ring fence looking rather less than watertight. However, to plug the gaps the government would have to confront the complexity of local accounting conventions, and it would be drawn into yet more detailed direction of local administration.

Indeed, for central government the new regime implies greater complexity and a greater administrative burden, arising from the need for more intervention at the local level in order to operate a more sensitive system of determinations. In addition, the decision to roll together general subsidy, rate fund contributions, and rent rebate subsidy will result in a system which is ostensibly simple but complicated to operate in practice.

Conclusion

In the first part of this chapter it was argued that the key problems in the reform of housing finance are to do with implementation, and that in practice successive governments have shown themselves to be more concerned with short-term feasibility than long-term durability or theoretical rectitude. The preoccupation with implementation is also due to the influence of policies other than housing finance, notably the continuing preference for home ownership and the control of public expenditure. The new regime for local authority housing finance can be understood within this context.

The stated objectives of the new regime are that it should be simpler, fairer, and more effective, but the analysis and discussion presented here suggest that it fails to meet even these modest objectives. There is a superficial simplicity involved in combining various forms of assistance into one subsidy, but the different elements will continue to be calculated separately, and, as has been argued above, central government will be drawn into a more complicated and interventionist relationship with local authorities. In this respect the stated objective of simplicity combined with consistency of incentives is shown to be contradictory: a simple policy applied to a differentiated set of local circumstances will produce varied outcomes, and a consistent pattern of outcomes requires a differentiated, sensitive set of policy inputs.

In terms of fairness the new regime is clearly defective in relation to both tenants and local authorities. In transferring the burden of rent rebates from the Exchequer to the HRA the new regime undermines the long-established principle that income maintenance is the responsibility of central government, drawing on resources from general taxation. The new system represents a redistribution of the cost of rebates for the poorest on to their rather less poor neighbours.

The new system is also unfair to local authorities to the extent that it treats them differently from private landlords. In the case of the private rented sector the whole basis of the government's policy is that profitability must be restored; income surpluses are seen as a right and proper feature of a healthy private market in rented housing. Whereas profit, or the prospect of it, is seen as essential for competition and efficiency in the private sector, in the public sector the argument is reversed and the government argues that surpluses must be removed because they represent a cushion to inefficiency.

Will the new regime be more effective in directing subsidy to areas where it is needed and provide an incentive to good management? The problem with the system is that, since it relies on financial leverage, it is more effective in forcing up rents than expenditure. Effective pressure on rents requires subsidy withdrawal, which implies less expenditure on management and maintenance. It was argued earlier in this chapter that the system relied on asymmetrical determinations, and that it is powerful for making authorities spend less, but much less effective for making them spend more. It is therefore difficult to interpret the new regime as an effective means of channelling resources to areas of greatest need.

But it is safe to conclude that improving the condition of the local authority housing stock is not a high priority for the government. Its primary aim is to continue to reduce the scale of public housing provision and, if higher rents were not reflected in improved housing services, then this would have the effect of further undermining council housing. The consultation paper. on the new regime was quite explicit in stating that 'Tenants will be given clear signals about the performance of their council's housing operation. They will be able to take better informed decisions about the alternatives the Government's housing policy is placing before them, and to decide whether to exercise the options the Government is giving them through the Right to Buy and Tenants' Choice.'[38]

Behind the stated objectives of greater simplicity, fairness, and effectiveness lies the barely hidden agenda of a government more concerned with attacking council housing and reducing the freedom of local authorities than with the need to construct a principled, coherent housing finance system. The new regime represents a second attempt to transfer the benefits of HRA surpluses to the Exchequer, following the collapse of the 1980 system. The new system has less coherence and integrity than the one it replaces, which was itself criticised as an unprincipled attack on housing subsidies. On this occasion the objective of greater control of local authority housing finance has led to the abandonment of the important distinction between subsidy and income maintenance. Lack of principle is also displayed in the way that local authorities are instructed to set rents in relation to value, but without any attempt to specify detailed criteria. The issue of affordability has proved to be extremely difficult for ministers to resolve, in both the council and housing association sectors.[39] Going beyond this there is the contradictory way in which local authorities are required to adopt different bases for income and expenditure. The point here is that the government is pushing authorities away from historic cost accounting conventions in which *income* is matched to expenditure, but it is moving to a situation in which income remains tied to expenditure while prices are set in relation to value.

Finally, to return to the themes of continuity, local autonomy, and residualisation, this chapter has indicated the extent to which the new regime represents a continuation of the 1980 system, reinforced by draconian new restrictions on local autonomy designed to turn the ratchet of residualisation. But because the new regime carries forward many of the deficiencies of the old system, including the short-term preoccupation with public expenditure, it can be predicted that it will generate 'anomalies' and its potency will decline within a relatively short period, precipitating yet another bout of legislation.

References

1 See R. Robinson, 'Housing tax expenditures, subsidies and the distribution of income', *The Manchester School*, June 1981, pp. 91–110. Also C. Whitehead,

'Neutrality between tenures: a critique of the HPR comparisons', *CES Review*, no. 2, December 1977, and 'Fiscal aspects of housing' in C. Sandford, C. Pond, and R. Walker (eds), *Taxation and Social Policy*, Heinemann Educational, London, 1980.

2 See also J. Ermisch, 'The Economics of British housing: present subsidies and options for reform', in *Inquiry into British Housing, Supplement*, NFHA, London, 1986, pp. 17–22

3 R. Berthoud and J. Ermisch, *Reshaping Benefits: The Political Arithmetic*, Policy Studies Institute, London 1978, p. 25.

4 J. Ermisch, 1986, op. cit., and *Housing Finance: Who Gains?*, Policy Studies Institute, London 1984.

5 A. B. Atkinson and M. A. King, 'Housing policy, taxation and reform', *Midland Bank Review*, March 1980, pp. 7–15.

6 *Inquiry into British Housing Report*, NFHA, London, 1985.

7 J. Hills, *Twenty-First Century Housing Subsidies: Durable Rent Fixing and Subsidy Arrangements for Social Housing*, Welfare State programme, paper No. 33, London School of Economics, 1988.

8 Housing Centre Trust, *Housing Finance Review: Evidence to the Secretary of State for the Environment*, London, 1975.

9 I. Kelly, *Heading for Rubble: the Political Need for Housing Finance Reform*, CHAS, London, 1986.

10 See also P. Malpass, 'Pricing and subsidy systems in social rented housing: assessing the policy options', *Housing Studies*, vol. 3, no 1, 1988, pp. 31–9.

11 S. Goss and S. Lansley, *What Price Housing*? SHAC, London, 1981.

12 Association of Metropolitan Authorities, *A New Deal for Homeowners and Tenants: A Proposal for a Housing Allowance Scheme*, AMA, London, 1987.

13 *Housing Policy: A Consultative Document*, HMSO, 1977, Cmnd. 6851, p. iv.

14 *Inquiry into British Housing*, Report, op. cit., p. 18.

15 J. Ermisch, 1986, op. cit., p. 20.

16 *Improving Council House Maintenance*, Audit Commission, HMSO, 1986.

17 *The Accounting Framework for Housing*, Coopers & Lybrand Associates, March 1987.

18 ibid., p. 41.

19 Conservative Party News Service, *Statement by Rt Hon. Nicholas Ridley: Conservative proposals for Housing*, 19 May 1987, mimeo.

20 Mr Waldegrave's speech to the Institute of Housing Annual Conference, 19 June 1987, mimeo.

21 *Housing: The Government's Proposals*, Cm. 214, HMSO, September 1987, p. 15.

22 ibid., p. 18.

23 ibid., p. 15.

24 CIPFA, *HMSO Revenue Account Statistics: Estimates, 1987–8*, 1987

25 P. Malpass, 'Ridley's one way ring-fence', *Roof,* September–October 1987, pp. 23–4.

26 *New Financial Regime for Local Authority Housing in England and Wales: A Consultation Paper*, Department of the Environment/Welsh Office, July 1988.

27 *Capital Expenditure and Finance: A Consultation Paper*, Department of the Environment/Welsh Office, July 1988.

28 M. Ward, 'Priced out', *Housing*, October 1988.

29 Department of the Environment letter to Local Authority Associations, 2 December 1988.

30 *New Financial Regime*, op. cit., p. 3.

31 ibid., p. 5.
32 ibid., p. 6.
33 ibid., pp. 8–9.
34 *New Financial Regime for Local Authority Housing in England and Wales: Note by the Department of the Environment*, 20 October 1988, para. 4.
35 *New Financial Regime: A Consultation Paper*, op. cit., pp. 5–6.
36 *Housing Revenue Accounts*, Report of the Working Party on the Housing Revenue Account, Ministry of Housing and Local Government, HMSO, 1969.
37 Audit Commission, *Managing the Crisis in Council Housing*, HMSO, 1986.
38 *New Financial Regime: A Consultation Paper*, op. cit., p. 7.
39 R. Bayley, 'The rent dilemma', *Housing*, October 1988, and 'Fair is not affordable', *Housing*, December 1988.

Chapter nine

At the end of the rainbow

Previous chapters have traced the development of rents and subsidies policy since the Second World War, and it is now necessary to draw out some conclusions. It has been shown that the mid-1950s period was the key turning-point, and that since then there has been considerable continuity in the direction of policy development. In particular, successive Conservative governments have sought to raise the level of council rents and to place greater emphasis on means-tested rent rebates. Labour governments in the 1960s and 1970s accepted the case for rebating, although their preference for maintaining output and their preoccupation with anti-inflation policy led to a rather softer line on general subsidy and rents. However, Labour failed to articulate a coherent alternative policy for housing finance, and a theme running through previous chapters is that Conservative governments have dominated the course of rents and subsidy policy. It has been during periods of Conservative government that policy has been carried forward in pursuit of the objective of a restructured subsidy system, based on income related assistance rather than across-the-board 'indiscriminate' subsidy; an important underlying assumption has been that council rents should be brought more into line with market rents.

Movement towards market related rents and income related subsidies is a trend that has occurred in other European countries,[1] and it is necessary to avoid interpretations which overemphasise political and economic factors within any particular country. Nevertheless, British social rented housing is distinctive in that the major providers are locally elected councils, and a feature of policy development, referred to throughout this book, has been the tendency for successive governments to become more assertive and interventionist in pursuit of rents and subsidy policy objectives. From the relatively gentle approach based on leverage and incentive, introduced in 1955–6, there have developed the systems of 1972, 1980, and 1989, each seeking in different ways to limit local autonomy in rent setting and to facilitate the early elimination of general subsidy.

In Chapter 2 it was argued that it is necessary to look at the long-term restructuring of housing tenure as a whole, and in Chapter 3 the point was made that developments in rents and subsidies policy had to be located in relation to the intensification of support for owner occupation and the increasing residualisation of council housing. In other words, the reshaping of rents and subsidies policy in the public sector exists within the wider setting of tenure restructuring. The objective of a system of market related rents and income related subsidies sits alongside the broader objective of a residualised public sector. Over many years rents and subsidies have been manipulated to reinforce the process of making renting from local authorities simultaneously less attractive to better-off households and more affordable for the less well off. The long-term continuity in rents and subsidies policy reflects its importance as an instrument of residualisation, and has to be understood in the context of the continuing refusal by governments of all political persuasions to confront the inequities of the subsidies awarded to home owners. Housing finance in general has been, and remains, skewed in a way which is intended to influence tenure choice rather than to promote tenure neutrality.

However, the nearer the goal of a thoroughly residualised public sector, and the higher the proportion of tenants who depend on rebate assistance, the less justification there is for continuing to raise rents. Whereas higher rents and wider use of rebates may have been effective policies during the *transition* to a residualised public sector, this approach is steadily losing credibility and is clearly inappropriate in certain respects in a situation where most tenants cannot afford to pay existing rents from their own resources. The rents and subsidy policy objective was also the means to the achievement of the tenure restructuring objective; the approach of a residualised public sector undermines the case for the policies which helped to bring it about.

In this sense rents and subsidies policy has reached the end of the rainbow. For a quarter of a century British governments used rents and subsidies to promote tenure restructuring, but in the 1980s it became clear that contradictions were emerging. Just when it seemed that the goal of a system based on market related rents and income related subsidies was on the brink of being achieved, the government discovered that this objective was no longer so desirable. At least four contributory factors can be identified. First, there can be no real market when two-thirds of tenants rely on housing benefit. In this situation it is impossible to determine market rents because the rents that consumers are willing to pay are effectively set by the Department of Social Security rather than by market forces. Second, the case for market related rents and income related subsidies rests in part on arguments about the efficiency of targeting assistance on those in greatest need. But means testing is administratively labour intensive and expensive, and the case for it diminishes as the proportion of tenants claiming help increases. Third, there is an element of perversity in pressing ahead with market related rents at a time when council housing is clearly becoming a residual welfare service for those who are unable to secure accommodation in the market.

Finally, the government has discovered that relating rents to current values generates public-expenditure problems and provokes conflict with local authorities over the determination of income and expenditure and the ownership of housing revenue account surpluses. Whereas market-related rents may have attractions in terms of cross tenure comparisons (especially for a government which aims to revive private renting), they also have a distorting impact on public expenditure and government relationships. This is largely because, in the current situation, market related rents generate, in many authorities, levels of gross income which are far higher than is required to cover expenditure on housing services. The government itself has recognised the problem in the way that it has backed away from a policy of market pricing in social rented housing since its aggressive approach in the early 1980s.

In these circumstances the goal of a coherent, fair, and durable framework for rents and subsidies has moved off into the distance once more. The problem arises from the way in which rents and subsidies policy is still geared to the objective of tenure restructuring, when what is required for the 1990s is an approach related to contemporary circumstances. In this sense the 'new regime' is flawed by the way it addresses the problems of yesterday rather than tomorrow. Indeed, it can be argued that housing finance as a whole in Britain is outdated as well as inequitable, to the extent that in owner occupation as well as council housing the subsidy system remains rooted in the era of transition. This perspective suggests that what is required in owner occupation is recognition of the needs of existing home owners facing the uncertainty and expense of repair and maintenance. Rather than giving indiscriminate mortgage interest tax relief, to push up demand (and prices), and then using interest rate increases to dampen demand, the government should consider further development of publicly funded advice agencies and a more generous grant system in order to preserve the quality of the existing stock of houses.

In relation to council housing at the present time, the implication is that what is required is a definition of affordability which pitches rents at a relatively low level, thereby minimising the need for means testing. Historic cost seems to present a much better basis for rent setting than current value, especially given the concentration of low-income households in the public sector. The problem with historic cost pricing, as earlier chapters repeatedly demonstrated, is that costs vary considerably from place to place, in a capricious manner, not necessarily related to quality of service. The main cause of variation is differences in debt charges per dwelling, and a coherent approach requires some means of dealing with the problem. One way of tackling it would be some form of national rent pooling, extending to the national level the advantages of pooling income and costs currently enjoyed at the local level. An alternative would be to transfer all outstanding and future debt charges to the Treasury, leaving local authorities to set rents to cover only the costs of day-to-day management and maintenance. Both of these options have serious disadvantages as well as some important advantages over the current system, and it is not necessary or appropriate to go into a detailed discussion here.[2] It is, however, relevant to note the urgency of tackling the need for new investment in social rented housing. While academics and would-be reformers have produced a series of blueprints for housing finance, the government has gone off in a different direction, motivated by considerations of feasibility and political advantage, and the output of new council houses has declined to the lowest levels for more than sixty years, contributing to a continuing rise in homelessness.[3] Bramley's research has demonstrated the scale of demand for social rented housing and the need for a substantial revival of new building, especially in the south of England,[4] and it is essential that a financial structure is established to enable that investment to take place in a way which generates genuinely affordable rents. More generally, it can be said that council housing has not been the failure that its critics have depicted in recent years, and that it is necessary to restore a sense of proportion in the debate. In financial terms local authority housing has immense advantages for consumers compared with the market sector, not least of which is the advantage of scale and the benefits of historic costs. Plans to break up and privatise council housing will irrevocably damage this desirable and distinctive feature of the sector.

Reshaping housing policy

This book has been written during 1988, a year of frenetic reshaping of housing policy, continuing a period of rapid change ushered in by the advent of the Thatcher revolution after the 1979 general election. The intention, however, has been to demonstrate the need for a historical perspective on contemporary events, to argue that it is necessary to take account of continuities as well as changes, and to establish an explanation of the present which is anchored in an understanding of the past. This is not to minimise the importance of change; on the contrary, by drawing out the long-term continuities in the direction of change it is shown that current trends are not just the ephemeral products of a particular government. Nor is this to be interpreted as an apology for the Thatcherite onslaught on council housing. It is a reminder that the changes imposed in the 1980s and those planned for the 1990s are rooted in trends that were well established before 1979, and that, therefore, they are all the more difficult to challenge.

The book is about the reshaping of housing policy, but it also attempts to reshape the way we conceive and analyse that process. The three themes of continuity, residualisation, and central–local relations provide a framework within which to make some concluding comments about the implications for thinking about and researching housing policy. On the theme of continuity, it emerges that a long-term study tends to highlight continuities and to relocate changes. A long-term perspective embraces events which tend not to be identified in research focused on major political or legislative controversies. It has been argued that the evidence on rents and subsidies points to 1955 as the key turning point, representing a major policy change, even though there was no primary legislation. What happened then was that the government of the day picked up and used as important policy instruments two devices, rent rebates and rent pooling, which had been introduced in legislation in the 1930s but which had hitherto made little impact.

This perspective casts a rather different light on the Housing Finance Act, 1972, which is often seen as an epoch-making event, and which has been acknowledged (in Chapter 3) as standing between the 'old' and 'new' systems of housing finance. The 1972 Act can be seen as an attempt to introduce new policy instruments to pursue established policy objectives. It was in this sense a major legislative event, but arguably not one associated with a major change of policy. The 1972 Act now emerges as an oddity, a digression from the established methods of influencing local authority rents policies. The rent pooling device used from 1955 to 1972 relied on financial leverage, which was the same principle adopted in the late 1970s as the replacement for the temporary 1975 Act.

On the question of continuity in housing finance, this book has put forward the view that there has been considerable underlying similarity in successive subsidy systems, and that the analytical task is to identify and explain the links rather than to mystify the situation by detailing the differences. In thinking about local authority housing finance the key analytical distinctions are those between historic cost pricing and current value pricing, between production subsidies and consumption subsidies, and between financial incentive and administrative-legal means of control. What has been shown in this book is that there has been a marked shift in emphasis over time, but until 1972 all subsidies were paid as production subsidies, although authorities were under growing pressure to distribute the benefits in the form of consumption subsidies (rebates). At the same time, pressures were building up for a break-out from the constraints of historic cost pricing. Since the 1972 Act there have been two further attempts to establish a basis for some form of current value pricing, with consumption subsidies playing the major role. In terms of central government's attempts to control what local authorities do about rents, it has been shown that financial incentive methods have predominated, and only the 1972 Act stands apart from this tradition. This way of looking at developments in housing finance provides a framework for analysis which is quite distinct from those approaches which emphasise the differences in successive subsidy systems. It represents an attempt to get away from the widely held view, even amongst housing specialists, that housing finance is immensely complex and difficult. Such a view holds back the development of the sort of informed debate which is essential for constructive policy development.

Turning to the issue of residualisation, there are two brief points to be made. First, the account of rents and subsidies policy since 1945 challenges the perception of residualisation as a recent trend, associated with the Thatcher revolution and the sale of council houses. The residualisation process has its origins in the restructuring of housing policy in the mid-1950s, and in Chapter 2 an attempt was made to link residualisation to the wider notion of the modernisation of housing provision. This relates to the second point, which refers to the suggestion by Forrest and Murie[5] (discussed in Chapter 1) that residualisation is a valuable descriptive concept but for explanation it is necessary to turn to the notion of marginalisation. Their position is grounded in the present situation, and it is certainly a valuable point to make that contemporary labour market trends and the concentration of the least well off in council housing make the tenure vulnerable to further erosion and reductions in quality of service provision. Forrest and Murie are here looking beyond housing for an explanation of changes within housing provision. The problem with this approach is that it neglects consideration of the historical processes by which so many of the least well off came to be concentrated in council housing, and it also undervalues factors from within housing itself which helped to bring about this situation.

The evidence of the development of rents and subsidies policy suggests that over many years housing policy was subject to pressures to make council housing less attractive to the better off and more affordable for the least well off. It has been argued in Chapter 2 that this must be linked to the wider restructuring of housing provision, which is itself to be understood in a way that takes account of labour market trends. However, the residualisation of council housing has more to do with full employment and rising living standards in the 1950s and 1960s, drawing away the better-off working class into home ownership. The residualised status of council housing reflects housing policies, over many years, in support of home ownership. And on the supply side, if Harloe is right to argue that home ownership is the modern form of the private housing market and the form which is most effective from the point of view of capital,[6] then residualisation has been driven, in part at least, by forces at work within the housing market itself. In short, a focus on the current situation and labour market factors is an inadequate explanation of how council housing came to be like it is, but residualisation, seen in historical perspective, does provide valuable purchase on the problem.

The third theme, concerned with relations between central and local government, has drawn attention to the growing assertiveness and interventionism of the centre. During the 1980s, relations between central and local government in general have been highly problematic, prompting a number of writers to refer to a crisis.[7] When the centre abolishes a whole class of authorities (as with the removal of the Greater London Council and the six metropolitan counties in 1986) and then introduces a highly unpopular poll tax to replace the centuries-old system of local rates, there is clearly some basis for this view. Housing cannot be separated from the wider crisis of local government, and, indeed, as the major service provided by most local authorities, housing has been at the centre of the attack on local government.

However, the analysis presented in previous chapters suggests that, first, the erosion of local autonomy has been continuing for many years, and second, it is not a straightforward process. It can be concluded that models of central–local relations which refer to partnership or agency relationships are too static in a period characterised by change. Nor is it sufficient to think in terms of a linear erosion of local autonomy. The history of rents and subsidies policy suggests the need for a more dynamic and interactive model, recognising that local authorities have resources to resist or evade central-government attempts to fetter their discretion. The relationship seems to invite analogies with limbo dancing, in the sense that central government repeatedly lowers the bar, believing that local authorities will be unable to get through, but when they do, albeit with increasing difficulty, the bar is lowered once more. It is interesting that studies of central–local relations in the 1980s give far more attention to council house sales than to rents and subsidies, although in some ways the latter is a more complex and rewarding area for research, pointing to the dynamic nature of the relationship.

The final point, and arguably the most important in terms of its implications for housing research and theory, concerns the need to look at implementation issues. The argument was developed in Chapter 8 that the housing finance literature was generally neglectful of implementation, yet governments were heavily influenced by this problem. At the same time the implementation literature tends to focus on rather different kinds of issues, more concerned with the politics of getting things done in situations where action depends upon mobilising numerous actors and agencies.[8] In the case of rents and subsidies the issue is not to do with bureaucratic discretion or administrative politics. Nor is implementation frustrated by difficulties of mobilisation. If the elected councillors decide that rents are to increase by a certain amount, then implementation can be taken for granted. The implementation issue is the problem faced by central government: how can it ensure that its policy objectives are matched by the outcomes at local level? It has been argued in this book that this is especially difficult, given the variation in local circumstances and the extent of local authority commitment to autonomy in rent setting. It is not surprising then if governments, beset with competing priorities as well as problems of housing finance, settle for pragmatic short-term feasibility rather than long-term principled solutions. The evidence suggest that the 'new regime' for local authority housing finance will deliver what the government wants in the short term: less freedom for local authorities, more council house sales, lower public expenditure, and higher council house rents. But only for a few years. Then they will think of something else.

References

1   M. Ball, M. Harloe and M. Martens, *Housing and Social Change in Europe and the USA*, Routledge, London, 1988, Chapter 2; P. Wilmott and A. Murie, *Polarisation and Social Housing*, Policy Studies Institute, London, 1988, pp. 22–3; R. Flynn, 'Cutback contradictions in Dutch housing policy,' *Journal of Social Policy*, vol 15, no. 2, 1986; H. Priemus, 'Housing Allowances in the Netherlands', in P. Kemp (ed.), *The Future of Housing Benefits*, Centre for Housing Research, University of Glasgow, 1986.
2   P. Malpass, 'Pricing and subsidy systems in British social rented housing: assessing the policy options', *Housing Studies*, vol. 3, no. 1, 1988.
3   *Raise the Roof*, Shelter, London, 1988.
4   G. Bramley, 'The demand for social housing in England in the 1980s', *Housing Studies*, vol 4, no. 1, January 1989.
5   R. Forrest and A. Murie, *Selling the Welfare State: The Privatisation of Public Housing*, Routledge, London, 1988, p. 78.
6   M. Harloe, *Private Rented Housing in the United States and Europe*, Croom Helm, London, 1985, p. xxiii.
7   S. Duncan and M. Goodwin, *The Local State and Uneven Development*, Polity Press, Cambridge, 1988; S. Ranson, G. Jones, and K. Walsh (eds), *Between Centre and Locality*, Allen & Unwin, London, 1985; D. Blunkett and K. Jackson, *Democracy in Crisis*, Hogarth, London, 1985.
8   B. Houlihan, 'Policy implemetation and central–local government relations in England: the example of the sale of council houses and area improvement', *Housing Studies*, vol. 2, 1987, pp. 99–111.

Name index

Subject index